Evolving project leadership

Evolving project leadership

From command and control to engage and empower

by
Gordon MacKay
MBA, BSc(Hons) BA(Hons) MAPM MInstLM

Association for Project Management

Association for Project Management
Ibis House, Regent Park
Summerleys Road, Princes Risborough
Buckinghamshire
HP27 9LE

© Association for Project Management 2021
© Gordon MacKay 2021 for figures 9 and 10.

First published 2021

All rights reserved. No part of this publication may be reproduced, stored in a retrieval system, or transmitted, in any form or by any means, without the express permission in writing of the Association for Project Management. Within the UK exceptions are allowed in respect of any fair dealing for the purposes of research or private study, or criticism or review, as permitted under the Copyright, Designs and Patents Act, 1988, or in the case of reprographic reproduction in accordance with the terms of the licenses issued by the Copyright Licensing Agency. Enquiries concerning reproduction outside these terms and in other countries should be sent to the Rights Department, Association for Project Management at the address above.

The author, Gordon MacKay, has asserted his moral right under the Copyright, Designs and Patents Act, 1988 and subsequent amendments to be identified as the author of this work.

British Library Cataloguing in Publication Data is available.
Paperback ISBN: 978-1-913305-12-3
eISBN: 978-1-913305-14-7

Cover design by Croft Design Associates
Typeset by RefineCatch Limited, Bungay, Suffolk
in 11/14pt Foundry Sans

Contents

Preface viii

Introduction 1

1 The changing face of project leadership 7
   1.1 Leadership behaviours in crisis must not be the norm 11
   1.2 Primitive leadership: its origin and function 13
   1.3 The role of the organisational in supporting project leadership 20
   1.4 Transformation of project management is essential to the very survival of the profession as a credible enabler in delivery 23
   1.5 Assertiveness costs: A challenge to traditional leadership 28
   1.6 The SCARF Model from the elevation of the leader to release of potential 34
   1.7 No follower = No leadership 35
   1.8 Teams and their members follow leaders who inspire, and merit the title bestowed 40
   1.9 Learning outcomes 43

2 Why command and control is inadequate 45
   2.1 New technology: Its impact and significance for project management 46
   2.2 Environment ascendant 48
   2.3 The new function of project management in leadership 51
   2.4 Learning outcomes 52

3 Project leaders deliver teams 53
   3.1 The challenge of increasing, emergent complexity 55
   3.2 The necessity for empowerment and therefore coaching 55
   3.3 Treating employees as customers fosters engagement and ownership 56
   3.4 Mentor or coach? 58
   3.5 Too busy to coach 59
   3.6 Modelling stakeholder engagement 60
   3.7 Calling to account 62

Contents

3.8	Emotional intelligence nurtures resilience	64
3.9	The GROW Model	65
3.10	Changing minds: Shifting perspectives	68
3.11	Learning outcomes	74

4 Introducing the Triple Catalyst Model — **75**

4.1	What criteria can assess project leadership capability, and how are they applied?	76
4.2	Organisational intelligence	78
4.3	Judgement and decision making	79
4.4	Creating project culture and environment	80
4.5	The Triple Catalyst for project management leadership	82
4.6	The hard truth about 'soft skills'	85
4.7	The Nine Steps to project team delivery and project leadership	90
4.8	Learning outcomes	90

5 Organisational foundations enabling and supporting the project leader journey — **93**

5.1	An informed focus for change	95
5.2	A psychological understanding of resistance	95
5.3	Insight, ready or not: the 'nudge' to aporia; more powerful than 'shove'	96
5.4	Stories articulate lived experience with the immediacy of a 3D virtual reality	97
5.5	Insight for the willing	97
5.6	The subordinate nudge and power of expectation	98
5.7	Organisational influence on project leadership culture through hiring standards	100
5.8	The counter-productive result of traditional project management interview and assessment	101
5.9	Organisational responsibility for appropriate project management assessment and selection	104
5.10	Learning outcomes	105

6 Steps 1 to 3: Insight: informing situational awareness — **107**

6.1	Situational awareness	107
6.2	Insight Step 1. Self as leader, strengths and weaknesses now	108
6.3	Insight Step 2. Team as individuals, strengths and weaknesses now	121

		6.4	Insight Step 3. The integrated project team as a unified team: collaborativeness	145
		6.5	Learning outcomes	155
7	**Steps 4 to 6: Foresight**			**157**
		7.1	The second catalyst: 'Foresight'	157
		7.2	Foresight Step 4. Developing personal leadership behaviours	159
		7.3	Foresight Step 5. Team members	176
		7.4	Foresight Step 6. Team to synergy	182
		7.5	Reporting	184
		7.6	Team meetings	184
		7.7	Learning outcomes	184
8	**Steps 7 to 9: Vision: informing and communicating situational understanding**			**187**
		8.1	The third catalyst: 'Vision'	187
		8.2	Vision Step 7. Personal transformation	189
		8.3	Vision Step 8. Empowering team members	193
		8.4	Vision Step 9. Measured informed ongoing intervention	196
		8.5	Situational understanding	201
		8.6	Learning outcomes	202
9	**Organisational transformation**			**203**
		9.1	Selecting, assessing and developing project leaders	204
		9.2	Project leadership behaviours, what good does and does not look like	205
		9.3	Facilitation skills	208
		9.4	Learning outcomes	214
10	**The power of project leadership**			**215**
		10.1	Team perceptions and role: how empowering followers fosters engagement	216
		10.2	Embedding the Vision	218
		10.3	Setting the standard	223
		10.4	The power of project leadership	227
		10.5	Insight and Foresight inform a new Vision	228

Appendix: Project leadership behavioural assessment   **229**

Index   **233**

Preface

*"**How would you measure or assess project leadership behaviours**?"*

When originally asked this question, having assessed many projects for complexity, I assumed that assessing leadership behaviours would be straightforward. After all, the *APM Body of Knowledge 7th edition* definition clearly states that good leadership 'inspires and aligns for a common cause'. How hard can it be to test for that? All I had to do was identify project leadership behaviours that achieve this, and then assess for evidence of their application.

In reality it was far from straightforward. First, I discovered that the behaviours most associated with leadership as generally applied are not at all what project leadership requires. It also turned out that the *kind* of leadership required has, in any case, changed, and in ways that are all too often unacknowledged.

This book presents the practitioner with two journeys. The first establishes a vision of what, in fact, good project leadership must do if it is to be effective. The second offers concrete steps to achieving this.

For those willing to get behind stereotypes and assumptions, it also offers a personal journey of discovery, leading to a richer, deeper appreciation of how what is required in delivery of both project management and leadership is evolving.

This need for personal 'continuing professional development' will be shown in turn to drive the continuing 'profession' development that is now necessary to meet demands from increasingly complex delivery environments. Similarly, only an 'empowered' team, collaborating across all disciplines, has the agility and expertise equal to such emergent complexity.

The research underpinning this book draws on many disciplines, and both professional and academic literature. It is also informed by personal experience. From Royal Naval engineering apprentice, and 20 years in project management, including line management of 1,200 staff, I witnessed, experienced and learned from leadership, both good and bad. Both prompt my ongoing commitment to fostering the good in myself and others.

Clarifying what is needed of project leadership; digging beneath surface assumptions as never before, I discovered scientific evidence showing that traditional portrayals of assertive 'command and control' leadership are far from inspiring; they actually alienate, disenfranchise and often antagonise.

Neuroscience offers insights rooted in evidence-based research, challenging the efficacy of command-and-control behaviours in particular. It consistently shows that such behaviours actively *inhibit* performance. They not only disincline others either to follow or collaborate, but they actually render them less *able* to! They 'inspire' failure.

How was I to equate or reconcile these contradictory portrayals implying that threatening behaviour could be 'inspiring'? And how, I also wondered, came such behaviours to be associated with 'leadership' in the first place? Uncovering the now much-needed vision of project leadership that follows, provided often unexpected answers to these questions.

I am surprised by the extent to which such clichés and stereotypes of leadership persist. They generally gloss over what it is like to be on the receiving end. Would those promoting such behaviours be 'inspired' if treated that way? Would most people?

I therefore challenge the validity of such behaviours imported without scrutiny into the practice of project management. This prompted a profound shift in my personal understanding, of both project management and project *leadership*. I had to ask what specifically project leadership behaviours must *do*; what they must achieve.

One powerful realisation informing my awareness of what project leadership behaviours must achieve had an unlikely source. The demands imposed by the COVID-19 pandemic mirror those of project delivery in inherently complex, volatile environments. They drive home the message that, just as responding to a pandemic requires agility, collaboration and the full engagement of all, so, too, does project delivery.

Carrying out hundreds of interviews and assessments with project managers encouraged a deep respect for those exhibiting the form of leadership promoted here. I have also, as I am sure many will relate to, observed and experienced, first-hand, those command-and-control behaviours posing as leadership, that felt threatening and fell far short of inspiring trust and loyalty.

My growing awareness of the prevalence of such misrepresentations of leadership prompted an earnest desire to expose and call out such behaviours for what they are.

This then informs the vision of effective project leadership required for the delivery of effective teams. The returns on offer are out of all proportion to the investment required in establishing project leadership in team delivery.

Preface

The benefits of a leadership that fosters and realises the potential of all will, in addition, set such a compelling standard as will inspire emulation far beyond our profession.

The Association for Project Management has been instrumental in supporting me throughout this endeavour, and the challenges the COVID-19 pandemic has imposed. To James Simons, Ros James and Clare Georgy in particular, and all who reviewed early drafts, along with the patient support of my partner Paula from concept to publication, I owe and express my sincere gratitude.

Gordon MacKay
MBA, BSc(Hons) BA(Hons)
MAPM MInstLM

We are grateful to the following for permission to reproduce copyright material:

The figures 'Performance Curve model' and the 'GROW Model' from *Coaching for Performance the Principles and Practice of Leadership, 5/e* by Sir John Whitmore, 2017, pp.95, 96. Reproduced with permission of Nicholas Brealey Publishing, an imprint of Hodder and Stoughton Limited, Carmelite House, 50 Victoria Embankment, London imprint, EC4Y 0DZ; and the figure 'Conflict Situations' based on Dr. Ralph Kilmann's version of the TKI Conflict Model, http://www.kilmanndiagnostics.com/overview-thomas-kilmann-conflict-mode-instrument-tki, copyright © 2009–2020 by Kilmann Diagnostics. All rights reserved.

In some instances we have been unable to trace the owners of copyright material, and we would appreciate any information that would enable us to do so.

Introduction

This book offers a structured path to effective project management, leadership and team delivery.

Fundamental changes in the nature of the delivery environment have effectively reframed the very role and function of the project manager. They present compelling drivers necessitating a fundamentally new approach to delivery adopting more fit-for-purpose project leadership behaviours.

Building on neuroscience it will be shown why traditional portrayals of 'heroic leadership', such as alpha-male dominance behaviours (command and control), are actually counter-productive in project delivery. An effective vision for project leadership must replace such behaviours by those nurturing and empowering team agility, synergy and collaboration.

Whether they are an aspiring project leader, an experienced professional, or anyone seeking insights into effective project leadership, a common thread is the practitioner's own willingness and ability to adapt. It demands an increased awareness and acknowledgement that their role is more about effecting collaborative working than commanding and controlling.

To address this, the book is structured in the following way:

- **CHAPTERS 1–3:** We begin by showing how the function of project leadership has changed, calling traditional leadership portrayals and assertive command-and-control behaviours to account.
- **CHAPTERS 4–5:** We present a new way of thinking about and exercising project leadership, and a path to achieving a harmonious style that is more in keeping with today's project environment.
- **CHAPTERS 6–8:** We look at how the move to a more collaborative style of leadership can have much wider benefits for project teams and project-based organisations, and ultimately for project success.
- **Chapter 9–10:** We highlight how the establishment of project leadership at the individual, team and organisational level liberates an agility and resilience in delivery traditional command and control stereotypes of leadership cannot equal.

Evolving project leadership

We explore the ascension in relevance of project 'leadership' in the project 'management' profession, finding it mirrors the ascendance of stakeholder 'engagement' over stakeholder 'management'.

Since both project management and project leadership are relatively new professions, the distinguishing characteristics of each are explored to demonstrate the increasing relevance of the latter. From this, effective project leadership competences are then identified, established and expanded upon.

Command-and-control (C&C) type behaviours have long been associated with traditional leadership, but are they relevant in project management today?

Honest scrutiny informed by scientific research reveals, as will be shown, that they are, more often than not, a liability. This reveals a clear and present need to adopt a new vision as to the most effective form project leadership should take.

This uncovering and exploration of previously unquestioned assumptions prompts an increasing need to act. Just as form follows function, the path to project leadership must be forged with a compelling vision of its new destination, 'what good looks like', now, in project leadership.

Exploring how this vision of project leadership might be realised informed the creation of both an effective model and structured path for project managers aspiring to realise their individual potential in project leadership.

But, as will be shown, simply focusing on project management is not enough, if the full benefits and power of project leadership is to be realised. The persistent cost of negative behaviours adversely affects *all* engaged in project delivery, so this too must be addressed at the organisational level.

What leadership has been and now is, continues to evolve

Generic forms of leadership and associated behaviours have evolved over time. Within them, as with the evolution of all human behaviours, vestiges and remnants of less useful or even counter-productive behaviours do inevitably persist, reflecting their diverse cultures and evolutionary origins.

Readers bring diverse knowledge, experience and assumptions to the concept of 'leadership'. So, to establish common ground, it is important to clarify how today's behaviours and forms of traditional leadership were, and continue to be, heavily influenced by their evolutionary origins. Even at the individual level, current attitudes and assumptions towards leadership have roots, but these are rarely examined.

Introduction

Seeds sown and accepted in childhood persist. Unquestioned, they continue to pervade adult portrayals of leadership. Parents, teachers and others in authority populated our imagination; defining what we thought we could, should or should not do, or even 'be'

During that impressionable stage, ahead of any developed sense of self, those 'in charge', defined what 'leadership' looked like, and how it felt to be a 'follower'. This early unexamined, unquestioned, utterly naïve sense of what leadership looked and felt like has a profound effect on what is later accepted and expected.

Both knowledge and experience of leadership is continually informed and reinforced through each culture's legacy of inspiring stories, myths and legends. Vividly portrayed, they become almost inseparable from our inner characterisation of what leadership looks like. This gradually accumulated sense of what leadership *is* remains largely unconscious; it is rarely brought to conscious attention or examined by the adult mind. For most, in fact, no reason to query traditional associations between assertive 'command-and-control' behaviours and leadership, whether in the world at large or in project management, may ever have arisen. Until now.

This book begins by doing just that, calling traditional leadership portrayals and assertive, command-and-control behaviours to account. Project leadership can then be framed in a way that accounts for its changed function in contemporary project management delivery.

Although unsettling, reflecting maturely through the eyes of an experienced adult on things one accepted without question as a child presents opportunities for a significant evolution in personal development.

At this point the reader is encouraged to take a moment to reflect on the following questions:

- Think of a fictional portrayal of leadership. What did they say and do?
- Imagine yourself as one of the 'led'. How would it feel to be spoken or so told what to do?
- Recall one in your life who has inspired you to be or do more than you thought you could be or do. What did they say? How did they speak to you?
- Compare these two examples. How does your experience of being inspired relate to the traditional portrayal?

This potentially challenging exercise in reflection reveals one's willingness and ability to revisit untested assumptions, and to be open to seeing things beyond the habitual.

Evolving project leadership

Learning and developing project leadership competence *requires* one to be open to change: a certain willingness to 'test personal assumptions', to consciously seek out and be open to insights alternative perspectives can offer.

Becoming what the Association for Project Management (APM) promotes as a 'reflective practitioner' nurtures this inner fearlessness when it comes to reviewing assumptions in the light of new evidence, and is essential to effective engagement in project delivery. Developing this core competence should be writ large on the 'To Do' list; whether taking on a new project, or considering proposed changes to scope etc.

The way project management supports team delivery will be shown to have relevance for all engaged as stakeholders, regardless of experience, seniority or background. For effective project leadership will be shown to be as much about the relations the project leader establishes as the particular behaviours that can be observed.

Certainly, the organisational and cultural changes necessary to realise effective project leadership will require wider engagement and influence wherever project delivery is practised. This will extend from Human Resources, engaged in selection and recruitment, through to the ongoing development of effective teams, as well as project leaders.

For the latter, the journey to competent leadership in project management presents a uniquely personal challenge for each project practitioner aspiring to project leadership: to consider anew what leadership really means to you, and why. It prompts the question whether the form of leadership aspired to matches what the role now demands.

Globally, forms of leadership change and evolve over time. This is reflected in contrasting leader/follower relationships spanning diverse cultures and ideologies.

Evolutionary traits still permeate portrayals of leadership as observed in any context where one individual seeks to dominate others. They can be seen on the sports field, in the office, in the political arena and even in wildlife documentaries. In each arena, however, one person's leader is another's dictator: those who are fêted as leaders by some, are seen as tyrants by others.

This should give any project practitioner aspiring to project leadership pause for thought in seeking to define the form of leadership most appropriate to project management.

Fortunately, the *APM Body of Knowledge 7th edition* helps remove ambiguity, for it defines leadership as '*the ability to establish vision and direction, to influence and align others towards a common purpose, and to empower and inspire people to achieve success*'.

Introduction

This is quite distinct from forms of leadership associated with simply telling others what to do, then 'calling to account' if they fail. It compels a very different focus, competence and capability.

Establishing vision and direction, influencing and aligning others towards common purposes, is fundamentally different from exerting or imposing power. It necessitates an ability to empower; not in the sense of abrogating power, 'giving it away', but rather, being actively engaged in a continuous process of encouraging, facilitating, nurturing; coaching for optimum team performance.

By investing in team empowerment, the resulting agility drives delegated and empowered delivery on multiple fronts, and so decreases the leader's own time spent reacting to tactical challenges. Their personal return on such investment offers the space and time secured to bring strategic intention to delivery.

Delegating the minutiae of day-to-day decision-making that others are increasingly more qualified to take, the leader's time is freed up to focus on team delivery, fostering and securing engagement from and between stakeholders.

Coaching, delegating and empowering the team returns situational awareness to the leader, just as aircraft or a ship's autopilot removes the drudgery of continual adjustments accounting for wind and tide. While the delivery team follows daily scheduled activities, the project leader is free to 'span the boundaries', ensuring the wider stakeholder engagement that the power of delegation releases.

In an increasingly complex and dynamic delivery environment, this book invites the aspiring project leader to really take on board that only an *empowered* integrated project team has the necessary agility to meet the demands of complex project delivery. This challenges many outdated assumptions around the nature of leadership itself, and project leadership in particular.

Having established the new role of leadership in project management, a structured approach is presented, offering concrete steps for project management and project delivery organisations alike to realise their potential in releasing the emerging power of project leadership.

1

The changing face of project leadership

The practitioner is invited to review and reflect on the changing nature of leadership and delivery environments. Responding to emergent complexity, driven by interdependent technologies in delivery, demands agility at rates that traditional command-and-control leadership cannot achieve.

This 'emergent complexity' demands a paradigm shift towards a more collaborative and empowering set of leadership behaviours within the integrated project team, and stakeholder relationships built on mutually acknowledged and respected interests.

- The need to distinguish project leadership from traditional forms.
- Changing nature of delivery environments.
    - AI and project data.
    - VUCA.
- Collaborative leadership.
- Paradigm shifts, eg stakeholder engagement supersedes management.

At first glance, the concept of 'project leadership' seems uncontentious. For many, 'it goes without saying'; it's *just* the application of 'traditional leadership', but in a 'project' setting. And since leadership is a concept familiar to all, there is not much more to be said.

Pressed a little further, one might be directed to traditional models reflecting various approaches or techniques. Some might even acknowledge the evolutionary roots of behaviours associated with leadership, a vast legacy with archetypal roots predating humanity itself.

This diversity of concepts around 'leadership' deserves close attention to ensure a common understanding and currency around its usage. On reflection it becomes apparent; just beneath the surface of terms project practitioners take largely for granted, there is significant ambiguity. General and traditional portrayals of 'management' and 'leadership' reflect wildly diverse contexts, and are manifested in behaviours that are not readily reconciled.

On this basis alone it is apparent that, before defining competent project leadership and how it is to be achieved, it is necessary to determine whether, and if so, how, project leadership differs from that exercised in other situations.

This chapter will show that when it comes to leadership, 'all that glitters is not gold', so by challenging unquestioned assumptions about traditional views and behaviours associated with leadership, it will make more apparent 'what good looks like' when it comes to project delivery.

But such definition is not readily or rightly obtained by focusing on the project leader's behaviour. For their behaviour should itself be defined by what they must *do* for effective delivery.

In fact, what the project manager must now do, in delivery, has itself changed significantly. The way projects are delivered, how they are delivered and who delivers them, and the contexts in which project delivery increasingly occurs – *all* have been and are changing.

Asking most project managers what they do will often result in stock answers reflecting adherence to process and baselines. This can bear surprisingly little relation to what would actually be observed, day to day, by watching their activities. Given what is now needed for successful delivery, it might well come as a surprise to discover that the time spent in securing successful stakeholder engagement, and coaching for delegation, significantly exceeds that exercised in directing, commanding and controlling their line-of-control reports.

The significance of these multi-dimensional changes must not be underestimated. Each affects all the others. The job and role description for a project manager exercising project leadership today seeks abilities and competences quite different from those before new technology spanned all disciplines in both delivery and deliverables.

This chapter will therefore focus on clarifying what project leadership is and should be, by first exposing what it is not, and why. It will be shown that much associated with traditional leadership, as promoted and presented, has no place in project delivery and its leadership.

Asked to give examples of leadership in the world at large, the faces and actions of many famous men and women will readily spring to mind. Vivid examples of great leadership may be exemplified in their words or actions. Dramatic accounts show the leader asserting their authority and expertise to impose conformity on their followers and direct them.

The observer is not generally prompted to consider how it would feel to find oneself a follower in such circumstances, or whether such behaviours depicted in fundamentally different and often extreme situations are relevant or even appropriate. On reflection, however, it soon becomes apparent that there is a tremendous difference when considering such behaviours in a project delivery environment as opposed to a battlefield or other crisis situation.

How does project leadership differ from traditional representations? Figure 1 marks the first step in illustrating how traditional and project leadership differs. It contrasts both, reflecting differing organisational structures and behaviours within each.

Subjecting the concept of project leadership, perhaps for the first time, to informed scrutiny, it might be assumed that *traditional* leadership behaviours, and their function, are of a kind with those appropriate to *project* leadership. Yet, as will be shown, this turns out to be a false assumption; a conflation of contrasting and in many ways contradictory manifestations of leadership behaviours, as shown in Figure 1. And they must be understood as such, if the true function and form of project leadership is to emerge.

Just as a journalist may tend to focus on crisis, conflict and controversy, so too, traditional narratives intended to exemplify leadership focus on 'dramatic' events, and personas typified in the stereotypes of steely-eyed, square-jawed heroes. Such portrayals of crisis tend to play down or ignore how the same leader, over extended periods of time, built up their reputation, inspiring trust and loyalty.

Traditional stereotypes of leadership conflate behaviours required in rare moments of extreme crisis with what is required to establish and earn the title of leader as bestowed by others.

They skew perceptions, distort them, and in so doing promote and exaggerate the relevance and effectiveness of command-and-control behaviours. They are projected as central to leadership generally when, more often than not, their true effectiveness is limited to extreme situations where the immediacy of peril precludes debate or question. Seldom is this ever justified in project leadership.

Exploring and differentiating between 'traditional' and 'project' leadership, it soon becomes clear that some behaviours traditionally associated with such 'leadership-in-extremis' are either redundant or counter-productive. They represent what Carl Sagan described as 'evolutionary baggage'. Identified as such, they can be set aside in favour of fit-for-purpose project leadership behaviours supporting collaborative, aligned delivery.

Evolving project leadership

Leadership style: Command and control (C&C)	Leadership style: Project
Traditional military, tribal coercive.	Cross functional and organizational, co-ordinator and facilitator.
Functional org. full team line-authoritty.	Matrix/projectized org. low if any direct line authority.
High education subject matter expert (SME).	Leader has relatively limited subject matter expertise.
High assertiveness.	Assertiveness – unwarranted.
Highly directive.	Low directive – high facilitation.
High dominance behavior.	Low dominance – high engagement/collaborative behaviors.
Stakeholder management.	Stakeholder engagement.

Traditional leadership ⟵⟶ **Project leadership**

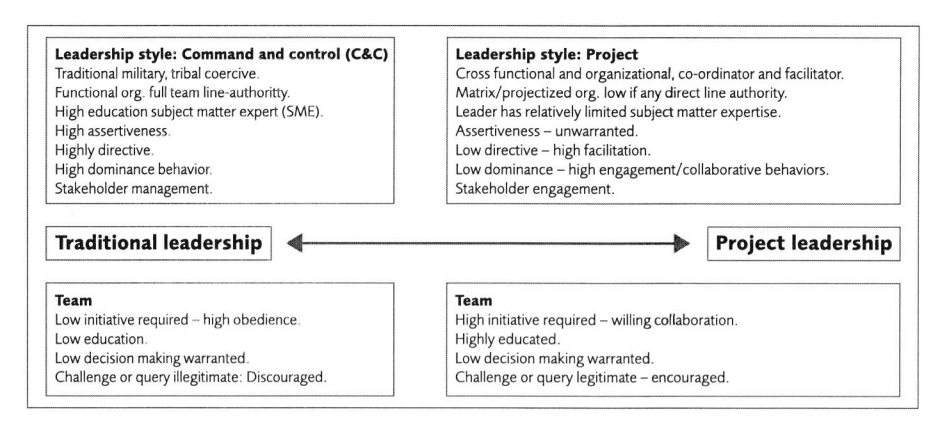

Team	Team
Low initiative required – high obedience.	High initiative required – willing collaboration.
Low education.	Highly educated.
Low decision making warranted.	Low decision making warranted.
Challenge or query illegitimate: Discouraged.	Challenge or query legitimate – encouraged.

Figure 1 Leadership styles: How form follows function

Traditional leadership, management and project leadership are discrete:

Leadership ≠ Management ≠ Project leadership.

For the project leader, attracting and inspiring personal commitment and engagement requires more than slavish, subservient obedience. Unlike management, where authority comes from a 'title', from above, where leadership *does* exist, authority is conferred *on* the leader *by the follower;* because it emerges from the follower, inside-out, rather than being imposed from the outside-in. Leadership behaviours communicate the availability of a relationship followers must be inclined or inspired to *want*. Leadership exists *only* when that relationship is mutual, two-way, binary.

Leadership ≠ Leadership behaviours.

Leadership = Mutual reciprocal <u>*relationship*</u> = (Follower **+** Leader).

The benefits of acquiring project leadership competences, underpinning and nurturing collaborative working, will reward the effort needed many times over. The diligent practitioner is also rewarded by experiencing, first-hand, the immense power of collaborative behaviours transforming delivery, organisational culture and themselves.

The effects of poor leadership behaviours generate a cascade of negative effects on culture and delivery alike. Their cost impacts on delivery capability and practice. The ongoing impact on impeded team member development and failure to collaborate are also compounded if exacerbated by counterproductive behaviours that undermine individual and team effectiveness.

This cost-benefit equation establishes a formidable case for developing and enhancing project leadership capability for both organisations and project managers alike.

Leadership behaviours in crisis must not be the norm

The above-mentioned promotion of leadership behaviours 'in extremis', as if they should be the norm, diverts focus from behaviours that actually enhance a team's long-term effectiveness and resilience.

Delivery constraints, and especially time, are often seized upon to persistently justify deferring and delaying coaching and individual or team development. This can result in all consideration of employee wellbeing and mental health over extended periods being discounted, not to mention the potentially catastrophic career consequences for those so 'victimised'. After a while, such excuses have a tendency to normalise what are effectively counter-productive behaviours that stunt individual and team development and become 'baked-in'.

Just as individuals shorn of self-esteem cannot realise their full potential, so teams not working collaboratively may deliver only short-term gains. Obedience based on fear cannot equal the effectiveness of a leader's investment in the development of an empowered, collaborative team founded on mutual respect. For however 'glorious' the tale, as will be shown, blind obedience in a project team is simply not fit for purpose in today's complex, subject matter expert-populated project environments.

To meet these demands, a core *function* of today's project leader is to develop *rapport*, eliciting trust and a sense of common purpose. They communicate a compelling '*vision*' substantiated by astute situational awareness embodied in '*Insight*', and '*Foresight*'. This narrative establishes and confers meaning and value that all in project delivery may readily buy into as active stakeholders.

This contrast between traditional and project leadership behaviours also serves to highlight how and why the motives and goals of some who aspire to project leadership are at odds with both its function and form. This contrast, in turn, raises questions and presents challenges for both individuals entering and those engaged in project management. It also serves to prompt the senior managerial and executive functions within organisations to review

Evolving project leadership

how their respective project management capability is both governed and developed.

Project management as a discrete discipline is a comparatively recent profession, although its roots and those of leadership behaviours are almost unimaginably ancient. Behaviours associated with leadership today emerge from diverse evolutionary origins. Understanding and taking them into account informs a balanced judgement as to their contemporary effect, relevance and effectiveness.

Evolutionary origins of leadership

World-wide, traditional portrayals and stories of 'leadership' are reflected in humanity's myths and legends. Ancient or modern, regardless of culture, often in the form of an epic journey, they evolved to engage, capture the imagination and foster admiration. Contemporary science and MRI scans of the brain show that even uttering the words 'Once upon a time . . .' have similar effects to those observed in hypnosis where the subject's higher brain function is effectively shut down.

The power of myth persists in and permeates all contemporary cultures. The props and scenery, the settings, vary wildly. But however vivid or memorable, when leadership is portrayed, it often reflects and promotes in the observer a hunger for fame, fortune and power. These narratives of leadership are kindled and crafted to inspire the imagination; to encourage emulation and aspiration.

It is rare that these behaviours are held up for scrutiny, but since for many they compete as relevant examples for application in project leadership they now must be. This exercise serves to ensure personal expectations and objectives are realistic, aligned, and congruent with what is shown to be required of the contemporary project leader.

As portrayals of leadership evolved with each new story and storyteller, some degree of moral ambiguity was inevitable. Dictators clearly 'lead' some, but are seen by non-followers as bad. Leadership is readily ascribed to heroes, warriors, Nobel Peace Prize winners, and tyrants.

This constellation of contradictory perceptions of leadership, as with many values imposed by others and absorbed as a child, are rarely exposed to critical adult examination. Consciously examining examples of previously unquestioned leadership behaviours, perhaps for the first time, one swiftly uncovers unexpectedly stark and confusing contradictions. They make clear that identifying *universal* leadership behaviours, or any attempt to 'measure' general leadership, is problematic.

Fortunately, however, effective 'project leadership' behaviours *can* be reduced to a subset of those encompassed under the historical and more widely lofted banner of 'leadership'. Like assaying gold from dross, both the necessary function and form of project leadership can be defined.

Primitive leadership: its origin and function

Leadership through dominance was favoured by natural selection when fitness was defined by a single metric: survival in a life-threatening environment. Unsurprisingly, examples of primitive leadership behaviours still extend throughout the entire animal kingdom.

The vestiges of such primitive behaviours continue to permeate mammal, hominid and human culture globally, even today. Even in the most civilised and relatively peaceful countries, consider the wealth and diversity of sports ranging from actual physical to mental conflict, with binary, win/lose outcomes and even violence. Globally developed countries constitutionally defend the right to bear arms and the perceived need to do so evidences and reflects threatening conditions sometimes equal to or even exceeding those prompting ancient survival behaviours.

The most fundamental of these instincts and corresponding fight-flight behaviours has characterised all terrestrial life since its emergence 3.5–4 billion years ago.

A wilful blindness to unconscious behaviours forged and validated in the fires of natural selection means they can neither be moderated nor informed. Emotional intelligence and its benefits for the enlightened and emotionally mature leader requires a fundamental ability to become aware of instincts as they arise, and a willingness to acknowledge and control them.

Our species also evolved behaviours fit-for-purpose in diverse physical *and social* environments. Evolving from mammal to hominid inevitably resulted in a spectrum of escalating dominance behaviours from expressive body language and audible signals such as growling, threatening or eventually physical violence.

In a world dominated by physical dangers and challenges, evolution understandably selected in favour of the strongest, fastest, and best warrior; The alpha female or male. It is worth noting however, that in other contexts, species evolution selected in favour of co-operation and collaboration. This supports the case that the form that effective leadership behaviours take must be correlated with the environment and context they are deployed in, as well as their specific function.

The absence of verbal language, as Homo sapiens emerged some 315,000 years ago, meant all interactions and communications were limited, and critically, the ability to rationalise or articulate internally (reason), was absent. Yet the human body still generates those same ancient emotional responses as it did then. Gut instincts precede conscious thought and take precedence. Time and again, it is shown that opinions may reflect instinctive feelings one seeks to justify 'after the fact' in circular arguments closed to reason: "He cut me up because he is a terrible person" – "He is a terrible person because he cut me up"

As highlighted by Antonio Damasio in *The Strange Order of Things* (2018), more than 500 million neurones in the gut's enteric nervous system (ENS) predated the skull, and those that make up the brain we have today. Then, as today, it provided the instantaneous 'towards' or 'away-from' reflex, predicting threat or reward.

Signals from the ENS enter our brain via the amygdala atop the spinal cord. It is the common gateway for all nervous system inbound signals. It triggers fight/flight reactions and base emotions, informing feelings. The most basic of these still compel movement towards, or movement away-from. Such behaviours predate the terrestrial life from which humans evolved four billion years ago and can still be seen operating in primitive, seaborne organisms around the world.

The visceral power for the project leader of the actual effect these ancient mechanisms still have cannot be underestimated.

They were supremely fit-for-purpose then, in environments where they flourished and were reinforced. These instincts and reactions are as viscerally powerful now as then – the biology is undeniable. Equally, their relevance for those aspiring to project leadership is immediate and visceral.

Adding to the contemporary power of these ancient mechanisms of emotion, the human brain is now exposed to volumes of data and information far beyond that which informed its evolution.

What effect can be expected on individual performance as individuals are increasingly subjected to and expected to make sense of it all? Consider, in western society, by adulthood, the average child processes orders of magnitude more information, and has met and interacted with more humans of differing cultures, than those previous generations encountered in an entire, generally much shorter, lifetime.

Historically, the average human might, in a lifetime, meet and interact only with those of their own and immediate tribes or eventually, villages. Today, by comparison, whether through social media, commuting in a major city, in the workplace, or even simply shopping, individuals may interact with hundreds if not thousands of others daily. As the COVID-19 pandemic so graphically illustrates, the vectors triggered by each interaction trigger many more in a cascade of influence and consequence.

Increased delivery environment complexity is also reflected in the idea of 'six degrees of separation', also known as the 'six handshakes rule'. If I shake hands with one person, who shakes hands with everyone they know, and each of them shakes hands with everyone they know and so on, then, in six iterations this 'social network' will encompass humanity itself. Similarly, in project delivery, altering the way one item performs can send signals or behave in ways that affect many others. This bears no comparison to the traditional world of project delivery in predictable, stable environments.

Consider the investment in and influence of advertising alone; the multiple platforms and media through which its agendas are engineered and delivered to influence and persuade; the language, both of body and verbal and images used. All intentionally target these ancient, often pre-conscious triggers, successfully triggering behaviours the conscious mind may not even be aware of or acknowledge.

To deny the significance of these factors, whether considering the impact of behaviours on and of leaders, or team members, is to set on one side that which, more than any other influence, can hamper, impede or foster successful stakeholder engagement.

Little wonder, then, that politicians, marketing campaigns, and those in high office, wittingly or not, seek to, and demonstrably do, influence others by activating subconscious triggers to trust and follow, to choose fight or flight. Untold billions of pounds are spent to encourage the consumption of goods and services. Although individuals may shy away from acknowledging that they have been subliminally influenced, the statistics at scale are undeniable.

Campfire storytellers, down countless generations, since long before movies, television, or even the written word, exploited emotions over reason to mesmerise and capture the imagination of their audience.

Leaders portrayed, were usually male and military, often in combat scenarios threatening life and limb. Their behaviours, and the language describing them, just like the great action heroes of today, popularised domineering behaviours and body language, confusing them with many now automatically associated with leadership. Rousing stories were, and are, passed on down the countless generations by word of mouth, precisely because they exploit, prioritise and trigger primitive human emotions over reason. Such undisguised primal responses can also be seen when the home team scores at any sporting event.

It is because of this unquestioned adoption and unquestioning acceptance of traditional 'dominance behaviours' passed off as 'leadership', that few question the applicability, relevance or validity of such behaviours in project management generally.

Fewer still would react well if spoken to or treated in the way so-called leaders on-screen speak to and treat others. Take many celebrities hailed as 'leaders', yet who treat the majority with contempt. How would most project professionals feel, or behave, if so treated?

Although aggressive assertiveness is increasingly challenged in the workplace, there are still those supporting such behaviours who offer what at first seems like a challenging argument in their favour.

Imagine that it is half time in a crucial football game, played on the national or even international stage. Your side are two-nil down. The team files off the pitch to the changing rooms visibly dejected, heads down, their own fans casting disappointed or even angry glances and comments in their direction.

The manager, jacket undone, collar and tie loosened, bursts into the changing room. He heads straight for the lead player – the one with the highest record of goal scoring. Squaring up to him, leaning forward until his face is inches away, hands on hips, or else gesticulating wildly, he shouts his disappointment at the player's failure to perform, letting his team and thousands of paying fans down – failing to live up to expectations. If the player is foolish enough to meet his eye or challenge, they are peremptorily and dismissively swept aside. The tirade continues as all present stand or slump in silence.

A pause. The manager looks deep into the player's eyes. "This is your last chance, your last stand. If you fail, the world will see and know you for a failure!" Another pause. "Think of the team! Think of the fans who have supported you! Think of your own family and children!" He sees the player's eyes narrowing, lifting, head still down signalling deference, to make full contact, his jaw becomes more set, determination replaces hopelessness.

> *Choosing this moment, the manager turns, making firm eye contact with all the players. He calls out the same message to all, steps aggressively towards any suggestion of challenge until he is sure the shame has hit home.*
>
> *Then he challenges them all too. His tone and body language teeter throughout on the edge of unpredictability. He looks as if he might lose all control at any moment. The tension in the air is palpable, as is the humiliation he lays on all for letting him, themselves, and the fans down.*
>
> *Again, the manager moves from humiliation verging on personal insult to a deep challenge, inspiring the response of defiance and a rising up both as individuals and then as a team working together to show the world the fruit of their efforts in coming so far . . .*
>
> *The team returns to the pitch and plays as never before; single-minded and determined, acting as one. With a little good fortune, they win. The fact that they played as well as they did, however, is not so much down to fortune as the reaction and calculated response the manager succeeded in evoking and inspiring.*

So, does this serve to undermine the argument that project leadership is not served well by such assertive and aggressive behaviours? Surely it makes clear the power such a leader has to draw the very best out of their team? Why should any project leader not be inspired by it and treat their team in the same way for stunning results?

Indeed, such an argument is readily adopted by those who believe a particular role or position bestows a licence and justifies such behaviours. Those with such a mindset, however, are also unlikely to consider how they would feel or respond to being treated like that, or the potential longer-term effects of such behaviours on others.

Clarity emerges when you can take a step back from such instinctive, 'trained', automatic responses. Why was the behaviour so effective, and why should such an approach *not* be valid for the project leader looking to inspire their team to greater efforts?

Consider, again, that half-time confrontation. What characterises the players' mood and its effect on their ability to perform at their best? They are despondent and physically tired. They are likely all too aware of, or fixated by, their own imminent failure in the next 45 minutes.

Given access to medical data about the physical condition of the players, what would be revealed about the biological effect of the manager's tirade?

It can readily be expected that an analysis of the players' blood would reveal they all receive a liberal dose of adrenalin, and with that, their neurological higher 'executive function' is decreased. They spend less time thinking about and dwelling on things. This means that they are less inclined, or even *able*, to dwell on fear of failure.

Adrenalin surges their attention into the 'now'. It plays directly into the manager's conscious intent: to facilitate trained responses and patterns of play unimpeded by rumination, or any superfluous mental distraction. The players enter 'Flow', that uninhibited performance drawing on countless hours of experience and practice. The player is effectively liberated from over-thinking and looking into the future – they are immersed in the 'now', as that same adrenalin kick serves to further enhance performance by directing blood to muscles in preference to the brain.

This biological perspective on the effect of the manager's tirade explains the increased physical performance of players both as individuals and as a team over the next 45 minutes.

In extolling its virtues as an approach to soliciting enhanced performance from a sports team, focus is not often turned to consider the effect on the players if the game is lost.

Even if the game has been won, the lead player might well find some resentment lingering beneath the surface at the way they were humiliated and let down by one whom they had been striving to please, in front of the entire team. An ill-advised phrase uttered by the manager will linger in the player's mind until the next time they fail or fall short. Then that phrase will re-emerge to haunt, taunt and handicap, because, without the manager there to trigger part two, the 'affirmation' is all too easily lost.

This effect is known as the 'nocebo effect' and is the opposite of the more widely known 'placebo effect', when a patient is led to believe a sugar-pill is a remedy, and it works for them. The nocebo effect is also in evidence when a manager or person in authority expresses lack of faith in someone, and they find that their performance is subsequently inhibited.

The above example casts into sharp contrast how varying contexts dictate the function of leadership and the varying forms it must adopt to be effective. Any physically demanding environment, ranging from the battlefield to sport, where individuals or the team are physically and biologically 'under fire', is *not* best served by behaviours that trigger threat responses. And this applies all the more when it comes to day-to-day project delivery.

While the traditional commander in the battlefield relies on unquestioning obedience and, along with the football manager, wittingly or not, inhibits neurological function, this is the very *last* thing the project manager seeks or needs! The adverse effects of triggering threat responses will be covered in more detail later, in relation to the application of the David Rock SCARF Model.

Despite increasing promotion and awareness of what Daniel Goleman termed emotional intelligence[1], – the ability to moderate primitive instinctive and emotional reactions – it is notoriously hard to achieve and sustain. Beneath the veneer of organisational life and individual consciousness, primitive threat and reward response behaviours and language affect perceptions and behaviours to a far greater degree than most people realise. A powerful example of these visceral, unconscious triggers and emotional responses is readily available to every motorist who has experienced, while in a neutral state, some perception of another road user being too close, acting in a way they see as inconsiderate or cutting closely in front with little or no warning.

The trillions of pounds spent on commercial advertising, along with the now-famous concept of *Nudge*, highlighted by Richard H Thaler and Cass R Sunstein, and the above-mentioned placebo and nocebo effect, all testify to the negative effects of forms of leadership not intelligently mapped to their effective function.

Primitive emotions readily hijack our conversations. Despite superficial civility, the aggressive body language, facial expressions and verbal patterns familiar to our ancient ancestors still trigger the same instinctive responses they always have.

Given the demonstrable evolutionary heritage of dominance behaviours, it is not surprising that traditional leadership functions emphasise command-and-control behaviours, body language, and speech, especially where the context benefits from strong, centralised leadership. They *can* be effective in the environments described above, and wherever the leader enjoys some elevated vantage point overseeing the full field of endeavour, whether it be a workface, battlefront or sport. In such cases, the workforce is not expected to exercise any autonomy or initiative, but simply to respond obediently to the commander.

Despite readily available, evidence-based research, a blind eye continues to be turned in many organisational settings to the persistence of counter-productive, primitive 'dominance' behaviours.

---

[1] 'Primal Leadership: Unleashing the Power of Emotional Intelligence' (2013) D. Goleman R. Boyatzis. A. McKee.

Evolving project leadership

Ignoring these behaviours means their effect is largely hidden, rarely brought into the open, or discussed. Meanwhile, selection from junior management to senior executive favours traditional, strongly masculine behaviours[2]. In interview or job selection, physical characteristics such as height, a deep voice and even a strong jaw-line, have all been shown to carry a disproportionate weight.

Paradoxically, these negative characteristics do attract those all too keen to escape responsibility by passing it on to another.

Psychologists refer to this tendency as co-dependency. A mature project leadership approach to this reluctance to take ownership will not exploit, as those inclined to dominant behaviours might, but rather coach to encourage greater self-confidence, and hence willingness to take responsibility.

Where project leadership is positively supported by organisational processes, encouraging self-development instead of actively inhibiting personal growth, then examples of unrealised potential will reduce significantly.

The role of the organisation in supporting project leadership

Senior management and Human Resources departments can both play their part in supporting and literally promoting traditional, stereotypical command-and-control leadership behaviours.

Ask individuals two metres tall, of deep voice, or even square of jaw what weight such characteristics might carry in selection or interview, and denial will likely be prompt and adamant, or even disdainful. Nonetheless, the statistics are undeniable. Those characteristics really do make a difference.

Equally clearly, promoting anyone with such traits or characteristics, however charismatic, says nothing at all about their ability to *lead* effectively – not, certainly, in today's complex project delivery environments. After all, in project delivery, the ability to render the team compliant by force of charisma will do nothing to facilitate agile, empowered team responses to complexity.

---

[2] https://www.researchgate.net/publication/256015132_Voice_Pitch_and_the_Labor_Market_Success_of_Male_Chief_Executive_Officers https://research-repository.st-andrews.ac.uk/bitstream/handle/10023/4440/DanielRe_PhDThesis.pdf?sequence=3&isAllowed=y

Human Resources departments can therefore play a huge part in consciously taking account of these factors, and taking care to select against such outdated and actively counter-productive criteria in selection.

The project management capability (PMC) function or project management office (PMO), must also play its part in reviewing the personal attributes necessary and to be sought in recruitment and selection for effective project leadership.

By now it is clear that the advocacy of behaviours traditionally sought in team exercise scenarios where one individual 'dominates' the group, and thereby signals leadership potential, is redundant. Rather, the focus for project leadership selection should now be on identifying the low-profile 'enabler and facilitator', fostering the collective to release the power of collaboration.

No longer should project leadership selection through group exercises seek out the one who attempts or succeeds in controlling others or asserting themselves by force of will. Rather, the key characteristics to be sought are an ability to solicit engagement by all participants in the group – acting as a magnet and glue, encouraging, fostering and nurturing the best contribution from all and the emergence of a collective identity.

Supporting this growing awareness, a surge in literature based around the work of Daniel Goleman promotes emotional intelligence (EI) and the emotion-moderating, calming benefits of mindfulness. They also offer measures established to parallel the well-known metric of IQ; the intelligence quotient. The new metric, known as the EQ, or emotional intelligence quotient, calibrates a spectrum of emotional intelligence from zero to high functional and emotional empathy. At the zero end of the spectrum, the psychopathic narcissist operates without empathy or conscience, while the functional narcissist may predict and exploit the effects of their behaviours on others without remorse.

As will be shown, the absence of empathy and the necessary project leadership skills they enable means that while many have gravitated towards project management attracted by the authority to dominate others that traditional C&C confers, their disposition is now counter-productive and a liability to all. For projectised organisations and HR departments alike, this presents a formidable challenge, for, as with the 'Peter Principle', by which people are promoted to the level of their incompetence, the results of actively selecting in favour of traits and characteristics now shown to be of negative effect must be addressed.

Humankind: A Hopeful History (2020) by Rutger Bregman parallels these findings by overturning traditional narratives suggesting that individuals left alone always revert to selfish behaviours, as epitomised in William Golding's *Lord of the Flies* (1954), where children left alone on a desert island revert to bestial behaviours. In fact, Bregman now unearths extensive evidence showing that, on the contrary, the evolution-favoured tendency is actually towards collaboration.

In medicine, too, the body's innate immune and recovery capacity is now understood to be far more effective than active intervention.

What these examples all show is that in organisations, individuals and even biology, where such complex systems are in place, it is far more effective to nurture the existing positive dynamics and forces rather than deploying traditional, uni-dimensional and linear approaches.

The project leader imposing command and control in delivery environments marked by emergent complexity and distributed delivery teams is doomed to failure.

The increasing awareness of the cost of C&C is prompting a diminishing respect and tolerance of traditional, testosterone-fuelled male dominance behaviours. This growing awareness of EQ through stories exemplifying the benefits of its practice, increasingly throw into sharp relief emotionally *un*-intelligent language and behaviours. Meanwhile, apprentices and students representing the next generation of project management have been observed looking askance at what are increasingly recognised as outdated notions of leadership.

Movements in favour of equality, diversity and mental health all now contribute to greater expectations, that project leaders should show due consideration of others in these particular areas, and that, more generally, those seeking to positively influence and recruit willing followers should do the same.

Of all the COVID-19 pandemic's diverse impacts on organisational working practices, that of working from home (WFH), has been singular and profound, in ways yet to be fully realised. Among them, it seems readily apparent that diminished physical visibility of reportees means traditional eyes-on management becomes increasingly impotent, while those inspiring loyalty truly benefit.

Removing the mantle of respectability conferred on some behaviours by the *label* of leadership now exposes them for what they are, and the damage they can do.

One striking example of a behaviour long associated with, and seen as central to or characteristic of leadership is that of 'assertiveness'. An online search for videos or companies offering assertiveness training offers literally millions of results. Many a training provider eagerly promotes and characterises assertiveness as a core component of leadership. Equally, non-assertiveness is portrayed as synonymous with 'weakness'. Assertiveness is presented as a pre-requisite for leadership. To lack assertiveness, it is suggested, is to be ineffectual, and by association, impotent as a leader.

The single most pressing need and most effective enhancement in project delivery

The move from traditional project management to project leadership is a once-in-a-generation paradigm shift in project delivery. It is of a significance and effect never before seen in the profession and, unless it is addressed, the problems which ignorance, denial or a failure to act will give rise to will only increase.

Since the project management capability function exists to enable and maximise team effectiveness through empowerment and collaborative working, it arguably has no more pressing challenge or priority.

In project management terminology, the difference in 'scope' between 'leadership', and 'project leadership' is immense.

The challenge faced by every project management capability function to promote empowered, collaborative project leadership is indeed formidable. Transformation initiatives inevitably meet with resistance. But in this case it is especially difficult, for its very focus is those who would normally lead it: project managers. Some will recognise and embrace the need for change; others will not.

Transformation of project management through project leadership is essential to the very survival of the profession as a credible enabler in delivery

It is not an optional extra. The discipline of project management has never faced a more compelling need to transform, for the very function of project management has itself been reframed. The case has altered; the field of play, the rules, the very game itself have changed. There is not one ball in play, but many. The project manager is not directing a linear path to delivery. For this reason, traditional schedules and Gantt charts fail to convey the system-dynamic of many dependencies and interdependencies manifesting as delivery complexity. That which can be planned for, and anticipated, is invariably overtaken by emergent challenges and unavoidable changes imposed by working environments less predicable than ever before.

The pressure on project managers to deliver in these conditions without adequate support or relevant training is immense. The lack of clarity around the form effective leadership should take is reflected in misleading key performance indicators and measures of assessment.

Measures of project delivery performance do not necessarily correlate with competence in project leadership. Adopting the model for project leadership development that follows will both offer a route to competence and also provide measures that can be practically assessed and calibrated.

Self-help books generally find a ready audience in those willing to undergo some personal 'transformation' and evolution. But a real problem in the realisation of project leadership is inevitable for those who are unwilling to relinquish their traditional outlook and their command-and-control behaviours.

Again, just as the selection and appointment of candidates into roles necessitating project leadership behaviours must be recalibrated to reflect the more facilitative and influencing competences required, so too the organisational leadership must play a key part in transforming the existing population of project professionals in order to select against negative behaviours.

Obstacles to change – the executive challenge

While encouraging a transformation in project delivery favouring the benefits of informed project leadership, the organisation faces the simultaneous challenge of fostering and nurturing the new community of project leaders, while tackling the embedded culture and individuals unwilling or unable to embrace the demands and so realise the power of project leadership.

The roots of any individual's disposition, their ability to develop and grow, begin in childhood and become established through adolescence and into adulthood. Maslow's 'Hierarchy of Needs' emphasised the developmental importance of self-esteem on the route to personal self-actualisation. On this path, esteem-from-others forms a valued component. Psychology and psychiatry offer many insights into this period of growth, and although the language and concepts may not be familiar in project management, understanding the behaviours they prompt offers key insights for the development of fit-for-purpose project leadership.

Across the full diversity of human cultures, an absence of self-esteem in the early formative years can inhibit growth through childhood and beyond.

In later life, if the formation of self-esteem and identity or 'self-construal' has been hampered, this can also result in deficits in empathy. This lack can in turn be complemented by a disposition and behaviours *over*-compensating for inner insecurities. These may present in a project manager in over-confidence and narcissistic, ego-centric behaviours. It is inevitable that some have inherent limits to personal growth. This includes an inability to develop project leadership competence with emotional maturity and emotional intelligence and empathy. The same applies to the soft skills depending on them.

There is no known guaranteed fix, 'cure' or 'remedy' for those with a deficit in empathy. Unlike interventions of medical science, whether focused on disease or physical injury, there are no bio-markers; nothing visible to the naked eye or through a microscope that psychology or psychiatry can direct attention to in order to 'correct' such a deficit. For some, a growth and transition to interdependence is simply not viable, given today's limited scientific understanding in this area.

The significance and challenge of this for organisations where those with such a deficit are resident is obvious and far reaching. It is rarely acknowledged, never mind addressed. For centuries, or even millennia, traditional portrayals of heroic or charismatic leadership lent licence to those most personally insecure, projecting over-confidence and assertiveness, rather than empathy, or practising emotional intelligence. If anything, putting the needs of the team, or those in it, first would be dismissed as a sign of weakness in their regime and form of leadership.

For many organisations with a project management function, the negative, counter-productive impact of project managers' assertive behaviours on performance is rarely even recognised, never mind acknowledged or addressed. Where there are *real* casualties, they are dismissed as some inherent weakness in the victim, rather than a direct result of ill-considered and tacitly or explicitly condoned C&C behaviours.

Few employees survive a career without, at some point, having been on the receiving end of behaviours that humiliate, or in some sense demean. Threatening behaviours, under the guise of assertiveness, effect the very opposite of the function the project leader is fundamentally called upon to fulfil. Despite this demonstrable and widely scientifically evidenced fact, behaviours such as *'calling a subordinate to account'* are still widely accepted, promoted and unquestioned as both legitimate and necessary.

Consider a situation where, in your line manager's estimation, your performance has fallen short. They take you to one side and 'call you to account'. The stern expression, the assertive body language and tone of voice dominate your perception, triggering ancient, physical fight-or-flight reactions.

When they show no interest or desire to understand *your* intent, or the effort you have made, how well disposed are you to see *them* as a 'leader', inspiring loyalty, rather than a demeaning obedience?

On the other hand, imagine a similar occasion where you are invited to sit, not face-to-face, but at an angle to each other. You are invited to explain the course of events from your own perspective.

Which of these two approaches fosters a perception of being 'led'? Which inspires the sense of another communicating due respect, appreciating and taking on board your view and perspective?

Which would *you* see as a 'leader'?

The multi-dimensional, cumulative negative effect of the first kind of behaviour continues to be a very real problem. Increasingly, however, millennials will vote with their feet when faced with them. The costs in terms of project delivery are multi-dimensional, because they are repercussive and team members may move to their next project in some sense demotivated or even scarred. The example set by a poor project manager may even be copied by some who know no better.

The global analytics and advisory firm, Gallup, has discovered that 75 per cent of people leave their jobs because of their line manager. The immediate cost to their company includes overheads in replacement and lost productivity. But imagine what this amounts to when the loss in team effectiveness that this implies is also taken into account? Consider the impact as individuals find any attempt to develop and realise their potential frustrated, or attempts to collaborate portrayed as undermining the manager's authority.

Faced with such a prospect, senior management might decide to take action; to identify managers actively inhibiting collaborative potential. To gain feedback on the status of the project management community, they might require all managers to undertake mandatory, externally moderated 360° assessments. Accurate results would indeed help to identify teams benefiting from some level of assessment and intervention. But due account would have to be taken of the likely response of those with good reason to fear the results.

Not only would management encounter direct resistance to implementation, but also subsequent denial of the feedback generated by the team, peers and management, perhaps suggesting their team is incompetent or 'out to get them'. The team might understandably be reluctant to speak out, given that they might still be working under their manager, labouring under loss of face and associated resentment.

Any initiative intended to assess soft skills, empathy, emotional intelligence and the like, always presents as a real threat to those ambitious for power. Preoccupied with self-promotion, seeking increasing control over others, their typical dismissal of these skills would be that they are un-masculine; signalling weakness. Still more challenging for them, the development of insight into self necessitates a conscious, deliberate examination of their personal motives. And as those motives are likely to be that they are over-compensating for personal insecurities, the threat their exposure presents will simply drive their resistance higher.

At an organisational level, there is one ready indicator of those whose behaviours are primarily self-promotional. Their efforts and the work-time they deploy in seeking self-promotion are *observable,* and far exceed that exercised in actual project delivery.

It is an ancient cross-species technique: those lower in the pecking order seek to ingratiate themselves to the leader. ever seeking to establish alliances with those perceived to hold more power. Those lower in any hierarchy or social group, some with narcissistic or sociopathic tendencies, actively engineer opportunities to rub shoulders with the leader. They then seek to influence others around them by 'being seen' from below as a friend of those above, while from above, as a willing ally. In today's organisations such behaviours are as prevalent as ever.

Progressive and mature senior management and leadership are becoming wise to the costs of vaulting ambition for the promotion of self over others, which inevitably places self-interest ahead of the team, the organisation or indeed, anyone or anything else, including principles. They are becoming aware that it invariably comes at a cost to others, the organisation, its stakeholders and all working for them. They recognise such approaches, overtures, and attempts at influence for exactly what they are.

A major challenge now faced at the level of senior organisational management is therefore to establish an organisational culture that does *not* reward or encourage such self-promoting behaviours, but instead recognises those promoting collaboration, excellence and the benefit to all. They must discern the fundamental difference in outlook between those keen to 'take charge', as compared with those more concerned to 'take care' of the team, and the compelling difference such empowering delivery can make.

Stories are a powerful way to change perspectives, offering the reader an opportunity to see their world through different eyes. This in turn enriches insight and understanding. A graphic illustration of how counter-productive traditional, assertive leadership behaviours can be is provided in the following account. Most will recall similar experiences. Although set in the context of a team-building exercise rather than the workplace, it graphically characterises many project delivery environments where collaborative working is undermined by traditional command-and-control behaviours.

Assertiveness costs: a challenge to traditional leadership

The following narrative is based on real events. It brings the reader to a moment capturing, with some immediacy, what happens when traditional leadership behaviours are enacted in a context for which they are not fit. Although not a project delivery environment per se, the lessons about leadership in this example apply in every human arena where the title or banner of leadership is more often than not an excuse for behaviours that are evidently anything but.

> *The venue is a facilitated off-site event attended by an 'observer' who becomes aware that more is going on than might be immediately obvious. Forty attendees are present, and the manner of their arrival and introduction duly observed.*
>
> *Close attention is paid to each as they speak, for they are all strangers to the observer, who becomes aware that four attendees present themselves in a particularly 'assertive' manner. Some of their behaviour seems a little artificial or even contrived – it is as if they adopt postures and speak in ways encouraging others' subordination and subservience.*
>
> *Their body language, tone, and manner of speaking all contrive to communicate an assumption of their own authority and importance. Mere opinions are communicated with a finality that discourages question. The gravity of their superior view on any subject is emphasised by drawn-out phrases and long, 'meaningful' pauses, a raising of the chin or lowering of the head, or else intense staring from beneath lowered brows. The expression of others spoken to in this way appears guardedly neutral, and eye contact with the speaker is noted as minimal, or lowered when they become the object of the speaker's gaze.*
>
> *It is recalled by the observer that before the facilitator arrived, one of the men made, what seemed at the time, a very deliberate attempt to emphasise*

his authority and superiority by putting his feet upon another chair, while clasping hands behind his head. His comments seemed designed to accentuate the lower status of those around him.

Following introductions by all, the facilitator gives a talk covering various aspects of teamwork before inviting everyone to split into groups using several distributed flip-charts to discuss a variety of subjects. Unexpectedly, then, he points to one where the place of 'assertiveness' in project management and leadership is to be discussed.

The observer notes this, as everyone stands and heads to their chosen corner. The observer then focuses on those gravitating to the assertiveness flipchart where, it is noted with some surprise, all four identified as 'assertive' are gathered. There they all express their certainty that this quality and its behaviours are central to their ability to take charge and get things done. Its absence signals weakness, and actively invites disrespect from others. Leadership without assertiveness is clearly unthinkable.

Later in the day, the facilitator leaves the room before returning with several large canvas bags, each of which, he explains, holds a selection of unmarked planks of varying length with slots cut in various places. A single A4 drawing is provided, showing the completed assemblage. The teams are told to invite the timekeeper with stopwatch when the manner of construction has been agreed and practised. The winning group will be those who can create the 'bookshelf' layout in the shortest time from a standing pile of planks.

The observer joins a group including one of the noted four and, keen to watch how the task unfolds, they hold up the A4 sheet for all to see. Immediately the group enthusiastically engages with the task and confers; discussing ways to assemble the planks.

Throughout the discussion, the observer sustains low-key observation on the one among them who advocates assertiveness. Surreptitiously, they glance from left to right and back again; clearly unsettled by not being the centre of attention, not deferred to, or asked for guidance, and discomfited by the variety and number of solutions coming from all sides and team members.

Suddenly, and in a very measured and deliberate way, they reach out and, gripping the top of the sheet, firmly pull it from the observer's hands towards themselves. With a deep voice cutting through all others, they start telling people what to do; some taking the planks and dividing them up, others to match planks to the picture and label them, and so on.

Evolving project leadership

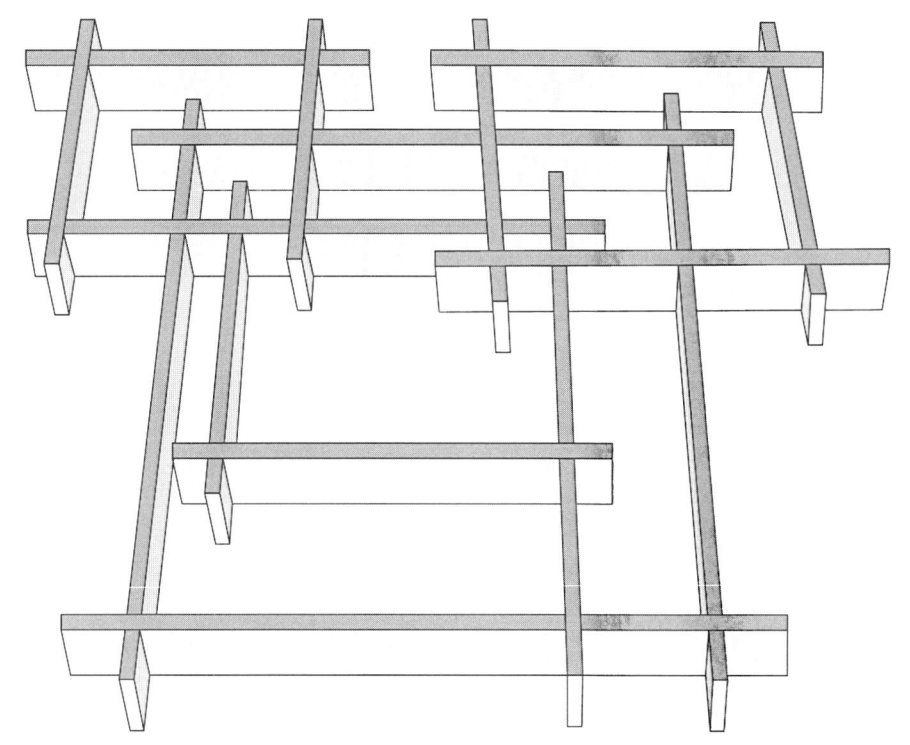

Figure 2 The bookshelf problem

    In this moment, it is as though two commentaries are running simultaneously for the observer. In one, white lab-coated observers with clipboards are nudging each other while exclaiming in hushed tones what a splendid example of assertive leadership they have seen as that person 'took control' of both the situation and the group.

    The other commentary is in stark contrast to the first. The observer is aware they have just witnessed, first-hand, an enthusiastic team working effectively and enthusiastically. Now not only was the group synergy effectively 'lobotomised', but members have been simultaneously alienated, disenfranchised, and effectively antagonised. Eyes were rolling upwards, lips pursed, bodies and eyes turning away. The observer stands back as team members follow the leader's directions. It is clear they have no alternative but to comply, or else challenge this self-appointed, assertive leader and risk being branded as 'disruptive' or, ironically, 'not a team player'.

> *Some time later they call the timekeeper, and, on their word, stopwatch started, each pulls labelled planks from the pile, assembling them according to the now labelled A4 sheet. In what seems a reasonable time the planks are assembled, and the observer notes, and is moderately impressed to see, that despite what seemed like an ill-fated effort, the planks were assembled in a little over 20 seconds.*

How often are many endeavours and projects completed and taken over the line, credited to strong, directive leadership? Sometimes the leader's behaviours are openly accepted to be less than inspiring, but they 'got the job done', and, it is suggested, or at least implied, that others would not have done.

At this point, and on reflection, one might understandably relinquish any misgivings, for there is no denying that the task was successfully completed. Then the facilitator re-enters the room, inviting all to "come next door, where another group have adopted a different approach – you may find this interesting."

> *Passing through the door, everyone spreads out along the edges of the room, as in the centre another group all take up positions in a circle around the pile of planks before dropping on to one knee, facing inwards. The timekeeper steps forwards and calling, "three, two, one, go!" starts the stopwatch.*
>
> *Immediately, team member 'number one' reaches out and takes several planks, then places them outside the circle where, now 'world expert' in his own particular assemblage, he proceeds to assemble them. His move is followed in rapid succession by all the other team members, each doing the same until the pile is gone.*
>
> *Each individual assemblage completed in moments, they all turn their bodies to face inwards, ready to contribute to the group. As soon as 'number one' is ready, they place their assemblage within the circle, followed by each connecting their assemblage to the whole. As the final assemblage is connected, all shout "Stop!" and the stopwatch is halted. The timekeeper turns to all assembled and declares the result: "Six seconds"!*

This story shows how dominant behaviours can limit the expression of both individual and team potential, and then make matters even worse by disenfranchising, alienating and antagonising the team. As will be shown shortly, the SCARF Model highlights these costs to great effect. Their significance has far-reaching consequences in any balanced consideration of the behaviours most appropriate 'with the end in mind', in project leadership.

The psychological impact on others when command and control is imposed, when they feel bound to avert their eyes and lower their heads in submission, is rarely noted. People will conceal their true feelings in the moment, despite the fire of real and long-lasting resentment that has been lit. For many leaders who depend on the authority of their position, the sentiments or feelings of their 'obliged followers' are of little or no interest. They are not concerned, nor are they ever called to account, for the 'opportunity cost' their attitudes and behaviours incur. What is hidden from sight, as in the above example, is the unaccounted-for costs arising from unrealised individual and group potential and all the associated benefits that are lost.

Many behaviours, like assertiveness, that have so long been associated with 'leadership', on closer examination turn out actually to be less productive, or even counter-productive. This is especially true where C&C dominance behaviours are deployed in environments that actually need and benefit from empowered teams of diverse expertise. This is of course of immense significance for project leadership, where such environments are increasingly typical of project delivery.

Fortunately, understanding and appreciating the evolutionary underpinnings of assertiveness, and its historical association with traditional leadership behaviours, offers empowering insights for the present day. Appreciating how many precursors of common human dominance behaviours can be observed mirrored in animals, especially primates, is the first step towards understanding that these behaviours might possibly not be appropriate or effective in contemporary human environments and contexts.

Indeed, while the very function of traditional leadership behaviours is to elevate the leader *over* others: constituting a licence to direct, command and control, it is now possible to take a step back and ask if such behaviours are compatible with project leadership.

The *APM Body of Knowledge 7th edition* characterises leadership by reference to 'influence' and 'inspiration', rather than domination.

In exploring the APM definition of leadership it is insightful to consider the adjectives used, and compare them with those of traditional command-and-control leadership:

- *"Providing **vision, direction, feedback** and **support** so people can do their best work."*

The changing face of project leadership

- *"The ability to establish **vision** and **direction**, to **influence** and **align** others towards a common purpose, and to **empower** and **inspire** people to achieve success."*

APM Body of Knowledge 7th edition

Those advocating traditional leadership behaviours might declare that an assertive alpha male does indeed *"establish vision and direction, thereby influencing and aligning others"*. But for the avoidance of doubt, establishing and aligning are not, as many traditional leadership behaviours are, about establishing vision by imposing it on others, nor is it about aligning others in a forceful way, from the outside in.

These requirements quite explicitly include '*how*' this *vision* and *direction* is to be communicated and achieved. E*mpowering* and *inspiring* followers requires, not a one-way external imposition of authority and power, through command and control or domination, but a more reciprocal, two-way relationship, characterised by mutual respect. Coaching, at the heart of project leadership, then results in an empowerment working from the inside out; inspiring mutual commitment and the loyalty characteristic of both leaders and followers.

This paradigm of project leadership is also reflected in the *APM Body of Knowledge 7th edition* where it is made clear both how and why stakeholder *engagement* supersedes stakeholder *management*.

Under Section 3, People and behaviours, it states:

> '*Stakeholders, those individuals or groups who have an interest or role in the project, programme or portfolio, or are impacted by it, cannot by definition be 'managed'. Rather, depending on their stake, and the role that ideally, they will play, the people involved in the work, from sponsor to team member, are part of the effort to keep the stakeholder appropriately **engaged** and **influenced** to do the right thing.*'

Working collaboratively requires the project leader, along with all stakeholders, to behave in a way that reflects a 'desire to meet the needs of others', balanced against a 'desire to meet personal needs' (*APM Body of Knowledge 7th edition*). This means that the project leader must demonstrate by their words and deeds appropriate regard for the needs of others if they are to achieve collaboration. This in turn necessarily precludes the imposition of command-and-control behaviours.

Evolving project leadership

Traditionally, to those attracted to assertive leadership behaviours, having the power to make and impose decisions on others communicates superior status. For this, they seize upon any and every opportunity to demonstrate and reinforce their position-power and status. As such, the 'licence' to practise such behaviours has been zealously guarded by those for whom leadership is synonymous with command-and-control behaviours. The autonomy of others is actively managed and minimised to avoid the emergence of any challenges threatening the imposed status quo. These behaviours reflect no regard for the interests or needs of any but the leader.

We have now placed various portrayals of leadership in a deep historical context. Reaching far into evolutionary history, such portrayals illustrate the origins and efficacy of behaviours geared primarily towards survival in a variety of environments starkly at odds with those faced by project leadership today.

The SCARF Model: from the elevation of the leader to release of potential

In 2008 David Rock published SCARF: a brain-based model for collaborating with and influencing others' (*NeuroLeadership Journal*).

Rock identified perceptions fundamental in triggering the ancient evolutionary reactions of 'fight or flight': to 'approach' and engage with, or 'avoid' and flee. The model is especially powerful in bringing home the adverse impact on those who feel under threat.

Each element of the SCARF Model captures a perceptual filter that is immensely sensitive to anything in the environment that is seen to threaten or undermine them.

- **S**tatus – Perceived security of position relative to others.
- **C**ertainty – Perception of a predictable and navigable outlook.
- **A**utonomy – Perceived freedom to act and respond without undue constraint.
- **R**elatedness – Perceived to be accepted and respected in social group.
- **F**airness – Perceived equity of treatment with others in group.

This model presents the leader traditionally concerned with asserting authority through command-and-control behaviours with an uncomfortable truth: that behaviours threatening any of these perceptions are not only ineffective, but counter-productive.

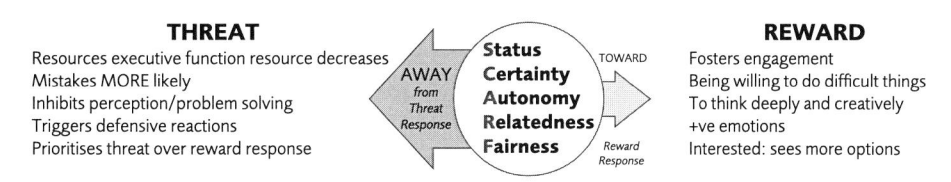

THREAT
Resources executive function resource decreases
Mistakes MORE likely
Inhibits perception/problem solving
Triggers defensive reactions
Prioritises threat over reward response

AWAY from Threat Response

Status
Certainty
Autonomy
Relatedness
Fairness

TOWARD

Reward Response

REWARD
Fosters engagement
Being willing to do difficult things
To think deeply and creatively
+ve emotions
Interested: sees more options

The enteric nervous system in humans consists of some 500 million neurons…
'The Strange Order of Things' (2019) Antonio Damasio

Gut feelings arbitrate, moderate, and determine perceptions: influence what we do and fail to 'see'.

More often than we recognise, disposition governs perception.

Often gut feelings precede the reasons we think up for them.

Figure 3 The SCARF Model of social threats and rewards David Rock

This, then, is one of the fundamental drivers that differentiate traditional heroic, or command-and-control leadership behaviours, from those that are effective in the specific context of project leadership, especially over time.

This latter consideration recognises that directing does have a place in extreme or proscribed 'battlefield' circumstances, or more mundanely in the 'unconscious incompetence' stage of learning to operate safely and effectively in a role or new working environment.

In addition to the negative effect of command-and-control behaviours over time, in what follows, a closer consideration as to the nature of the project delivery environment will further inform and endorse the need for a significant shift away from a traditional command-and-control approach to project leadership, and stakeholder engagement in particular.

No follower = No leadership

The title is *conferred* and *bestowed* by those inspired to team membership i.e. *There is no leader without a willing follower.*

Narratives and stories claiming or implying a portrayal of leadership often ignore this basic requirement. If an individual is commanded and controlled, obliged to 'obey without question', this is not leadership, but a form of tyranny.

This holds as true for project leadership as for any leader, whether on the battlefield, in government, or in any other sphere of human activity. So, why do followers follow? After all, anyone claiming leadership for themselves whose leadership is not endorsed by willing followership must, by definition, be deluded.

Evolving project leadership

For some in positions of power, a sense of 'entitlement' is assumed – that they have acquired a 'right' to their position. This confers a licence to treat or speak to others in ways that would be judged presumptuous in other, or social, settings. Equally, they would deem it presumptuous or even insubordinate to speak to the leader as they do to others.

Those strongly advocating traditional, command-and-control assertive behaviours towards subordinates are not usually well disposed to being treated in the same manner as they feel entitled to treat others. How likely are those advocating assertiveness to accept being so treated or 'led' themselves?

For some, an entitlement to treat others as *they* would *not* be treated is what entices them to management and leadership in the first place. This is a key characteristic of those who depend on esteem-from-others and should be actively selected against in the assessment of effective project leadership behaviours.

This demand for respect *by* the leader is all too often not reciprocated towards the follower. In such circumstances, team member compliance might be achieved on the basis of the self-declared leader's position or job title, but this is a 'transactional relationship' more characteristic of management than leadership.

This divergence highlights the difference between project management and true project leadership.

The kind of un-empathic behaviours described above are demonstrably to the detriment of their target, but they also harm the manager and the project, since the loyalty and commitment bestowed on them by the team member will likely be correspondingly undermined and diminished.

Transactional command-and-control behaviours evidence a telling characteristic found also in totalitarian regimes. There, too, those obliged to follow must comply without question or challenge. Significantly, the *flow of information* from leader to obliged-followers is predominantly one-way.

Historically, unitary information that flows one-way from leaders to subordinates has had bad consequences for the leader. The suppression of both reciprocal communication and empowerment of stakeholders in decision making undermines the resilience and cumulative intelligence necessary to project delivery in increasingly complex environments. Similarly, a reluctance to challenge or query has had catastrophic consequences – think of Chernobyl, or the Challenger and Columbia NASA missions.

Significantly, the contemporary project delivery environment is increasingly characterised by a fundamentally different dynamic from those in the past, and leadership behaviours perhaps effective elsewhere are increasingly not fit for purpose.

The changing face of project leadership

Within living memory, a project manager with expertise in engineering or civil engineering could competently sustain direct control across the entire project. Today, information and data flow between diverse and multiple workfaces that may be either physical or digital, and the rate of decision making within projects, has risen exponentially both in volume and required expertise. This means that a greater level of diversely devolved delegation is required across organisations and at multiple levels within each.

In such project delivery environments, it is immediately clear that the team member, as 'follower', is in a fundamentally different role from that found where obedience to predominantly one-way direction from a leader might be effective.

The devolved and cascaded decision making necessary in complex, multi-disciplinary and cross-organisational boundary delivery, as embedded in the recent emergence of 'lean' and 'agile', is now fast becoming the norm within waterfall delivery environments. It may also be the case that these different approaches can be found deployed within the same project at different stages of the life cycle.

There are many reasons individuals give up personal autonomy in respect for a leader. In extreme cases, some even sacrifice their live, or bestow 'leadership' on those for whom their welfare may be a secondary, or non-existent, consideration. Such leadership will always be found in cults, religions, nation states, and far more widely; wherever those concerned with self-promotion and self-aggrandisement flourish. Human dispositions towards leadership in all its forms vary widely, and it is certainly true that for some there is an inclination towards a form of co-dependency which means they are readily exploited by those seeking what psychologists call 'narcissistic supply'.

In developing project leadership at the organisational level, therefore, it is important to take due account of the need to nurture and foster the progression of those of such a disposition away from the need for 'direction', such that, through coaching and mentoring, they too can grow to take ownership in delegation rather than being dependent on others.

Project leaders must nurture relationships, not of exploitation or direction, but their very opposite; a leadership encouraging the realisation of individual potential along the Hersey Blanchard 'Growth curve' from direction, to ownership and delegation, so empowered to contribute fully in collaborative working. Sir John Whitmore referred to this as 'co-creation', collaboration at a level where a team "is aware it is greater than the sum of its parts".[1]

---

[1] Sir John Whitmore *'Coaching for Performance the Principles and Practice of Leadership'* (2017 5th edition)

Evolving project leadership

History readily provides many classic situations where strongly assertive leadership served to bring many homogenously skilled workers or soldiers together to 'act as one', in a concerted effort. Today, however, it is increasingly evident that project leadership brings together disparate, widely-skilled teams much as an orchestra conductor must co-ordinate diverse instruments contributing to a symphony.

Beyond facilitating the immediate project delivery team, the project leader must extend their influence to many stakeholders who may be crucial to delivery, but over whom the project manager has no line management authority whatsoever.

A project manager deploying traditional leadership behaviours and 'telling' a stakeholder what to do is unlikely to command or elicit respect – quite the opposite, in fact. Such an approach not only alienates and antagonises but, where the stakeholder is a key gatekeeper, may trigger indignation and resentment that could significantly impede delivery. Such behaviours signal to stakeholders that their own interests are of no concern to the project manager.

As the *APM Body of Knowledge 7th edition* makes clear, there is an ever-increasing awareness and recognition that since stakeholders cannot, by definition, be 'managed', the responsibility of the project leader is to engage and influence them so that *they* engage with the project. This engagement is not a case of the project manager 'engaging' *with* the stakeholder as a galleon might turn broadside to 'engage' with the enemy. Rather, it demands the project leader's wit, ability and competence in securing a level of effective rapport. That is fundamental if the project leader is to ensure a given stakeholder will in return wish to become engaged with the project.

Many schools of leadership now compete for attention and commercial support. Given the above, it is not surprising that many traditional stereotypes of leadership behaviour persist, not least because in many situations they have an effect in the same way that ancient alpha-male dominance behaviours did. Where those behaviours are promoted, of course there is little discussion of the repercussive effects of such behaviours in generating resentment and the scourge they represent in inhibiting and handicapping individual and group potential.

In the field of literature, too, books on leadership abound. Here again, leadership qualities are ascribed to selfish tyrants, dictators, saints and sporting heroes, warriors and Nobel Peace Prize winners. Behaviours are described that present immediate and visceral emotional responses as the hero takes charge and saves the day. Here, too, there is little consideration for the effect of such behaviours on the follower, other than immediate and at least apparent obedience and compliance. Given the possibility, as outlined above, that in many cases the

The changing face of project leadership

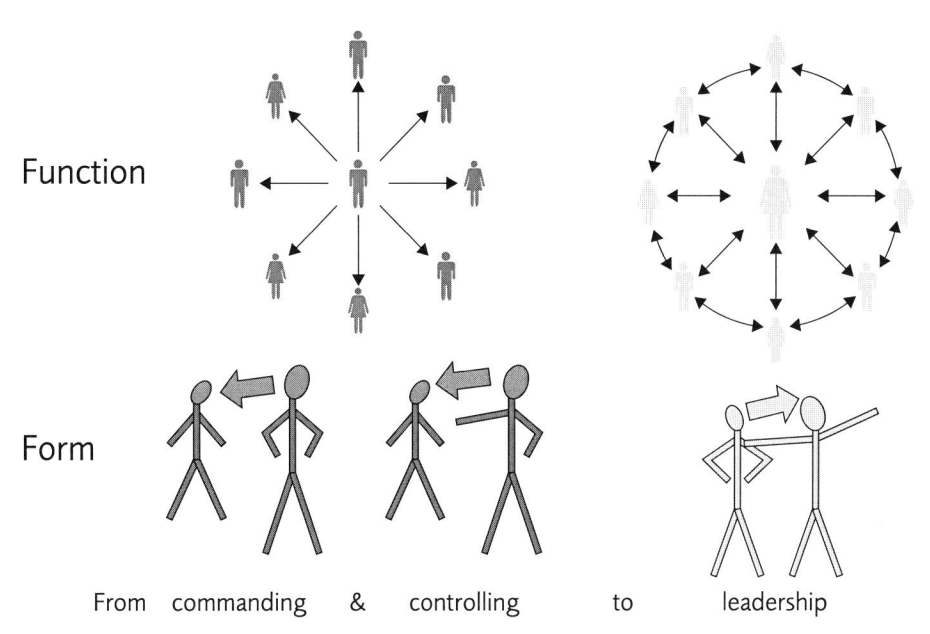

Function

Form

From commanding & controlling to leadership

Figure 4 Leadership function and form

emergence of individual potential, and therefore enhanced group potential, has been ignored or avoided, there is good reason to pause and take stock.

Where leadership behaviours are promoted, then, without due attention to the kind of relationship they create, and whether their effect on the follower is demonstrably appropriate to the context, they may well not be fit for purpose.

Writing about leadership usually focuses on what the aspiring leader should do; how *they* should behave and 'act'. The focus is on the leader's behaviour. As a result, little attention is given to the relationship with the team member, or the nature of leadership characteristics fit-for-purpose for a given context.

Furthermore, when it comes to 'acting out' such behaviours, some coaches encourage aspiring leaders to 'fake it till you make it'. Similarly, a simultaneously humorous and breath-taking old adage suggests: 'Authenticity is the most important quality for a leader today. Fake that and you've got it made!' Both approaches might have the merit of establishing a leader-follower relationship but, as in any relationship, appearances will only carry one so far. The energy demanded of those obliged to maintain appearances, like covering up lies, invariably increases with time, so eventually inhibiting the ability to perform. Meanwhile, those with an authentic commitment to the wellbeing of the team secure cumulative trust and rapport, and hence excel.

Teams and their members follow leaders who inspire, and merit the title bestowed

What must project leaders do in order to merit the title of project leader as bestowed by the team? In books and training on the subject of leadership there is a preoccupation with leadership behaviours to the exclusion of their purpose in terms of effect on the follower, and the end to which that effect is intended to be appropriate. This is widespread.

What such an approach also fails to do is take due account of *why* followers follow. If leadership exists only where followers are inspired to follow, then ignoring this central question and how a potential leader might behave and operate is like selling a product with no regard for the end-user's wants or needs. In one sense, the team member is the leader's customer, for a failure to influence and inspire means the 'product' of being able to relate to a leader as such, is not delivered by the would-be leader.

The would-be leader must take due account of the fact that not all customers have the same wants or needs or are motivated in the same way.

Leadership behaviour and communications must be perceived by the potential follower in a way they can relate to.

In the domain of project leadership, with today's more enlightened focus on equality, the leader must also take cognizance of the fact that their team is likely to be made up of people of various and disparate dispositions; individuals embracing various orientations towards gender, being of differing nationality or culture, and holding a mosaic of political or religious beliefs, or none. Taking account of all these factors is a critical step that should inform all the project leader's communications, while both building a collaborative team and securing engaged stakeholders.

But such diversity across the delivery team does not diminish what the project team and project leadership *do* have in common and which crucially defines them. All, regardless of disposition and outlook, are governed by common rules, regulations, national and international laws, all informing, constraining or demanding behaviours in any given business, organisation or corporation. Each may have local processes and administrative structures in place, establishing frameworks and operating environment. In the project delivery environment, these constraints and requirements, in addition, will be specific to a given workface in terms of access, what can or cannot be done, when and how. They drive a set of common behaviours ensuring compliance in the management and practice of health and safety, risk, quality etc.

Success in project delivery will reflect, to a greater or lesser extent, across the entire project team – for they all have a stake in its success. So the project leader should endeavour to ensure each member of the team understands what constitutes success and is aligned to its realisation. To achieve maximum performance, the project manager, as leader, must plan how they will engage and influence team members, both as individuals and as a group. This demands an approach based on keen, unbiased observation and really getting to know the team. This is a world away from mere management, giving unilateral orders, demanding obedience without question. Such a dictatorial style would be likely to mean that the team has no real understanding of *why* something is to be done. And of course, that will result in a workforce that lacks any form of resilience or ability to adapt to changing conditions.

True engagement exists when the leader's investment in time and empathy is reciprocated, such that the follower engages not merely willingly, but knowingly. In other words, the follower becomes fully aware of what they need to do and why; they take ownership and responsibility. To get to this point, a vision needs to have been effectively communicated, so that it is shared. It needs to have meaning and value for the followers, so that, so motivated and informed, they are empowered to play their part in its realisation.

Effectively communicating the vision plays a crucial part in creating the conditions under which a distinguishing characteristic and vital component of the leader-follower relationship can emerge: inspiration. For this to happen, the vision for the project needs to be presented in such a way that the follower finds or recognises within it something vital and meaningful for them personally – so that they wish to adopt it as their own.

This is like the mutual resonance experienced when rapport is achieved. Something is held in common, forming a binding connection. The significance of this in defining what characterises followers in a project team is that it confirms and endorses the view that, as with the clear distinction between project leadership and traditional leadership, there is a distinction to be made between a vision that is fit for purpose and likely to inspire followership across a project team, and that of a more general nature.

Inspiration, like leadership, can manifest itself in many ways, to the point where it is so diffuse as to elude ready or consistent definition. In response to music or a work of art, one person might be inspired to gaze vacantly into space, while another might find their appreciation and orientation to life itself transformed. What characterises inspiration in a project delivery environment, however, is distinctive. It does not manifest itself in either of these 'polar' ways. Rather, it aligns the follower with the larger vision for the project, and motivates them to take ownership of their own personal objectives contributing to its realisation.

This focus on why followers follow, responding to leader behaviours and thereby endorsing the existence of a leader-follower relationship, results in an enhanced appreciation of what, specifically, the project leader must 'do' in a project delivery environment, and so helps determine appropriate behaviours to serve that end.

The *APM Body of Knowledge 7th edition*, p.125, illustrates the leader's role in setting goals for team members and stakeholders that incorporate the vision, direction and momentum required, along with the motivation, support and development that team members will need for their achievement.

While the project's goals, and those of the team members, are external to the individual, the project leader's goal in motivation has an internal focus. It calls for a considered and structured approach to ensure team members' individual goals are communicated to them in a way that is meaningful, such that the follower is inclined to adopt and embrace them as their own.

The process the project leader must adopt is closely related to that of engaging other stakeholders, for they too must be approached in a personalised and focused manner inclining them to alignment with the project's goals.

From all this, it is apparent that approaches to leadership that focus on the adoption of certain external behaviours without relating them to followers' needs and, especially in a project delivery environment, what they expect, are likely to miss the mark.

In building a richer appreciation of what the project leader must do to be accepted in such a context, it is now clear that any attitude towards leadership that emphasises command and control, or telling and directing, evidences a clear and fundamental ignorance and misunderstanding as to the project manager's role as leader.

'Why followers follow' matters. Traditional leadership served to secure trust in the leaders, such that followers would obey them without question. They were inspired to such a level of confidence that they gave up their autonomy to do as they were told, as direct extensions of the leader's will. They adopted the leader's vision as their own. The attraction of such a relationship has, for time immemorial, always been that hard decisions could be deferred to (and blamed on) the leader, so followers could abrogate any personal responsibility. Thus, hard decisions and responsibilities are passed to the leader, and any anxiety arising from unknowns or uncertainties are dispelled by belief in the leader's supreme self-confidence and decisiveness.

Project leadership also requires a level of trust and confidence in the leader, but this relationship, by contrast, is characterised by a *mutuality* of respect often not apparent in accounts of traditional leadership or traditional leadership behaviours. The emphasis is more often on the asserted entitlement of the leader to respect and obedience from the follower. This is a relationship quite at odds with any effective relationship the contemporary project leader should expect with the members of their team.

Project leadership places a strong emphasis on the leader's empowerment of followers, reflecting a far greater degree of delegation than direction.

This shift in and of itself also places on the leader a direct and unambiguous responsibility: to 'lead as they would be led' – to serve in the capacity of coach or mentor as the follower needs, reflecting their stage of personal development.

Understanding this responsibility also serves to ensure that the ability to secure followership is not compromised by acts that erode and undermine the potential of team members. As will become apparent, some traditional behaviours that humiliate one team member can also alienate others.

Chapter 1 Learning outcomes

1. Traditional portrayals of leadership cannot be directly applied to project management.
2. The loss of line authority as delivery teams extend across multiple organisations limits command and control authority. Assertiveness has limited utility.
3. With loss of line authority, the project manager must be able to secure engagement from team members through influence and credible authentic leadership.
4. Delivery teams increasingly populated by highly qualified team members require the project manager's engagement in securing their effective inter-engagement.
5. Leadership represents a mutual, reciprocal relationship.
6. The project leader must recognise and distance themselves from outdated and ineffective behaviours more suited to a battle or sports field.

2

Why command and control is inadequate

Exploring the implications of evolving project delivery *environments*.

Interdependent technology increasingly permeates every facet of project delivery, in turn increasing 'emergent complexity'.

This drives the need for a fundamental reassessment of the function of the project manager: the promotion of leadership over management behaviours.

In light of the global effects of the COVID-19 pandemic, burgeoning climate change and unprecedented species extinctions, it is clearer now than at any time in human history that there is a burning need to review and reflect on the changing nature of project environments and their impact on delivery.

These changes have impacted both project delivery and deliverables in ways that promote the discipline of project leadership as a remedy.

When considering all environmental factors, technology is the first thing to consider – as it now permeates all political, economic, sociological, legal and wider biosphere environments.

Underpinning much of this book, and informing significant changes in emphasis and focus in the *APM Body of Knowledge 7th edition*, are the ongoing revolutions, not simply in technology but in multiple technologies. Technology permeates every facet of delivery, monopolising communications and interconnecting previously isolated deliverables, so driving huge increases in project delivery complexity.

The following section summarises the key elements characterising these changes, as highlighted in *Business Reporter*[1].

---

[1] *Business Reporter* special report, UK 2030, published in the *Sunday Telegraph* July 2017

Evolving project leadership

New technology: Its impact and significance for project management

Under the heading of 'Mapping out the future', *Business Reporter* highlights the following areas impacting on project delivery'. They include:

- *Digital revolution*: Burgeoning AI will pervade society, while physical and mental 'augmentation' may even redefine what it is to be human.
- *Digital impact on construction*: Driven by demand and the realisation of energy efficiencies.
- *Globalisation and virtual teams*: The matrix organisation is supplemented by virtual teams, so raising the bar for project leadership.
- *Diverse workforce:* Greater gender equality in project management and cross-generational workforces.
- *The gig economy*: Challenges to job security, loyalty and training.
- *Changing corporate culture*: Changing technology demands continuous development.
- *Co-opetition*: Alliances between competitors sharing costs and crowd-sourced funds.

Expanding upon these insights, further developments can be anticipated:

a) **Increasing use of AI**:

Technologies generating data and information are moderated by increasingly sophisticated forms of artificial intelligence (AI). AI is now anticipated to take three forms. First, artificial general intelligence (AGI), is the human-equivalent AI, where a machine can perform intellectual tasks to the same standard as humans. Artificial superintelligence (ASI), when it happens, will be able to outstrip humans, as the machine comes to outperform any human physically and mentally. With artificial narrow intelligence (ANI), a subset of human skills can be replicated. It is possible to see such capabilities already, for example, in some forms of transport, ranging from cars to boats to aircraft.

In project management, it is not expected that any form of artificial intelligence will be equal to conducting the *role* of the project manager any time soon, but in some areas it already does greatly enhance the ability to calibrate progress against the parameters of cost, time, quality and scope through intelligent programmes generating schedules and tracking earned value and related measures of performance.

b) Increasing interconnectivity

More significant is the move from technology being an isolated deliverable, sending a single or limited range of signals to intelligent software monitoring multiple sensors, and generating project-specific information on which the project manager can make decisions. It is like the move from a spreadsheet recording stored data, with some limited ability to interpret and generate information on which the project manager can act, to being able to draw upon historical project data, recognising patterns or other learnings based on experience in delivery far exceeding that of any given project manager.

c) Increasing amount of complexity and project data

Already even relatively small projects generate more information than many far larger projects did in history. Making sense of all this demands a level of diverse expertise that traditional 'command-and-control' leadership cannot equal. In what follows, this will be explored further, as the characteristics defining the modern project delivery environment are considered in more detail.

While projects are traditionally portrayed as delivering change in stable, business-as-usual operational environments, increasingly they are dynamic, inter-connected and reactive: systemic. The above report drives home the message that the function of the project manager has radically changed.

While technology once controlled or reported on a single item, for example, some element of civil, mechanical or electrical engineering, today the level of interconnectivity is such that any proposed intervention or change to one item likely has a repercussive, 'cascade' effect.

The designers of aircraft have always faced such systemic challenges. Any change to weight or required speed affects wing and engine size, and each in turn can affect the other, in a spiral of knock-on effects, until some equilibrium is reached.

In what follows, such increasing complexity in project delivery will further illustrate the challenges project leadership now faces, and the increasingly diverse competences needed to meet them effectively.

Project leadership is now defined and constrained by its function within project delivery environments, as defined by increasing, technology-driven complexity. In project management, the environment has traditionally been characterised as consisting of Political, Economic, Sociological, Technological, Legal and Environmental (PESTLE) factors. Just as *within* project delivery as described above, the pervading and increasing prevalence of new technologies, including artificial intelligence, now emerges from within, and bridges each of these factors.

These emergent challenges within and across delivery environments have now been variously described as 'messy' or VUCA (Volatile, Uncertain, Complex and Ambiguous)[1].

Such emergent complexity fundamentally influences the very function of the project leader, who must increasingly seek to anticipate and prepare for it by creating and nurturing an effective, resilient, empowered and collaborative team. By doing this, the project leader devolves the power to act to those best placed to decide and act on the most effective course of action. With that empowerment, they also ensure that those empowered are made aware of the limits of that power, and when it is appropriate to escalate decision making upwards.

Environment ascendant

The 'E' for 'Environment' in PESTLE is itself also demonstrably increasingly 'VUCA'. Climate change, as described in the *Intergovernmental Panel on Climate Change (IPCC) Special Report on Global Warming*, is already prompting global projects to address its potential effects, which range from flooding and wildfires to species extinction.

Awareness of, and sensitivity to, negative human impacts on the environment is now growing to such an extent worldwide, that the vast majority of projects must now evidence concrete efforts to minimise any detrimental effect on the environment both in delivery and waste disposal as well as in subsequent operations. The project leader will necessarily become a central point of accountability for such effects, to a level not previously experienced as necessary.

These effects are repercussive. Environmental concerns fill both national and social media daily. The actual effects of climate change will bring challenges to project delivery and generate the need for countless projects. The environmental drivers are, in turn, already impacting on political, economic, social, technology and legal factors, impacting cost, time, scope and quality. 'PESTLE' influences are increasingly impacting the project manager's iron triangle of cost, time and quality, in turn challenging scope.

Such interdependencies are of course familiar to the project manager, to whom responsibility falls to challenge, mitigate and balance them. That has not changed. What has changed is how repercussive any change is, as well as the sensitivity to it in the delivery environment.

Consider also the comparative volumes of data generated in project delivery historically and now.

When the 146m high, 4,500-year-old civil engineering project known as the Great Pyramid of Cheops was constructed, how much papyrus was generated? How much data analysis, reporting, H&S, risk assessment, legal requirements? By way of comparison, imagine if every email, drawing, or other document relating to a relatively small project were to be printed out and stacked next to the papyri . . .

Following Moore's Law, where computing power doubles every two years, the exponentially increasing volume of data generated, including emails, reports, spreadsheets and drawings in an average project, if printed, would present a formidable sight indeed.

With so much data being generated by an individual project, the project manager can only process a small subset of all that is required. Reports 'by exception' incrementally filter out decisions that can be made by other subject matter experts, so that they can focus on issues deemed to require project manager level intervention. There is an analogy to be drawn here between traditional leadership and project leadership in that, just as in computing, linear processing was superseded by parallel processing, in the same way an empowered project team working collaboratively can address emergent and diverse challenges far more effectively than any single decision maker can.

Similarly, whereas the project workface, or locations where construction occurs, was traditionally a specific geographical location, it is now often digitally distributed and, in some sense, 'virtual', with teams or individuals remote from the physical location able to observe and influence delivery.

As referenced at the beginning of this chapter, the *'Special report UK2030'*[2] under the heading of 'Mapping out the future' highlights "trends and drivers in society, technology, economic, environment and politics [that] will have global impacts on the way we deliver change through projects".

The report summarises this 'brave new world' by stating that managing all these factors in project delivery will require "leadership, ethical behaviour and the integration of specialists".

The fact is, the project manager cannot hope to keep abreast of all the new technologies emerging across all disciplines – whether installed as deliverables or engaged in delivery – which gives us yet another reason that traditional, linear, top-down chain of command is not fit for purpose in today's project environment.

Evolving project leadership

Subject matter experts (SMEs) populate inter-disciplinary teams, where the project leader's key role is often to be what Howard Aldrich, of Cornell University, writing in the 1970s, called a 'boundary spanner'. They are both the glue and the human link spanning the organisation's internal and external boundaries. This function requires the project leader, as in all stakeholder engagement and influencing, to communicate in ways those SMEs can relate to. This skill is integral to the process of establishing collaborative working and turns upon the project leader's ability to establish rapport with a diverse group of cross-disciplinary stakeholders.

Establishing such rapport requires, in turn, yet another project leadership attribute not generally high on the list of those practising traditional leadership behaviours – the ability to practise empathy, to appreciate and understand the world through the eyes of a stakeholder, their priorities, triggers and sensitivities.

The project leader is increasingly in the role of 'servant leader' but this is not to be confused with any notion of 'subservience'. Rather, their role is to facilitate the realisation of collaborative synergy; to light a fire of commitment within the integrated project team.

So, we have seen that evolving project delivery environments radically reframe the function of the project manager. But simply focusing on the project manager, and promoting their function as 'leader', is, as we have also seen, not enough, as it fails to address ambiguities inherent in the very concept of leadership as generally portrayed and understood.

There is a large population of project managers who would assert that they are *already* leaders and have nothing to learn. This is especially true of those from a military background, who are entrenched in the view that theirs is the very epitome of leadership.

While such resistance may be difficult to address or overcome, it is too important not to be addressed at the organisational level. For organisational leaders to consider and adopt a different approach, they must be convinced of the need to do so – of both the efficacy of a different approach, and any proposed route to competence.

At the level of senior management or a project management capability function, engagement must reach far beyond training, hiring and development policies. It entails a cultural transformation in both leadership behaviours and team engagement.

This might start with a look at some of the existing fallacies and misconceptions surrounding leadership, so let's now explore the function and form of project leadership in more detail.

The new function of project management in leadership

The most effective designs are those where form follows function. The most effective form of leadership in project delivery will therefore reflect its function. A focus exclusively on function will determine what the purpose of good leadership in project delivery is, if not how competence is acquired. It has the merit of starting with the end in mind, defining a destination, but how to get there is another question.

'Being there', the 'end' that project leadership must focus on, and which every behaviour's effectiveness must therefore be measured against, is the establishment and nurturing of a team of professionals, working collaboratively, realising and releasing the synergy of their individual and group potential, where the output of the whole is greater than the sum of its parts.

'Getting there', achieving project leadership, in practical terms, and in sharp contrast to heroic, traditional leadership, the project leader is preoccupied not with *self*-empowerment, but with exercising behaviours geared towards realising the collaborative working potential of the project delivery team and, beyond them, to attracting and securing fully engaged stakeholders. It is a move from 'me', to 'we'.

The way the project leader achieves this team synergy must also take account of emergent technological complexity appropriate to delivery environments; the specific context in which each project is delivered. Such environments are, as has been shown, increasingly permeated by interdependent technologies monitoring and moderating both delivery and deliverables.

This sounds complex, and it is, for the project manager as a project leader no longer stands at the top of a hierarchy cascading commands downward, nor yet at the centre of a web radiating uni-directional commands outwards. Rather, the project leader is co-ordinating disparate disciplines and effecting communications between 'nodes', nurturing multi-disciplinary collaboration, resilience and agility.

It is not a linear dependency, with all the team looking to the leader, but a multi-dimensional, systemic, and therefore inter-dependent set of professional relationships between highly qualified SMEs. Just as in project management, cost, time, quality and scope are interdependent, so too project leadership must take a systemic rather than a linear approach to delivery.

Any proposed change to agreed delivery must prompt a fresh, multi-variate review of stakeholders affected. For example, while 'what' is affected might be covered by changes measured in cost, time, quality and scope, wider questions of 'who, where, when, why and how' might reveal a wider web of dependencies and inter-dependencies.

So, dynamic ongoing change in the project delivery environment has radically changed the project manager's job and role description. What they are responsible and accountable for delivering may still be assessed against traditional measures of cost, time scope and quality, but their part in achieving this must change fundamentally.

It has now been shown how the context or playing field has changed, and with it the rules affecting how the game should be played. So, what does the most appropriate form of leadership for contemporary project delivery environments look like?

What behaviours will an effective project leader deploy, and to what end?

What skills are most central and necessary to project leadership, and can they be developed?

Equally, in light of all the above, what traditional leadership behaviours must the project leader now recognise as unhelpful, even counter-productive, and therefore discard as baggage?

Chapter 2 Learning outcomes

1. Delivery environments characterised by greater technological interdependencies mean a single change or issue has multiple knock-on effects requiring delegated, expert decision making.
2. The function of the project manager is no longer that of the single subject matter expert managing all and making all decisions in relation to delivery. Rather, it is one of facilitating collaborative, distributed processes to effect resilience and rapid response.
3. The new function of the project manager is to facilitate and serve the team as a collective unit.
4. The aspiring project leader will recognise their vital function in orchestrating the realisation of a collaborative delivery team.
5. The project leader must recognise that the title of leader is not imposed, but bestowed, and must be earned.

3

Project leaders deliver teams

Emergent constraints and demands in delivery establish a compelling demand for leadership in a form maximising resilience and agility in delivery.

This brings to centre stage the previously downplayed function of coaching, with attendant competence in so-called 'soft skills', including empathy and emotional intelligence.

The practitioner is urged to recognise the vast return on investment in team delivery from a team coached to realise their individual and collective potential.

This section begins with the recognition that 'project management' is, increasingly, a contradiction in terms. Managerial 'command and control' does not inspire or, engage, nor does it foster the synergy of collaborative working.

The function of delivery to cost, time, quality and scope remains. But, the function *in* delivery is to adopt a form fit for purpose in increasingly VUCA external and internal delivery environments. This chapter expands on the new function of project leadership – what it seeks to achieve as underpinned by

PROJECT MANAGEMENT
FUNCTIONAL
ORG STRUCTURE

PM full line authority
Command and control
PM centralised expertise
In-house delivery

PROJECT LEADERSHIP
PROJECTISED MATRIX
ORG STRUCTURE

PM little line authority
Team engagement/ownership collaboration
Devolved multi-disciplinary expertise
Sub-contracted-out delivery

Figure 5 Project leadership, changing context, changing function

relevant contemporary theory. It is followed by a structured approach for the aspirant and practising project leader to apply, in order to establish effective project leadership.

The function of project leadership is to empower and facilitate the realisation of individual and team potential, and the emergence of collaborative team synergy.

Just as the function and form of 'stakeholder management' shifts towards 'stakeholder *engagement*', so too, now, successful project delivery requires a move from 'project *management*' to a function and congruent form resulting in a fully 'engaged', collaborative team. What 'engages' the team, and all project stakeholders? Project *leadership*.

As we have seen from the SCARF Model, project leadership is not well served by traditional command-and-control behaviours. So what *is* needed? What are the drivers and function of leadership in a project environment? Given any highly educated, multi-disciplinary project delivery team, what *can* inform the function to be fulfilled and the behaviours appropriate to achieve it?

The function of project leadership is to engage the entire project team and all the project's stakeholders. But this is not engagement in the sense of Patrick O'Brian's 'Jack Aubrey' raising the gun ports to 'engage the enemy'. Its focus is not so much on engaging with them, as about getting them, as stakeholders, to engage with the project leader, the project and other stakeholders.

The project leader must also 'negotiate and influence' stakeholders. '. . . *the people involved in the work, from sponsor to team member, are part of the effort to keep the stakeholder appropriately engaged and influenced to do the right things*". Here too, 'stakeholder engagement' is defined as "*The systematic identification, analysis, planning and implementation of actions designed to influence stakeholders'. APM Body of Knowledge 7th edition.*

As with stakeholder management being about getting *them* to engage, so with influence the focus is on helping stakeholders find their own best way to engage with the project, rather than directing or telling. To achieve such influence, the project leader and team through coaching will need to develop *contextual and cultural awareness, communication and conflict resolution skills*.

The *rate* at which complexity in project delivery continues to increase reflects the occurrence of events arising in the environment that simply could not have been anticipated, never mind measured the "unknown unknowns – the ones we don't know we don't know", as the former US Defence Secretary, Donald Rumsfeld, is often quoted as saying.

The challenge of increasing, emergent complexity

Unknown unknowns are like black swans. Everyone knows all swans are white, until the day a black swan paddles into view. The history of science is rich with anecdotes of unexpected discoveries giving rise to entire industries. They range from the now ubiquitous Post-it note emerging from the development of a 'failed' glue that 'doesn't stick', to the accidental discovery of penicillin.

What all such stories have in common is that they were the result of 'emergent complexity'; where bringing 'A' and 'B' together resulted in something unplanned and unexpected.

Time and again, scrutiny of failure to deliver projects – especially within the constraint of 'time', reveals such 'emergent' complexity; issues and impacts arising unexpectedly during delivery that simply could not have been anticipated at the outset. Turbulent environments where any change triggers a cascade of others are a classic source of emergent complexity, and there's no more resonant example of this than the appearance of one isolated case of COVID-19. Like the classic example from chaos theory, this was like the fluttering of the butterfly wings that resulted in a hurricane sweeping across the entire world.

If it is to be effective, project leadership must adapt to take account of this kind of complexity. This section therefore addresses the question of what characterises fit-for-purpose leadership in such a dynamic environment. What does 'good' look like?

While some endeavours requiring many players benefit from centralised command and control, in general the contemporary project delivery environment is populated by SMEs' diverse skills and stakeholders more qualified than the project manager in their respective domains.

The necessity for empowerment and therefore coaching

What this environment, and the wide diversity of increasing technical specialisations *does* call for, is a far more empowered and autonomous delivery team, working collaboratively.

Working alongside engaged stakeholders, such a team benefits from the intelligence, not of a single authority figure, but the combined input of all SMEs.

Treating employees as customers fosters engagement and ownership

Employees generally, and a new generation of project team members, stakeholders and customers are now increasingly sensitive, aware and demanding when it comes to ethics and values. This shift means there is far less tolerance for behaviours that are perceived to undermine an individual's basic self-esteem, and hence their performance.

Meanwhile, outside the work environment, it is no coincidence that sales of self-help books are soaring, while there is ever less tolerance for gender stereotyping, and increasing support for the individual's right to self-expression and respect.

This heightened awareness underpins expectations that the workplace should offer value and meaning; that leadership itself should reciprocate the respect it expects or even demands of others. Classic models such as Maslow's 'Hierarchy of Needs' reflect these basic requisites for good mental health, and organisations are increasingly acknowledging and reflecting this in their HR policies.

This means project leadership must now account for a more dynamic and unpredictable environment, coupled with the expectations of a more discerning and educated employee base.

The paradigm shift in what good and bad leadership 'looks like' takes the project leader beyond self-interested preoccupation with their personal status and recognition, and project delivery/deliverables, to a focus on developing others. In the interests of effecting and promoting collaboration benefiting all stakeholders, the project leader must move from being primarily concerned with 'me, me, me', to a mutually empowering focus on 'we'.

As Whitmore's sub-title to *Coaching for performance: the principles and practice of coaching and leadership* (2017) captures, the principles of leadership are now realised through 'coaching for success', within and across both the project team and stakeholders, both establishing and nurturing a culture of mutual respect and collaboration.

Coaching effectively unlocks people's potential. It is worth noting how closely this resonates with the APM definition of leadership in "providing vision, direction, feedback and support so people can do their best work".

The project leader's function is fulfilled through the realisation and release of individual and group potential of those they work with, so achieving a critical mass of effectively collaborating team members.

Just as project leadership is evolving to account for emerging changes and associated challenges in the delivery environment, so too it is increasingly apparent that, to be fully competent, project leaders themselves need to evolve on a personal level.

This changing aspect of the project leader is reflected both by Sir John Whitmore in his Performance Curve model, and in Stephen Covey's '*7 Habits of Highly Effective People*' (2004). Both highlight the progressive steps individuals must take to evolve in maturity, from the 'dependence' of the child on parents and teachers, through the acquisition of self-confidence and self-esteem to eventual 'interdependence'.

Whitmore characterises Maslow's 'Esteem from others' stage as reflecting the immature leader's concern, or even preoccupation, with their own *entitlement* to 'status and recognition' conferred by others. As a leadership style, this is all about 'me, me, me'; a demand for obedience and deference from others to bolster their own self-importance. Making the point that such a "leadership style must evolve" to the next level, Whitmore notes, "They are often arrogant, assertive, domineering, and self-important" (Op Cit p19).

Much of this book is intended to support the route to the stage of interdependence. However, what Whitmore describes as a 'subtle shift' is needed to facilitate the evolution from the leader's state of achieving 'independence', to that of 'interdependence' against Maslow's Hierarchy of Needs.

Both Covey and Whitmore drive home the point that this transformation occurs with emotional maturity, as the individual becomes less obsessed with 'me-me-me' and evolves to recognise the power of 'we'. The preceding, immature emotional needs associated with 'independence' are "displaced by a subtle shift to the need for self-esteem, or, as I prefer to call it, self-belief (the bedrock of coaching and the prerequisite for high performance)."

This shift, however subtle, is transformative for both the individual concerned and those they lead. In what follows, the reader prepared to embrace the need for an evolution in leadership behaviours, will be introduced to such a path, potentially leading to a paradigm shift in individual, project, and organisational effectiveness.

Synergy is best developed when, instead of one brain 'dictating' to the team, the effective project leader facilitates the emergence of empowered, collaborative teamwork. This occurs as the project leader intentionally engineers effective team unity.

Compare what happens when a group of people in separate rooms address a problem separately, with the outcome when they are all together, collaborating and engaging positively and non-assertively. It is an environment characterised by exclamations of "Yes and . . .", rather than "No, but . . .". It is about engaging creatively and productively with each other's ideas.

For this reason alone, traditional and heroic leadership models are under tremendous pressure, and redundant in all but the most extreme circumstances. Through empowerment, the competent project leader creates and nurtures agility and resilience in the team, matching the challenges of a VUCA environment. The single most powerful tool driving this evolution is coaching.

Mentor or coach?

Distinguishing the role and nature of 'mentor' and 'coach', Whitmore clarifies that, whereas the mentor may be quite directive, the coach is concerned to nurture self-belief and self-esteem, rather than fostering a relationship where the student becomes dependent on direction. This relates equally to the project leader's role in nurturing members of the team to take real ownership for their own development through the acquisition of knowledge and competence.

As coach, pure and simple, it is not necessary to be a 'subject matter expert' in the sense necessary to communicate knowledge. Rather, coaching focuses on "unlocking people's potential to maximise their performance" (Op Cit Whitmore 2019). This means the project leader will aim to coach reports as quickly as practicable, beyond a telling or directing leadership style, to encourage ongoing development until the power of delegation can be bestowed.

Coaching seeks to realise the individual's inner potential, rather than imposing mechanistic behaviours associated with 'blind obedience' from the outside in. In the world of technology, this distinction is paralleled in ongoing attempts to move from artificial and mechanistic intelligence to general intelligence, where decisions are improved and competence increases through learning from experience, rather than just doing the same thing over and over because a circumstance matches some basic learned pattern.

'Interference' is an effect highlighted by Whitmore that occurs when innate learning capabilities are compromised or even inhibited by instruction imposed on another or others. Most people can relate to this phenomenon, particularly when, for example, a time or context for learning is imposed that is at odds with the learner's own preference. The project leader must take account of this by actively encouraging the team to engage in conscious self-reflection; identifying and pursuing the most effective learning style for *them*.

The capacity of aspirant and operational project leaders alike for self-reflection, and having the discipline necessary for development, means they will become familiar with methods to support this process. Well known models, such as organisationally approved '360-degree feedback' mechanisms, and the 'Johari Window Model' can play their part, informing individuals of any gaps between their self-perception and that of others.

Despite compelling arguments and hard evidence demonstrating the importance and centrality of coaching for effective project leadership, the prospect of finding time for coaching can be quite daunting. But, as with the formation of many good habits in life, one can readily anticipate and hence be prepared to address the regular excuses for deferring action. For a project manager striving to meet the stringent demands of delivery, where time is the greatest driver, it is understandable that the addition of coaching might seem an unaffordable luxury, but a closer look is warranted . . .

Too busy to coach?

The prospect of scheduling coaching activity on top of an already hectic and demanding schedule might seem a formidable, not to mention unwelcome, overhead for any project manager under pressure to deliver.

They are likely to declare that they are already working flat-out; clearly and readily evidenced by the fact of a fully booked-up daily schedule for weeks ahead.

However, this view reflects a real misapprehension as to how coaching should be practised, and anyway, the reality is that few would escape being caught out beneath the gaze of a full time-and-motion study. How often, in issuing any decision or directive to line management, does the project manager consider how this might be done in such a way that, having explained the basis for the decision made, it could be delegated next time around?

In fact, in practice, coaching does not even demand that the project manager should schedule regular meetings of any significant length. It can take place in and around existing activities, and consist of brief, anticipatory and retrospective conversations. These conversations have as their focus an intention to empower and delegate responsibility. In other words, the cost of time spent should, by definition, result in time saved through delegation.

Before a meeting, the coach might, for example, encourage the coachee to consider or say how *they* might address what is now to be done, or how something might have been done differently.

The first time this happens, such a question will be something of a surprise for the coachee. Perhaps for some time they have only been used to being *told* what to do, or largely ignored. In many cases their opinion will never have been invited or sought.

So, to save any counter-productive embarrassment or humiliation, the empathic coach merely invites the coachee to 'consider' their point of view rather than asking them to express it at this early stage. They ask them to think how they might have conducted the meeting or approached the issue, without expecting them to voice it, unless they want to.

Even before getting to this, the leader might offer a private explanation underpinning their own perspective or approach. This communicates a degree of respect and trust to the coachee, and builds rapport, besides encouraging the coachee to, in future, give thought to and prepare before meetings to anticipate issues, and support sought outcomes.

From now on, the remembrance of this prompts and encourages the coachee to become used to proactively anticipating events and how they would deal with them, as well as reflecting on what has happened, to learn from experience. Often, surprisingly quickly, a few such brief conversations help the coach and coachee to understand more about each other's approach to things, and to gain rapport.

This is an essential component in all collaboration, as well as being a necessary foundation for the establishment of a leader-follower relationship. The erstwhile 'servant' is suddenly being treated as an, at least potential, future leader; their self-esteem is nurtured, and, most importantly for the project leader, they feel respected and encouraged.

This dynamic grows and gains a momentum and power far beyond the *seconds* taken to ask a simple question that does not even require an answer.

Modelling stakeholder engagement

In the 1950s, Eric Berne developed the theory of 'Transactional Analysis'. This theory offers valuable insights into ways the project leader can anticipate or assess ongoing interactions with other stakeholders in project delivery. The actual process of consciously doing this prompts the project leader to step away from their own emotional engagement in any given scenario in order to gain a fresh perspective on it.

Figure 6 Parent, adult child model based on Eric Berne, '*Transactional Analysis*'

The model suggests interpersonal relationships can be mapped against three predominating ego states; that of the 'parent', 'adult' and 'child'. It is a powerful approach, not least because it is so intuitive.

The 'parent' ego state can be graphically envisaged as standing and 'telling', hands on hips. Another image might show the leader as parent, arm outstretched, pointing assertively in the direction to be travelled. The 'child' ego state is characterised by a hands-on-hips stance emanating a sense of moral judgement.

Finally, the 'adult' is encouraging as, hand on the other's shoulder, they point the way without confrontation. The leader as 'adult' does not confront, but stands beside the subject, pointing the way, or else is seated but, rather than sitting opposite the subject, sits beside them.

Crucially, avoiding face-to-face, head-to-head, 'confrontational' body language, the focus remains on what is to be done 'out there' and how, rather than dominating the subject's field of view and distracting them by the dominating presence or behaviours of the leader.

As with any potentially confrontational situation, the ability to externalise and depersonalise debate makes for more rational discussion.

These graphic examples represent an attitude to directing and coaching, intentionally avoiding stereotypical, assertive or confrontational forms of body language or tone of voice.

As coach, pure and simple, it is not necessary to be a 'subject matter expert' in the sense necessary to communicate knowledge. Rather, coaching is all about "unlocking people's potential to maximise their performance" (Op Cit Whitmore 2019). This means the project leader will aim to mentor reports as quickly as practicable; beyond a 'telling' or moderated 'directing' leadership style to coach and encourage ongoing development until the empowerment of delegation can be bestowed.

Evolving project leadership

It is easy to imagine the petulant child being admonished by the assertive parent, or the intervening adult urging the parent to nurture, rather than control, encouraging rather than suppressing and inhibiting.

With this lens, the project leader is empowered to understand a given situation, and also what has happened or might happen. To this understanding they can bring their own intention: what approach will have the desired effect on the other or others? Being more aware of what is happening and how they might influence others offers insights into how they might moderate outcomes by their own measured responses and interventions. What does this mean in the real, down-to-earth situations project leaders find themselves in?

Consider a situation where there has been some failure in performance. It is not difficult to recall instances from childhood onwards where an authority figure seems to have judged and ruled with no consideration given to the corrosive impact of their words and behaviours.

For some, anything presenting as a failure by a subordinate offers a licence to exercise command-and-control behaviours, enforcing their authority over the majority with no consideration of their actual effect on the individual.

For those attempting to assert authority and dominance in any group, and this ranges across the evolutionary history of all primates, such instances present as an almost irresistible temptation. This is especially true where the aspirant leader suffers from personal insecurity.

Most can recall occasions when the most vulnerable in the group was picked on, making an example of them for the sole purpose of asserting a would-be leader's dominance. There are signs such bullying behaviours are increasingly recognised for what they are, and they have no place for those aspiring to project leadership.

Calling to account

An ability to 'hold subordinates to account' is portrayed as central to traditional leadership. The phrase immediately suggests that the subject is made helpless, completely at the mercy of someone without sympathy. It triggers the single most basic and debilitating emotional response of all – fear. This is the very opposite of behaviour that inspires individuals to realise their potential.

Unfortunately, some relish any opportunity to dominate others. Their sense of self is primarily based on a job title or role. For them, the authority offered by a licence to dominate others and 'hold them to account' is irresistible.

Project leadership is not about instilling fear or dominating others. In fact, project leadership actually calls such behaviours to account, for they are both unnecessary and actively counter-productive.

Those who do associate project management with command-and-control behaviours will likely react strongly to any suggestion that 'holding others to account' is not a necessary or central function of the project leader. This long-unquestioned way of behaving should now be exposed as detrimental and a weakness of character, both personally and professionally.

The following questions serve to reframe this issue and offer a more positive perspective.

> *Would 'holding others to account' be necessary were followers committed and loyal to their leader?*
>
> *Would 'holding others to account' be necessary were followers already doing their best?*
>
> *If a leader has to 'call to account', does this not imply, by definition, a failure in leadership?*

Or again, considering the detrimental and counter-productive results that, according to the SCARF Model, 'calling to account' is likely to trigger, is this really worthy of being deemed a leadership behaviour in project leadership, or any other kind of leadership?

What outcome is sought by such behaviours? Is a positive outcome not more important than someone's need to assert authority and dominance over another?

The effective project leader sees through these ineffective dominance behaviours. They are empowered to resist both their temptation and others' expectations, seeing any perceived failure as an opportunity, not to humiliate and undermine, as in an arena of conflict, but as a platform and stepping stone to enhanced performance.

Instead of confrontation, accusation, intimidating body language, stern demeanour and an aggressive tone of voice, the project leader challenges any perceived failure in performance very differently. Their approach seeks to uncover the reasons and motives, leading to a mutual appreciation of what has happened and why.

The leader, having avoided the trap of adopting the role of dominating parent or aggressive child will, by taking the role of adult, be far more likely to see the accused walk away empowered, learning from experience and better prepared to meet similar situations in future.

The application of emotional intelligence seeks influence far beyond a single measure of performance or behaviour. As a result, all parties walk away, not only with dignity, but with greater respect for the leader, who is now far more likely to be seen as such. In this way the individual is not only educated to avoid future failure, but, by their leader's example, is encouraged to treat others with respect and dignity.

And so, the project leader actively nurtures and encourages loyalty and commitment from others.

Followers will strive not to let them down, knowing that their leader perceives them not as a failure, but as capable of evolving towards a greater potential.

Emotional intelligence nurtures resilience

Emotional intelligence, or EQ, as made popular in Daniel Goleman's 1985 book, is a measure of maturity in understanding and moderating one's own emotions and then those of other individuals and the group.

Achieving emotional intelligence in its various manifestations can be one of the greatest sources of resilience and inspiration to greater achievement that any follower can have, and hence that any project leader can bestow. In multiple future scenarios, the accused and forgiven will be prompted to recall and draw upon this experience. It may not only serve to stiffen their own resolve, but to treat others in turn, as they have been treated. This works both ways, of course, and no doubt many an aggressive humiliator of those who fail has lived to regret their own, less humane approach.

The positive effects do not stop here, though. Observation or even awareness of such enlightened behaviours by the leader can cascade across the entire project delivery team. Each instance where the leader intervenes can become one of those stories so powerfully informing organisational culture, sometimes for years, or even follow individuals for their entire career.

To bring the above to life, you only have to recall instances in your own experience where one in authority acted in one or other of the ways described. Such an exercise will show you the power and longevity of the impressions formed when someone fails while trying, and their accompanying vulnerability is exploited.

When being found to be at fault is seized upon as an excuse to exhibit their power by one in authority, this incurs a double cost, impacting both the individual and the business. Not only is the subject diminished by one who is merely parading authority, but the lost opportunity to coach and develop the individual and thereby send positive cultural messages to the entire team is lost. The resulting corrosive fears actively inhibit ongoing individual performance and growth. Sadly, too, this can have repercussions for the individual's life, both professional and personal.

The importance of ensuring that performance criticism is not perceived as an attack on the individual cannot be overstated. When a leader communicates disrespect for those reporting to them, this becomes an act of self-harm, since the leader, far from reinforcing their authority, is in fact actively eroding and undermining the very basis on which they are perceived as leaders: mutual respect.

When someone sincerely tries to succeed, and fails, yet is humiliated for their trouble, this actually presents, and is experienced as, a betrayal of trust; a breach of the psychological contract established when a willing follower places their trust in a leader.

The GROW Model

One of the most widely adopted models offering a structured approach to coaching is the GROW Model created by Sir John Whitmore.

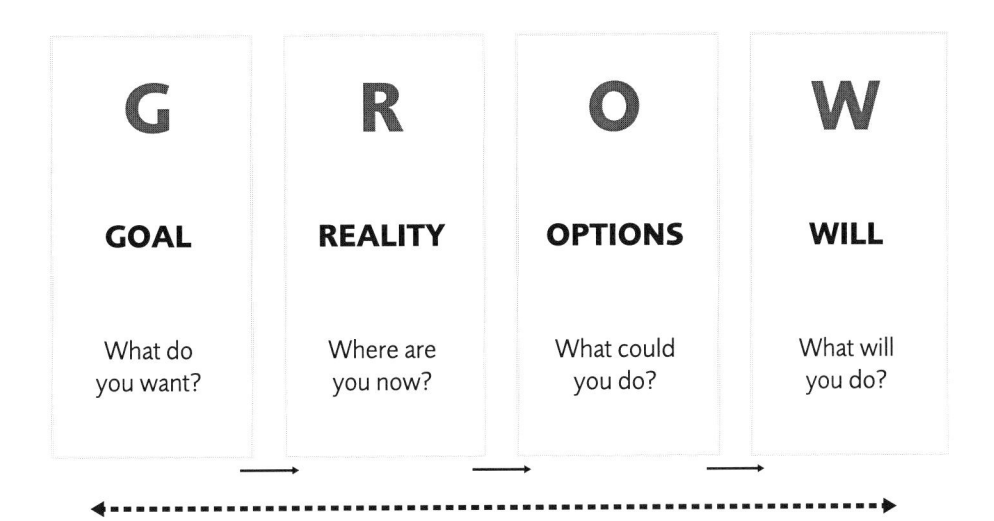

Figure 7 The coaching GROW Model©. J Whitmore (Op Cit)
https://www.coachingperformance.com/grow-model/
http://www.1000ventures.com/business_guide/crosscuttings/coaching_grow.html

'GROW' is an acronym for the four key stages in any successful coaching conversation:

1. **The goal**
   One trap the coach and coachee must avoid is that of limiting the selected goal to the existing context or environment. It is entirely appropriate that the selected goal should have an element of the visionary about it. In any given situation, the ability to raise the perspective to a different plane can serve to reframe the current situation, providing a fresh perspective that can be immensely powerful in its own right. And that is before the 'R', 'O', and 'W' are even considered!

   It is also vital that the project leader, working as coach, adopts an approach that encourages the other to articulate their deeply personal goal. It should be a goal with special resonance for the coachee, for this will, in due course, constitute a source of ongoing resilience, reigniting their enthusiasm when things are not going well.

   The goal should in some sense transcend what is now, the current environment or coachee. It might reflect the attainment of a new skillset or enhanced way to live and work. It might, in a project delivery environment, encompass the establishment of an improved culture and way of working, or a vision of how to achieve that.

   The goal should be one that weighs favourably against the anticipated cost and effort to be expended for its realisation. It would also be as well at this point to ensure these goals are challenging and inspiring.

2. **The reality**
   Situational awareness: What are the significant characteristics of the environment and/or situation, now? Where are we in relation to where we have come from, and where we wish to be? For the project leader or stakeholders, including team members, there may be some aspects of either that can be tapped into as a source of strength – a desire to move away from, or towards.

3. **The options**
   This is about the route from here to there; alternative ways to reach the same goal. This may include the need to consider the classic cost, time, quality and scope variables and those considerations that are fixed. The question should help both the coach and coachee to think outside the box – to bounce ideas around that might at first glance seem impracticable, but which might result in some unexpected ideas.

   Some options may follow the path of least resistance, while others may take the more direct line.

4. What will you do?
   Informed by steps one to three, it is now for the coachee to decide a way forward in light of what they have learned.

The 'GROW' coaching process mirrors the concepts, structures and processes of project management itself, driving a project from initial uncertainties to a desired end.

We will revisit the GROW Model in the next section. It offers support to the project leader, providing a structured approach to team member development, while prompting them to see their leader in an altogether new and positive light.

The shift in behaviours from those appropriate to heroic leadership and to those effective in project leadership is not an isolated case. There are also parallels to be drawn with the distinct difference in approach adopted by military authorities in dealing with emergent complexity in the challenges *they* face, and which have also 'evolved'. Whereas heroic styles of leadership were adequate in the traditional battlefield scenario, more recent conflicts exhibit a very different dynamic summed up by the term 'asymmetric warfare'.

The latter is characterised by situations where a traditional state and military institutions find themselves facing off against terrorist organisations. In this scenario, the enemy does not conveniently line up on a border or battlefield to face off against. There is no country, there are no airfields, to bomb or invade, for the enemy may well already be dispersed within the borders of the homeland. The enemy may be largely invisible and seek a low profile, mounting sporadic, unannounced attacks on the comparatively static bases and infrastructure of the state. The very disparate and unpredictable actions of terrorists acting largely without a clear and centralised command-and-control structure makes meeting this challenge unenviable for the commanders of troops drilled and trained to be directed, and respond to centralised control.

The response to such a scenario is mirrored by the different operational culture and processes in the elite corps of the Special Air Service (SAS) and Special Boat Service (SBS). Here the forces are highly trained to act with their own initiative. Working on first name terms with their leadership, there is a strong culture of open speech, challenge, and sharing insights and observations. Where practicable, decisions are informed by all involved, and leadership will often defer to those with 'eyes-on' any given scenario. To those raised and trained, living and working 24/7 year-round in a traditional military leader-led environment, it is highly disconcerting to witness such elite force discussions, where frankly expressed views seem to verge on the insubordinate.

Evolving project leadership

Once deployed, the situational awareness and understanding of the special forces is such that they are far more agile and resilient than traditional forces. The 'noise' incurred when people in complex, dynamic situations are obliged to seek direction from a remote, centralised command headquarters is vastly reduced. The objective is well established, but the means of reaching that goal is very much in the hands of those on the ground with eyes to see.

On reflection, it is not difficult to see that contemporary project delivery environments will also benefit from the realisation of real efficiencies through devolved decision making and empowerment. For this to happen, however, the project leader needs to embrace a substantially different role in the way they relate to their team.

At the heart of this subtle shift is the project leader's instrumental role in the empowerment of their team. But this can only occur following the leader's active role in preparing each team member for such delegation, and this correlates with the journey from Direction to Delegation offered by the Hersey Blanchard Model of Situational Leadership®.

The route and tools for this journey are laid out by Sir John Whitmore in *'Coaching for Performance: the principles of coaching and leadership'* (2019). The subtitle itself offers food for thought, since it so explicitly allies the practice and principles of coaching with leadership.

Changing minds: shifting perspectives

The role of the coach sometimes benefits from a skill Plato illustrated in a series of classic conversations known as the Socratic Dialogues.

Using a process called 'elenchus', Socrates drew out the unexpected implications of students' brashly asserted beliefs. Eventually, his questions led to the moment of 'aporia' as they ran out of arguments – that blank 'void' is informed by a reframing of previous understanding. As the pre-existing inconsistencies are reconciled – largely unconsciously – a new level of awareness emerges. This new consciousness often occurs in a rush as the contradictory and irreconcilable nature of their previous position is revealed. This is often referred to as the 'Aha' moment.

Known in psychology as 'cognitive dissonance', when such unsustainable positions crumble they often trigger potentially transformative moments. It is like a phenomenon in physics, when a minute flaw in a deeply chilled liquid triggers an almost instant 'phase change', and a small crystal of ice instantaneously spreads outwards in all directions. Similarly, in these moments, the individual can experience a profound change of mind, as a new, informed perspective supersedes what went before.

To personally appreciate the power of such a moment, imagine driving down the road, cars in front and behind, when suddenly an overtaking car cuts in.

Emotions, and even a sense of outrage, may be triggered as one is forced to veer and brake sharply. Anger and indignation feel entirely justified, as that vicious, circular argument spirals upwards to fully dominate consciousness: the driver is a bad person for doing this. Why did they do this? Because they are a bad person!

Suddenly your passenger exclaims: "*I know him! He's a surgeon from the hospital just down the road. He must be on call-out for an urgent operation!*"

In the briefest pause, these words, and all they signify, sink in. That seemingly unshakeable self-righteousness, outrage, and indignation of but a moment before vanish, although leaving a hollow, silent space. Such sudden shifts in consciousness and perception reflect a paradigm shift in perception.

In a similar manner to Socrates, the project leader, in coaching mode, can help those in their charge, as well as in the wider stakeholder community, to move from entrenched or previously unexamined positions or opinions.

But of course, using this valuable coaching tool effectively demands emotional intelligence, the ability to set aside any inner need to win an argument, prove the other wrong or score points. Instead, it requires one to start from a position of ignorance, seeking understanding, showing due respect for, and being curious to understand, the other's point of view.

Sir John Whitmore wrote the 5th edition of *Coaching for Performance* in 2017. Its sub-title, '*The principles and practice of coaching and leadership*', offers an explicit endorsement of the central nature of coaching in leadership, and this is especially applicable to project leadership.

Whitmore uses Maslow's 'Hierarchy of Needs' to illustrate yet another powerful reason that traditional command-and-control type behaviour is increasingly shown to be counterproductive. The point is made that, moving up the hierarchy, a sense of entitlement accompanies Maslow's 'self esteem' needs being met, what he calls the 'independence' stage on Whitmore's Performance Curve. This is reflected in the immature leader's focus on 'me', rather than the 'we' that only comes with achievement of 'interdependence' that correlates with fulfilment of Maslow's Self Actualisation need.

'The Performance Curve', as in Figure 8 following, relates to Maslow's 'Hierarchy of Needs', since as individuals mature towards leadership there is a

Evolving project leadership

correlation between the needs he identifies, and the levels through which individuals pass on their journey to leadership. The path from left to right on the Performance Curve mirrors the progression to 'Self Actualisation'. Starting from the basic biological need for 'food and water', the next needs are for 'shelter and safety', then 'belonging'.

It is, when progressing across Whitmore's curve between 'independence' and 'interdependence' that the significance for project leadership emerges. This progression mirrors Maslow's ascent from the Need for 'Esteem from Others' through 'Self Esteem' to 'Self Actualisation'.

In a culture exercising traditional styles of leadership, most leaders seek status and recognition that is characterised as being "often arrogant, assertive, domineering and self-important. They will do anything to get more pay; they don't need or deserve it, but it is a way [for them] of measuring and asserting their status" (Op Cit p20).

Behaviours of those aspiring to leadership at the 'Independence stage' of the performance curve, can be excessively pre-occupied with controlling others and their environment. All other considerations, including consideration of others, are secondary to this singular, overwhelming need. The resulting obsession betrays their deep, inner insecurity and uncertain sense of self-identity within. Without the job title, they feel they are nothing. Where 'self-esteem' depends on 'esteem from others', no effort, nor consideration of others, is spared to secure or protect their position, and by definition, their sense of identity.

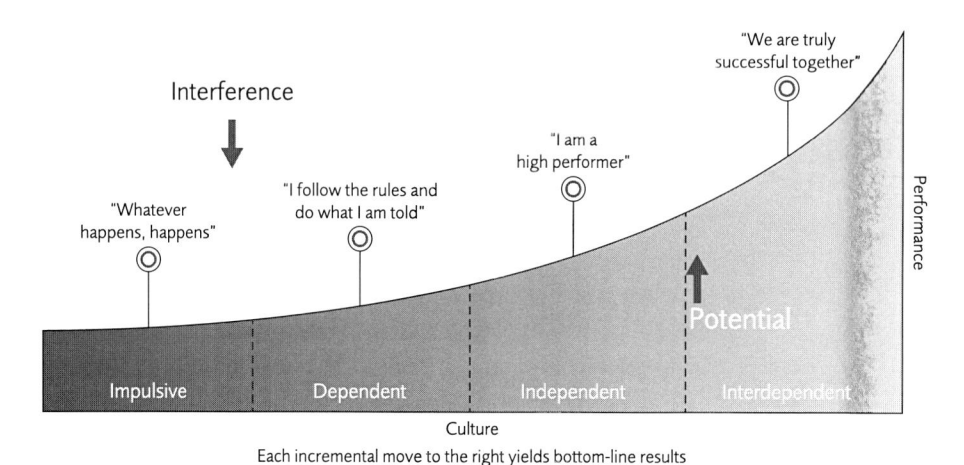

Figure 8 Performance Curve by Sir John Whitmore

Project leadership today necessitates a personal evolution beyond such self-interest or personal insecurities.

It is now clear that in a project environment those much-vaunted traditional leadership behaviours are both redundant and actively counter-productive. In all that follows, the focus will turn to a form of leadership and the means to its attainment that is fit-for-purpose in today's delivery environment.

Aspiring project leaders are presented with challenges very different from those in the wider field of traditional leadership. The skills demanded, as both Whitmore's and Covey's models clearly show, are those acquired by leaders who have transitioned from the traditional leadership stage of independence to that of interdependence. The product of these skills and competences are followers and collaborative teams that are agile and resilient in artificially intelligent delivery environments.

One way of describing those who *have* moved past the previously described leadership growth stage of 'independence', of being 'in-dependency' on others' esteem, to that of 'interdependence', is to see this transition as one of 'conversion': a fundamental change in world-view. This move, from demanding that others fall into orbit around 'me', to a self-effacing focus on 'we, the team', cannot be readily forced from the outside-in, but must be coaxed from the inside-out, by facilitating those able to make this crucial transition. Not all are.

The rest of this book focuses on the steps an aspirant project leader can follow by exhibiting particular behaviours, doing certain things. But while this offers real benefits in the delivery of any project, the disposition of the project manager in taking each step will have a real effect on the outcome.

For those hiding or disguising a psychological need for others' esteem; power, authority, and external validation by job title, the idea of admitting such motives, or the need for authenticity, will be threatening. Those promoting and approaching leadership by adopting assertive body language or power stances, adopting a philosophy of 'fake it till you make it', are increasingly recognised as phoney.

Those who aspire to project leadership, but who are labouring under a dated and increasingly discredited focus on self-promotion to the detriment of others, are increasingly exposed to organisational scrutiny. Both peers and subordinates' increasingly look askance at behaviours that are now recognised as saying and being more about the actor, than benefiting delivery.

Project leadership is more than behaviour. It is not merely about adopting a tone or form of communication. Nor is it about body language or behaviours asserting dominance over subordinates or stakeholders.

Evolving project leadership

The aspirant project leader raised in a culture intended to control and dominate must take stock. Be clear: neither the road ahead, nor its destination, are as they are portrayed in many stories and images of traditional leadership. But such stories, however prevalent and attention grabbing, seizing on the most primal of emotions, are *not* the only sources of insight.

Young people entering project management and many other organisational settings are showing increasing reluctance to be dictated to by the older generation. The emergence of Greta Thunberg as a campaigner against climate change denial exemplifies this questioning and refusal to be silenced.

To engage and influence stakeholders implies a process. That process requires both willingness and motivation to understand; to see what is to be done through the eyes of the stakeholder. This ability to see another point of view requires a genuine desire to set aside one's own perspective, priorities and agenda.

Those hampered by their own ego, by an overwhelming need to control or impose their own will on others, will find themselves impotent to initiate or effect such progress, and by exhibiting assertive behaviours, will end up polarising positions and alienate or antagonise the very stakeholders they need on side.

Called 'soft skills', the products of self-control and self-understanding are often dismissed by those who readily characterise their adoption as a sign of weakness. In reality, it is the inability to deploy these skills that constitutes both a weakness and liability.

The project leader unable to exercise control over their primal emotions and behaviours is not showing strength, but a weakness of character to the detriment of themselves and all.

As the neurological research underpinning David Rock's SCARF Model, described above, clearly shows, the assertive behaviours once promoted as exemplifying effectiveness and strength and central to leadership are now de-centred. Rather than being the defining behaviour and body language of project leadership, assertiveness is relegated to being called upon only as a last resort

There is no greater duty for anyone aspiring to project leadership than that of embracing and becoming proficient in the skills of emotional intelligence. They empower the ability, through empathy, for preconceptions to be influenced and informed. This is the basis necessary to establishing genuine rapport, mutual respect and understanding. Only on this foundation can the project leader expect to influence stakeholders and bring about their willing engagement.

So, now we have established what project leadership is not, let's turn to the task of understanding and applying a model and process that meets both the demands of the project delivery environment and those who operate in it, including stakeholders and the project delivery team.

This model builds on the 'eight project leadership survival skills' that follow as defined in the *APM Research Fund series, 'Project leadership: skills, behaviours, knowledge and values' (Oct. 2018)*:

1. Anticipating – being prepared for what could knock the project off course next.
2. Judgement and decision-making – making timely decisions with incomplete information.
3. Seeing it all – feeling the totality of what is going on inside and outside the project.
4. Building credibility and confidence – belief in the leadership and the team.
5. Being organisationally intelligent – knowing when and how to engage with the organisation.
6. Learning – being open-minded, and reflecting on and developing personal and team performance.
7. Resolving conflicts and collaborating – building a common purpose, despite the rules.
8. Creating the project culture and environment – deliberately defining and creating the culture and environment to succeed.

Survival skills are all about establishing a baseline – a bare minimum to demonstrate competence and offer a passable performance. What the following model offers is both a model and process that works on both the project leader and their followers in a transformative way that encourages and facilitates that paradigm shift from independence to interdependence: Stephen Covey's 'Public Victory'.

Chapter 3 Learning outcomes

1. Project leadership in team delivery is about creating teams who can deliver.
2. Team members are stakeholders whose willing engagement must be sought through the establishment of mutual respect, support and rapport.
3. The central function of the project leader is that of coach – fostering and encouraging engagement and collaboration with and between team members.
4. Coaching is not an added extra or nice-to-have. It is not the first activity to be dropped as pressure increases, but the last. The return in benefit outweighs invested time and effort by orders of magnitude.

Stakeholder engagement must be informed by the principle, 'lead as they would be led'.

4

Introducing the Triple Catalyst Model

The practitioner is introduced to the 'Triple Catalyst', a model offering a structured process where each catalyst drives a set of effective behaviours promoting project leadership, team formation and delivery.

Success in project delivery can be measured in many ways. Traditionally, a demonstrable adherence to agreed project health indicators – cost, time, quality and scope – would be taken to evidence competent project management. Yet these criteria do not measure leadership at all. They are like a doctor diagnosing and medicating for the secondary symptom of a headache, rather than identifying the brain tumour that is causing it.

Or again, imagine being told, a couple of decades ago, about a tool called 'Google', that gives virtually instantaneous access to expert knowledge across all arts and sciences. How far back in time might you expect it would be, with such access to data and knowledge, before you became a millionaire? Having such power at your fingertips – having access to such vast amounts of data and information, it seems eminently reasonable to imagine that it would be no time at all.

Ironically, despite such exponential increases in available technologies to generate, assess, measure and calibrate progress in delivery, so many projects fail to meet some or all targets, despite the availability of vast and immediate streams of *data* and *information*.

Now, just as then, however, information is of far more value if it offers foresight, rather than retrospective reports on progress to date. Effectiveness in project leadership, like project management, cannot be simply limited to measures of cost, time, quality and scope where all are increasingly subject to change and uncertainty.

Evolving project leadership

The causes of success or failure in project delivery lie in the effectiveness of proactive project leadership. And assessing this requires an entirely different metric.

What criteria can assess project leadership capability, and how are they applied?

The model for and approach to project leadership offered here presents an opportunity to establish genuine metrics that can be calibrated, and against which appropriate behaviours might be both identified and scored.

We have seen that for most people today, in this information-rich era, having vast amounts of data available offers *no* guarantee of success. This is equally true for the project manager – no matter how many reports, and however instantaneously they are generated, they offer no guarantee or promise of success in delivery. As discussed above, the complexifying factors in project delivery, and being able to navigate and even take advantage of them, lies with the ability to infer what is happening, what is to be done – and doing it.

Seasoned project managers can draw upon greater levels of expertise, materials and equipment than ever before, yet still, when measured against traditional criteria, they fall short – not occasionally, but regularly, and in some areas increasingly.

Once upon a time, in a stable environment, the leader could issue directives from a central location via a chain of command, with little likelihood or need for any of the recipients to communicate or interact with each other. The expert in the centre told everyone else what to do. Communication was linear and largely one-way: "Make it so, and confirm when it is done".

Today the case has altered beyond compare. On one hand, experts in every discipline are themselves required to commit to significant continuing professional development (CPD), while, at the same time, the Political, Economic, Sociological, Technological, Legal, and wider Environmental environment (PESTLE), is itself characterised as VUCA.

Communications are anything but linear, as highlighted above. Everyone is inter-communicating and copying others in, often generating cascades of effects undreamed of by the original sender.

Linear command and control does not work in a world of distributed experts and environmental turbulence.

So, it becomes clear that effective project leadership must occupy a paradigm very distinct from that occupied by traditional, command-and-control versions of leadership.

Introducing the Triple Catalyst Model

For the aspiring project leader, therefore, there is but one route to success, and that is through team empowerment. To create the relations, understanding and competences necessary across the entire field of delivery, and necessary to securing stakeholder engagement, a form of architecture is needed that empowers and primes the whole project team for success.

This architecture starts, as with all projects, with a design, and firm foundations on which project delivery can build.

The model that follows, and the process it prescribes, fulfils several functions simultaneously. By following its steps, the project leader will not only ignite the potential of the team, both as individuals and as a unity, releasing the synergy of collaboration, but will, by pursuing each step, find themselves acknowledged as project leaders.

To achieve this and realise its maximum effect, however, the aspiring project leader must make that 'subtle shift' that Sir John Whitmore described, and that Stephen Covey established as the necessary precursor to 'Public Victory', and that is the orientation towards others characterised by the move from the 'independent' stage of leadership development to 'interdependence'.

For those prepared to follow the spirit of this path – to embrace the necessary personal development and evolutionary transformation of self, it offers a powerful route to realising the personal potential that traditional leadership behaviours can literally only pretend to.

By setting aside any sense of personal entitlement that elevates 'me' over others, and instead focusing on establishing collaborative working, creating an ethos of 'we', project leadership will acquire an upwardly spiralling dynamic of agility and resilience that no centralised command-and-control structure can emulate or equal.

At the start of this section, we touched on the traditional project health indicators. By observing the model shortly to be introduced as the 'Triple Catalyst' and its corresponding 'Nine Steps to Delivery Team Leadership', the aspiring project leader will acquire a compelling insight into the engine driving project delivery – the integrated project team spanning all the disciplines needed and, vitally, themselves. The resulting overview gives an instant view of the health and potential of the parts making up that engine, providing indicators about the success in project delivery that are far more potent than traditional measures of earned value, scheduled performance or cost performance indices.

This insight into the project delivery team is similar to what you would find out about a vehicle after it had been through its MOT test. It would tell you about any issues with current performance, and its fitness for the journey ahead.

So, while traditional measures might indicate delivery against schedule, what is or is not working, being able to understand the status of the delivery team, the engine, is more powerful, because it can expose crucial indicators as to 'why'. To put this another way – whatever the status is now against traditional measures, if the project leader has assurance that the team itself is effective, they can be equally assured that the outcome will be the best it can be with the resources available, subject to emergent complexity.

Organisational intelligence

'Organisational intelligence' (or 'OI') is, to the organisation, what IQ is to the intellect, or EQ to emotional intelligence. It reflects a capacity for the organisation to acquire pertinent knowledge about the existing and anticipated environment, and then to strategically adapt for advantage. For the project leader, the acquisition and application of OI cannot take place from within the bubble of their own preconceptions. It necessitates a journey out of the comfort zone of assumptions to see through the eyes of others.

For the project leader, this organisational requirement necessitates the adoption of behaviours quite foreign to those in business-as-usual operational environments.

For those in operations, the circle of professional acquaintances is relatively small and stable. The project manager, by comparison, must regularly venture out as a 'boundary-spanner', stepping outside familiar environments and relationships to proactively engage with new stakeholders in unfamiliar environments, many carrying their own micro-cultures, even within the same organisation.

There will also be situations where the project manager is leading the way for the project in making 'first contact' with client stakeholders, and is responsible for establishing the 'wiring' for ongoing communications that are appropriate and effective by: consulting, informing, influencing and winning engagement reflecting the stakeholder's own level of power and influence.

Whether initiating a project or taking over at some point in the delivery life cycle, the organisationally intelligent project leader will be as keen to characterise the organisational and cultural context into which, the project will deliver, as they would be to investigate the underlying geology and conditions beneath a greenfield development. Both investigations characterise the foundations on which the project will build and deliver.

No matter how rigorous and insightful any scheduling, resourcing and procurement may be, if the owner or client controlling access and activity declines to facilitate or even actively frustrates delivery, the project manager will be in a hard place indeed. For, even if they contrive to escalate and in some way enforce compliance, they are still working in the other's territory and subject to the inevitable problems this will bring. Again, the traditional project leader finds their ability to perform requires them to act in ways quite at odds with the command-and-control leadership style. The only way forwards is to adopt both an emotionally and organisationally intelligent approach to identifying, as early as possible, those stakeholders presenting maximum influence and power, in order to map and prioritise their approach to securing engagement.

Recent APM research reinforces this message: "*Organisational intelligence is needed to attract and hang on to resource, to understand the wider organisational landscape and to build political awareness.*" (APM Research Fund series, *Project leadership: skills, behaviours, knowledge and values* (Oct 2018)).

Judgement and decision making

Just as baseline scope and management is fundamental to setting the vehicle of project delivery on the rails, so too the project manager must, in taking on a new role, endeavour to build a picture confirming their ability to deliver that takes into account the immediate environment and environs in an organisational and cultural sense. If significant roadblocks are to be encountered, it is better to identify them sooner rather than later. The project leader will then have time to adopt a winning approach or escalate the issues to inform a proactive, rather than reactive, response.

The project leader is responsible for delivery to cost, scope, quality and time, but there is another level of judgement and awareness they must cultivate and apply. Within a programme or portfolio, the success of the investment being made will be made against the return on that investment and the benefits it is intended to secure, or any negative outcomes it is designed to obviate or avoid. If, in exercising ongoing judgement, the project leader becomes aware of factors threatening the realisation of these benefits, it falls to them to ensure that those working at the strategic level of governance are in a position to make informed decisions.

APM research interviews showed "*. . . most saw project leaders as working on projects and project managers as working in projects, albeit that project*

Evolving project leadership

leaders needed the capability to zoom in and out of the detail as necessary." (APM Research Fund series, Project leadership: skills, behaviours, knowledge and values (Oct 2018). This reference to working *on* projects as opposed to working *in* them mirrors the above distinction between delivering to time and budget, while 'zooming out' reflects the ability to take a higher-level view, to see the wood for the trees.

Creating project culture and environment

Some see the project manager as a mere 'statistician', pulling together figures reflecting performance against a baseline, or else as an administrator, checking and signing off contractors' bills for work done, or sounding early warnings of additional cost, time, or scope.

Such portrayals, like those suggesting the centrality of assertive behaviours in leadership, distract attention from what really makes the difference between agile, collaborative and focused project teams, and those where each team member is focused on doing the minimum necessary to avoid 'being called to account'.

Neither is project leadership about establishing and managing frameworks, structures and processes, telling people what to do, for that is the realm of management. Rather, it is about empowering and inspiring, successfully enlisting others who willingly recognise you as their leader. Done well, it establishes relationships that underpin and drive effectiveness, agility and excellence in project delivery.

It was American politician and four-star general Colin Powell who noted that: "As a leader, you set the tone for your entire team." Those in a leadership position are particularly influential in setting the tone for the team.

The leader sets the tone, culture, values and style of working for all. It therefore falls on the project leader to embody the same values as they expect the team to work to. This is a significant responsibility, and was well captured by Dag Hammarskjöld, a former Secretary-General of the United Nations. He exhorted leaders to take to heart the following message, which is nowhere more true than in project leadership:

> "Your position never gives you the right to command.
>   It only imposes on you the duty of so living your life
>   that others can receive your orders without being humiliated"

What lends gravity to this affirmation is the way it strips away the *right* to command, the *right* to demand respect, loyalty and compliance of the follower, without a reciprocal obligation from the leader.

Instead, it places direct responsibility on the leader to earn and secure the status of leader in their followers' eyes. This denies a leadership policy of requiring their followers' blind obedience, but rather imposes the responsibility to coach them, such that they understand what must be done by making clear the 'why'. In this way followers are empowered, so reluctance or resistance is far less likely. This is how followers taking ownership is cultivated and stakeholders become engaged.

Securing such status in the eyes of the team requires a conscious shift away from command-and-control behaviours. Instead the project leader must adopt and exhibit competence in building productive relationships across diverse team members, founded on rapport, mutual respect and commitment. This commitment must be seen to be reciprocal and authentic. The model detailed in Chapter 4 will facilitate this.

Authenticity is a by-product of the acquisition of emotional intelligence, which itself comes with self-knowledge born of managing reactive emotions and behaviours.

The 'parent', 'adult' and 'child' in the Transactional Analysis model previously discussed offers a ready metaphor for emotional intelligence in the measured disposition and moderated behaviours of the 'adult'. Unlike the overly stern 'parent' or petulant 'child', the 'adult' attitude reflects practice and forbearance, to control and moderate the instinctual responses to others' behaviours and words.

The competent project leader is measured by their tone and behaviour, especially when others lose control around them. This takes practice and self-awareness. When the 'temperature' of the conversation increases, this may be reflected in the increasing 'pace' of any exchange, along with corresponding increased heart rate and faster, shallower breathing. Less oxygen reaches the brain, impairing its performance. The nervous system goes into fight-or-flight mode as the brain reverts to ancient primordial pathways, diverting resources from the higher levels of reasoning in preparation for physical conflict.

The project leader will not only deal with such situations when they occur unpredictably, but will on many occasions anticipate and pre-empt their occurrence. However, sometimes they might actually allow such situations to occur, within limits. As will be discussed in Chapter 6, there is a process of 'Forming Storming and Norming' as new teams come together, where the experienced project leader will allow the team to explore each other's boundaries within healthy limits.

Evolving project leadership

The project leader is the team's 'architect'. They must establish the foundations and groundwork, and then actively cultivate disparate individuals into a high-performing, collaborative team. The project leader's own behaviours and the example they set for their team is repercussive, with far-reaching ramifications. It is about "*the leader becoming the role model for and promoting behaviours setting the tone for the project culture, since the way the team behaves is very indicative of the leader's style*". (APM Research Fund series, Project leadership: skills, behaviours, knowledge and values (Oct 2018).

The Triple Catalyst Model has been developed to give the project leader both a framework and process to benefit themselves, each member of the project delivery team, and especially line reports. This development of self and the immediate team naturally leads to greater self-awareness and encourages greater emotional intelligence in the leader themselves.

Implicit in this process, and the example set by the leader, is the establishment of a culture of treating others as they would expect to be treated.

This expectation works as a powerful 'nudge', encouraging others to reciprocate and 'pass on' the respect shown to them. For the aspiring project leader, the adoption of the Triple Catalyst offers a structured path, nurturing the evolution of high-performing leadership and teams alike.

The Triple Catalyst for project management leadership

Project leadership is itself a 'catalyst'. It both realises and releases the potential of empowered, committed team members, securing full engagement from stakeholders and facilitating collaboratively aligned combined delivery.

The Triple Catalyst Model for project leadership, and the 'Nine Steps' it prompts (See Figures 9 and 10), provide a structured approach to releasing and realising synergy in project delivery. They also provide a dynamic metric, enabling project delivery organisations to calibrate the effectiveness of project delivery.

The triple catalysts of 'Vision' informed by 'Insight' and 'Foresight', are at the core of this book. They constitute a 'golden thread' running through the establishment and practice of project leadership. While project management is the vehicle of project delivery, project leadership is like fuel bringing the engine to life, realising and releasing the potential synergy residing within an otherwise lifeless engine.

Introducing the Triple Catalyst Model

```
                    VISION
                 What should be?
                 Self and team, CPD

                        Cost
                       Scope
                   Time     Quality

         INSIGHT              FORESIGHT
   Knowing & understanding:   Anticipating:
         What Is              What could be?
   Self and team: Functioning &  Self and team member
        development              potential
```

Awareness — *Understanding*

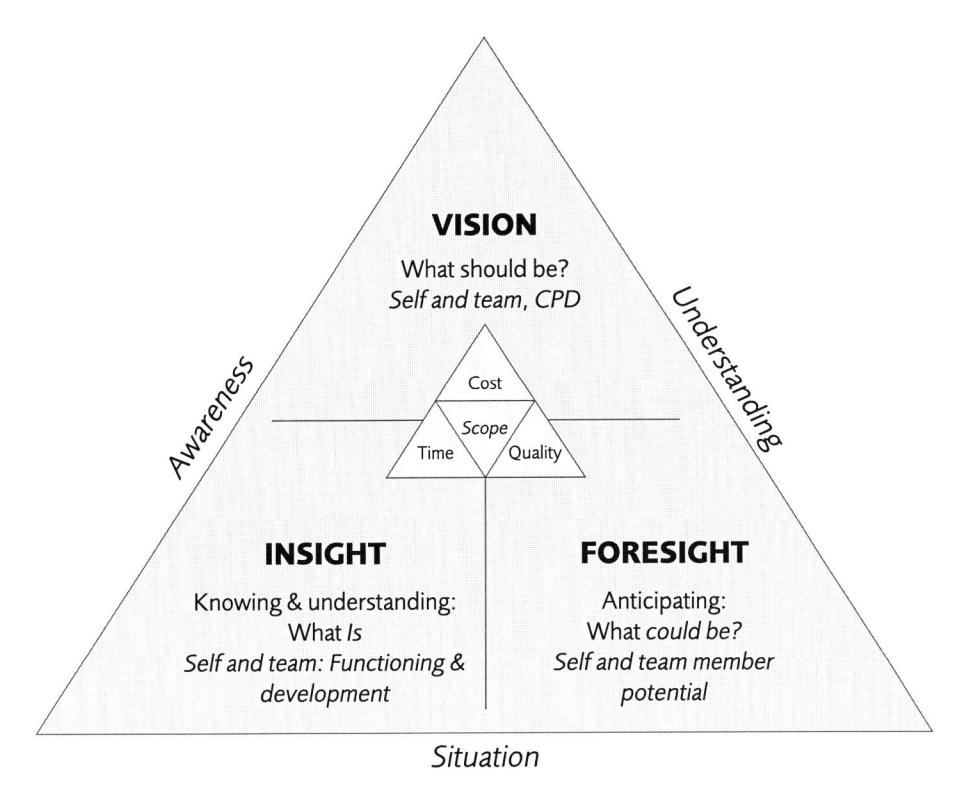

Situation

Figure 9 The project leader Triple Catalysts

The potentially transformative power of this approach far surpasses that of the traditional measures of performance – against cost, time, quality. All experienced project managers have been measured against these metrics. They know only too well that such measures never take into account the extent to which the project manager has exercised leadership in order to obtain the best possible performance from the team.

When projects fail according to the classic criteria, the true reasons for that failure may not lie with the project manager or delivery team at all. Leaving aside the the disservice that does to both of them, such a focus diverts attention away from the true causes of failure in the way aircraft manufacturers might attribute disasters to pilots.

Equally, many project delivery teams succeed in driving delivery across the line, but where it might have been far more effective never comes to light. In many project teams, experience suggests that members' potential is not realised, because of poor and ineffective project management.

Evolving project leadership

Worst of all, in project delivery organisations, and for all striving within them, poor project management results in a toxic delivery culture, actively eroding individual and team performance, and even affecting mental health. This has far-reaching implications and costs for all.

Due consideration for mental health and its promotion cannot be ignored, marginalised or treated as a peripheral concern in project management delivery, either at the organisational or individual level. An irresponsible project manager who does not exercise appropriate project leadership behaviours is a liability to all. The cost of poor project management is carried out of the workplace, into homes and future projects.

Behaviours that do not take account of the wellbeing of those managed are no less reprehensible than ignorance or wilful disregard of Health and Safety regulations. By any measure reflecting the impact of toxic behaviours, there are clear financial, economic and reputational repercussions for any organisation.

Nevertheless, rather than seeking genuine indicators of project leadership, organisations are frequently drawn by the growing ubiquity of IT and AI, which now offer continuous traditional measures of progress in project delivery.

The absence of identifying measures and the difficulty of calibrating 'leadership' is clear and understandable. After all, what is to be objectively measured, considering the diversity of recognised leaders and environments?

How would one measure the leadership of Sir Winston Churchill against that of Nelson Mandela, Mahatma Gandhi, Jacinda Aherne, Florence Nightingale or Sir Ernest Shackleton? Such diversity renders the identification of any one metric extremely problematic. Even the 'number of followers' bears little scrutiny, since what followers might 'do' for a given leader will likely vary greatly.

Attempting to focus on and determine leadership *behaviours* as a potential candidate for measurement, one is immediately faced, yet again, with the sheer diversity of settings or environments where leadership emerges. What seems or proves appropriate varies depending on participants and context. Again, the form leadership takes varies with its function in a given context and culture.

Can traditional leaders be characterised, ranking competence, one against another? Might success in leadership be measured by numbers of willing followers, or salary? Even were such measures applied, they would have little relevance in determining what makes *'project leadership'* good or bad.

What is to be measured?

Fortunately, it is the very distinction between traditional leadership and project leadership that offers a way forward, for it avoids the formidable obstacles that prevent universal measures being formulated. A tighter focus opens the way for the behaviours demanded in project leadership to be identified and, to a significant degree, both calibrated and assessed.

The very distinctive set of behaviours that remain, once the constraints identified in Sections 1 to 4 have been applied, indicate what the project leader must *do*, enabling and defining discrete steps in a process that can be demonstrably followed.

The project manager aspiring to leadership must engage in three key activities. They require acquisition of a set of challenging competences that have long laboured under the misnomer of 'soft skills'. They are in fact both 'hard', in the sense of challenging, and the product of a journey that those relying on the props of title or position-power fear to face.

The three activities each act as a 'Triple Catalyst' in their own, specific domain. The Cambridge Dictionary describes a catalyst as "an event or person that causes great change". This is the origin of the name for the Triple Catalyst Model, for that, indeed, is what they do.

The journey to project leadership reflects the shift from Covey and Whitmore's 'independence' to 'interdependence', and the Triple Catalyst will be shown to facilitate that journey.

To appreciate the power and importance of the skills called 'soft' in project management and leadership, it is important to first expose and then strip away the distortion this label imposes. The portrayal of skills securing others' engagement and followership, influencing both disposition and actions, as 'soft', is at best misleading, and at worst disingenuous.

The hard truth about 'soft skills'

'**Soft skills**' often identified include:
- Leadership
- Teamwork
- Communication skills
- Problem solving skills
- Work ethic
- Flexibility / adaptability
- Interpersonal skills.

Evolving project leadership

This list becomes even longer and even harder to dismiss as trivial when the above 'leadership' soft skills are broken down and identified, variously, to include:

Leadership soft skills:
- Empathy
- Empowerment
- Influencing
- Negotiating
- Delegating
- Creativity and innovation
- Honesty and integrity
- Inspiring others.

Just as any consensus on what leadership *'is'* falls apart under scrutiny, as project leadership turns out to be quite distinct from traditional leadership, so too, as the above list illustrates, the nature of skills described as 'soft' turns out, under closer consideration, to be anything but.

This is further reinforced when you consider that, while so-called 'hard skills' might be used to identify what is to be done and how (engineering design and construction) or what progress is made (project controls), actually making it happen falls to leadership, so it is here where the remit and contribution of the project manager as leader is front and centre.

For many advocating behaviours associated with traditional, heroic leadership, 'soft skills' are merely 'referred-out-to', as if marginal or an 'optional extra'; certainly subordinate to traditional leadership's central concern to promote assertiveness, to hold others to account.

There is a largely unacknowledged prejudice and bias when leadership skills are referred to as 'soft'. The Collins Dictionary provides a range of words and phrases associated with the adjective, including the following.

Collins Dictionary
Soft
In British English:
i.e.
- not hard; giving little or no resistance to pressure or weight
- easy to influence or impose upon
- prepared to compromise; not doctrinaire
- informal, derogatory, feeble or silly (often in the phrase soft in the head)
- unable to endure hardship, especially through too much pampering

- informal, requiring little exertion; easy, a soft job
- unprotected against attack, a soft target

And in American English:
i.e.
- not hard; giving little or no resistance to pressure or weight
- not hard for its kind; not as hard as is normal, desirable etc.
- weak or delicate; not strong or vigorous; esp., not able to endure hardship, as because of easy living
- having flabby muscles
- requiring little effort; easy
- easily impressed, influenced, or imposed upon.

It is impossible to dissociate the word 'soft' from the above connotations. It is not surprising, therefore, that 'soft skills' are often referred to in an off-hand or even faintly derogatory manner. They seem by definition to carry less weight than 'hard skills'.

For those that recognise their importance, however, becoming adept in these crucial skills can be actively promoted through the application of the Triple Catalyst and the process it invokes.

Compelling in effecting project leadership competence, these skills are hard both to secure and to master. Few could claim universal excellence in all contexts. Such excellence is the pursuit of a lifetime's continuing professional development.

The Triple Catalyst found in Figure 9 has nine discrete steps that prompt the project leader to achieve Insight, Foresight and Vision for self, each team member, and then the team as a collective.

Each step can be progressively documented, and greater competence will be effected and refined over time to meet emergent complexities in delivery. These Nine Steps are illustrated sequentially in Figure 10 on page 89.

In Figure 9, the central 'Iron Triangle' is represented to highlight the Triple Catalyst's ultimate focus.

Every project leader can be expected to show the leadership behaviours that are expressed in these steps and that are necessary to realise their own potential, along with that of individuals in their team and the group as a whole.

Insight, Foresight and Vision are essential project leader competences. Without them, delivery to the triple constraints cannot and will not, happen.

The project leader must apply Insight, 'what is' (the present), with a clear Vision of 'what should be' (intent), informed by Foresight 'what could be' (anticipation).

Insight, Foresight and Vision therefore represent the Triple Catalysts for the project leader; specific leadership behaviours prompting the employment of other supporting models and tools.

Evolving project leadership

> The competent project leader sequentially applies the Triple Catalysts of Insight, Foresight, and Vision, to self, team members and then the team as a whole.
>
> These nine steps prompt powerful project management leadership behaviours, aligning and empowering the wider project team and stakeholders and so supporting delivery within the Triple Constraints of cost, time and scope

By generating and applying Insight about themselves and their team, the competent project leader develops 'Situational awareness' of what *is*.

This, in turn, informs both Vision and Foresight, constituting the project leader's 'situational understanding', what could and should be, in developing both themselves and their team to deliver to cost, time and scope.

Establishing and communicating a clear Vision encourages collaborative team behaviours, but requires both a demonstrable clear Vision of 'ends', and the means and manner of their achievement.

The nine steps outlined in Figure 10 enable the effective project leader to determine the status and development of self, team members and the wider delivery team.

There is a systemic, even symbiotic, relationship between Insight, Foresight and Vision. Achieving and achieved, they each inform and are interdependent with the others.

Whereas with the Iron Triangle, any change to cost, time, quality, or scope affects the other elements, here, whether Insight, Foresight or Vision are informed, they *enrich* the others. Situational awareness, coupled with foresight and a vision of what is to be and how to get there, fosters greater situational understanding, and that in turn can feed back to enrich Insight.

Take as an example an individual – it could be a project team member or the project leader. Having developed a degree of insight into performance and competence in the current delivery environment, the next level fosters foresight to anticipate what will be needed down the line. The difference between performance and required competence now against what is going to be required informs a vision of the end state and what is to be done to achieve it. Once established and detailed, this bigger picture will then provide a greater Insight into the current situation.

Initially an individual may be seen to be performing competently – ownership and delegation of responsibilities may be complete, with line management quite comfortable. However, an appreciation of what is in prospect – it could be a new phase in the life cycle, or a new set of tasks in an unfamiliar delivery environment,

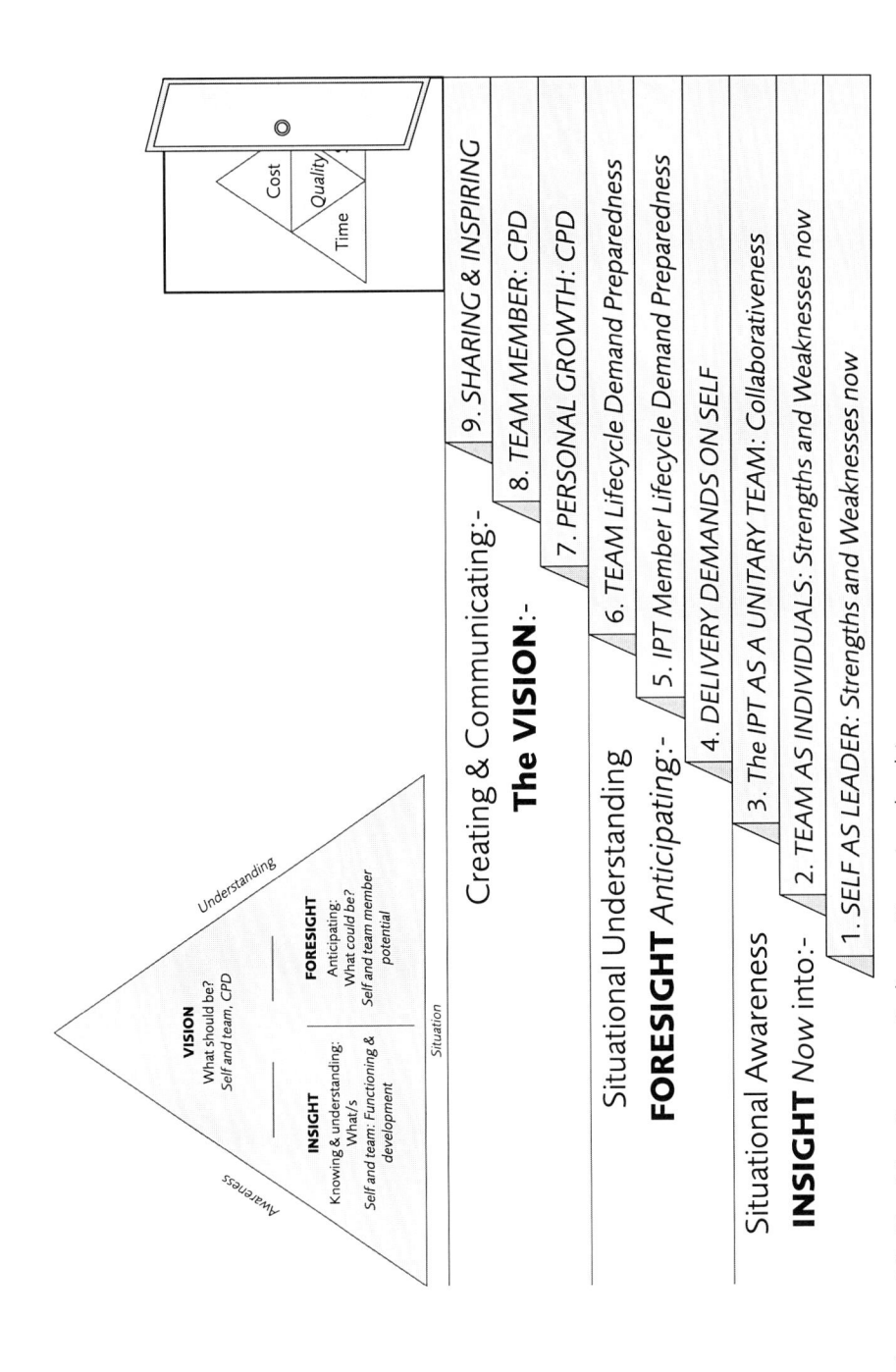

Figure 10 The Nine Steps to Delivery Team Leadership

or maybe even a new contractual relationship – all serve to bring to the fore the need to build-in appropriate development before the demand arises.

Following these steps benefits the project leader, the extended team and the business, in addition to facilitating the emergence of team 'synergy'.

In Figure 9, the central 'Iron Triangle' or 'Triple Constraint' is represented to highlight the 'Triple Catalyst's particular focus.

The Vision for, and target of, all project leader behaviours have, at their very core, a focus on delivering within these very specific triple constraints constituting 'what should be'. They fundamentally inform how it should be done and 'what good looks like' in project delivery.

Although the Iron Triangle is variously presented, as consisting of cost, time and, interchangeably, quality/scope[1], it is incumbent on the project leader to recognise that their fundamental and personal responsibility is to align and empower the delivery team, orienting them to work collaboratively; delivering within these specific constraints, however they are characterised.

While the triple constraint provides a focus on the end, the Triple Catalyst gives a focus on the means to that end: the integrated project team and the full and effective engagement and appropriate influencing of all stakeholders.

The Nine Steps to Project Team Delivery and Project Leadership

Figure 10, on page 89, shows nine steps acting as a sequential 'checklist' for the project leader to implement so enabling the delivery team to really 'take off' in collaborative working.

Each step is vital. Failing to address them all will undermine the project leader, limiting their ability to realise the potential of themselves and the wider team.

Insight, Foresight and Vision are focused through an iterative, successive focus on the project leader themselves, then the team members individually, and then the team as a collective unity.

Application of the Triple Catalyst and its Nine Steps is not a one-off task. It must, like any vehicle, be maintained and serviced by the project leader across the life cycle.

By understanding the need for these behaviours and embodying them, the project leader will discover new Insights into themselves and their team, informing Foresight into what is to be done, and the Vision to be communicated and shared.

What might not be immediately apparent, however, is the truly profound impact these behaviours can have on the way the project leader is perceived and the transformation in relationships it can precipitate.

Introducing the Triple Catalyst Model

By following the nine steps, it is inevitable that the relationships between the project leader, their reports and the wider delivery team as a whole will enter a whole new dimension of effectiveness.

This can be a real source of inspiration, as the project leader transforms a group of individuals into a team, and in so doing becomes, and is seen, not only as a project manager but as a true leader, "providing vision, direction, feedback and support so people can do their best work" *Body of Knowledge 7th edition*.

Application of the Triple Catalyst Model provides both a structure and platform for the project manager to practise core behaviours necessary to the establishment of project leadership. This marks, not the end of the journey or a final destination, but the establishment of fit-for-purpose, team relationship management and project leadership.

Facilitating collaboration, competent coaching, engaging with and influencing stakeholders to 'do the right things' and pre-empting or managing conflict; all are at the heart of day-to-day EQ-informed and responsive project management and leadership.

Insight, Foresight and Vision are focused through an iterative, successive focus on the project leader themselves, then the team members individually, and then the team as a collective unity.

Chapter 4 Learning outcomes

1. The Triple Catalyst fosters Insight, Foresight and Vision for the project leader, individual team members and as a collective unity.
2. To be effective, the Triple Catalyst must be supported at organisational level.
3. The project leader must exercise discernment, and ability to keep the larger picture in mind, including benefit delivery, especially in change management.
4. The project leader has a profound impact on delivery team culture. Their behaviours, tone of voice, and attitude have a disproportionate effect on all.
5. The Triple Catalyst prompts the Nine Steps to Project Leadership through the development of Insight, Foresight and Vision in relation to self, the team members and the team as a whole.
6. Implementing the Nine Steps requires the development of the hard 'soft skills' of empathy and emotional intelligence.

5

Organisational foundations enabling and supporting the project leader journey

In addition, the necessity of wider strategic and organisation support in structures and processes highlights the fact that the project manager will not achieve the full benefits of project leadership alone.

The project manager will not likely realise project leadership's benefits working in isolation. Wider organisational support in active strategy, structures and processes is vital, and while initiated top-down, must be nurtured at all levels.

Organisations promoting organisation-wide awareness and expectations of project leadership behaviours must extend this to project leader selection, performance assessment and promotion.

Key challenges in developing Insight

The development of grounded, informed situational awareness generates Insight into the current status of the team as a unit. It requires the project leader to scrutinise their *own* competence, before doing the same with each team member, then assessing the performance and collaborative effectiveness of the team as a whole.

At the organisational level, Insight prompts measures promoting reflective practice by all project managers. Lean enterprise organisational practices encourage ongoing review of processes, minimising waste and increasing value creation. So too, at the individual level, the reflective practitioner in project management is encouraged to consider how and if their way of working is as effective as it could or should be. Is it appropriate for their current environment?

From an organisational perspective, the promised benefits released by application of the Triple Catalyst include removing the ongoing sunk-cost of outmoded leadership styles. The additional benefits stemming from establishing empowered collaborative teams cannot be denied.

On the plus side, establishing expectations and organisational support for the practice of Insight is a powerful, compelling and welcome initiative for those accepting the need for change and growth. From these, at the individual level, there is no resistance; for them the next part of this book offers a clear and welcome path.

However, to realise the benefits the Triple Catalyst promises for the *entire* organisation and its stakeholders, it is crucial to ask *how* its adoption might be promoted and *embedded* at the *organisation level*, what challenges might emerge, and how they might best be resolved.

The challenge in promoting the practice of Insight at the organisational level, from the top down, is that there will be those who resist and even resent its adoption. Their attitudes and behaviours represent a real problem. For among project managers there will certainly be some who, far from welcoming the change, will feel not only their source of power but their very identity undermined.

They will resist the introspection, needed to exercise the practice of 'Insight', and all organisational drives to evidence or promote its recognition or adoption. For them, the team exists to do *their* bidding, and stakeholders, including the delivery team, should defer to their management. They were, from the start, attracted to the project management function by an ambition for power over others. They anticipated the role of project manager conferring a licence to exercise command-and-control behaviours.

Those at the 'independent' stage on the Leadership Performance Curve are in-dependence on esteem-from-others to support their ego-centric self-construal. They have much in common with the behaviours typical of a narcissist. Strongly advocating and deploying command-and-control behaviours at every opportunity, they are likely to reject any need to develop Insight and self-awareness. They are also likely to assert that the importance of their project is such that delivery must take precedence over personal considerations; delivery time constraints mean that coaching and team member development can and should be set aside.

With little empathy for those in their remit, they feel themselves justified in treating them as a means to an end. They project blame for shortcomings or deficits onto others. Meanwhile, any credit for work carried out by the team, they deem as their due entitlement. They invariably declare themselves as an exception to rules or norms, exempt from performance assessments, qualification standards, and any need for training.

There is, then, a very deep conflict between the organisational and strategic need for true project leadership, and those least willing, or able, to embrace it.

An informed focus for change

It is tempting to adopt a traditional approach to cultural change, by attempting to implement top-down management initiatives focusing tightly and specifically on the aberrant behaviours of the 'resistance' – those routinely exhibiting command-and-control behaviours, oblivious or in denial about their counter-productive effects.

However, the energy and time expended in focusing on this minority is likely to be wasted. If any change or lasting evolution is to occur in those actively resisting it, it will not be through imposition from the 'top down', or 'outside in'. What is required is a means to precipitate a revolution or paradigm shift in outlook and perspective, an inside-out transformation in their perception and behaviours. The attraction of command and control has always been promoted through heroic narratives and stories; at the very heart of its allure was the offer of an elevated identity, endowed with an almost mythical dimension. For those in-dependence on esteem for others, this is irresistible. For this reason, evolving a culture supportive of project leadership among those inclined towards traditional command and control necessitates the establishment of a new narrative – one that subverts and replaces the old with something more appealing. To do that requires some understanding of the psychology differentiating those who are in-dependence from the interdependent.

A psychological understanding of resistance

For those whose identity is in-dependence on traditional command-and-control authority, the conversion to interdependence presents as a fundamental challenge – even a threat. Reframing the function and form of leadership away from traditional dominance behaviours not only threatens their habitual form of self expression, but negates the self-image they derive from them.

For those in the interdependent stage of leadership, one's sense of self can be informed or supported by beliefs and values. For those whose self-esteem and very sense of identity is derived from a relation of dominance over others, if you remove the licence to dominate, while promoting empowerment of others, it will invite intense discomfort and hence resistance.

Where strong, identity-related beliefs are held, such as a sense of entitlement and demand for esteem from others, change will be contested. When such a change does succeed, it is often only after an individual's accumulated experience of personal expectations has been repeatedly contradicted or overturned. Imagine holding a perception about someone that is incrementally eroded, until a pivotal moment arrives when it seems the veil is torn away and a fundamental re-evaluation occurs.

This incremental increase in 'cognitive dissonance', the tension arising from simultaneously holding conflicting views, accumulates until the 'final straw breaks the camel's back'. Suddenly, the penny drops; the old world-view is upended and usurped; a new frame of reference is embraced. This is one way in which the movement from being 'In-dependence' on esteem-from-others can lead to awareness, and then leadership pursued and realised in the Covey and Whtmore's state of 'Interdependence'.

Insight, ready or not: the 'nudge' to aporia; more powerful than 'shove'

For those resisting the demotion of command-and-control behaviours, yet capable of change, a truly compelling route to such change is through an approach widely known as the 'nudge'.

Instinctive resistance can eventually be overcome by engineering cognitive dissonance between what is believed and what is experienced.

Step by step, the facts as they are experienced are shown to be increasingly at odds with previously held beliefs or prejudice. For example, suppose those achieving successful collaboration are publicly celebrated, endorsed by senior management, and held up as exemplars. Consider the effect of showing team members openly declaring their gratitude and loyalty to a leader who has respected them and helped them grow. A dawning awareness is fostered in the 'unconverted'.

Organisational foundations enabling and supporting the project leader journey

The organisation can be instrumental in shifting perceptions by widely supporting and championing 'what good looks like'; lauding the concrete benefits and examples of success.

Stories articulate lived experience with the immediacy of a 3D virtual reality

There is no greater force for driving and supporting culture change than the stories people tell. Stories arbitrate change, and articulate human experience with an immediacy that policies and procedures can never match.

With this in mind, at the organisational level, a way is prepared to avoid the costs associated with likely low return on effort invested in trying to change those averse to adopting fit-for-purpose project leadership behaviours.

Those demanding attention, spending as much or more time on self-promotion than on delivery, are not the real 'talent pool' – just the opposite. Those committed both to their team and collaborative, empowered delivery are least likely to claim personal credit at the expense of others. An authentic leader voices a vision they live by: "it's not about me, but us, achieving *that*, together". If they do seek credit, it is for the team. If there is failure, they first call themselves to account. If there is blame, they take responsibility.

Decisive leadership is needed to recognise, expose and so discourage egotistical, self-promoting behaviours, exposing and calling them out for what they are. Promotions and regrading are justified by team performance, not self-promotion.

Is the team performing effectively? Is it highly motivated, empowered, with ongoing individual professional development and the exercise of initiative? Do team members attribute their aspiration and inspiration to grow to one they are proud to call their leader?

Insight for the willing

For those of no prior opinion, position or prejudice, the establishment of new norms in project leadership behaviours are less problematic. Not being entrenched or holding a vested interest in the status quo, they are open to debate, argument and reason; more readily inclined to adopt a more facilitative, empowering approach to project leadership.

Positive leadership behaviours can be developed, exercised and evidenced as informed by the Triple Catalyst. But integrity and authenticity cannot be faked. The final measure of leadership effectiveness is the team, in their disposition and performance. True leadership can never be based on self-aggrandising behaviours, including self-promotion.

For this reason, growing from 'independence' to 'interdependence' is a fundamental, qualifying prerequisite for project leadership. In the next section, the step of developing 'Insight into self' represents, in a crucial sense, a 'guarded-threshold' to discovering and releasing the inner qualities necessary to personal, as well as team leadership.

The transformation from toxic to productive project management culture, like all successful personal or cultural change, is not best served from the top down, by imposing new processes. Culture eats process for breakfast. Learning to light a fire, one soon discovers that it is not best achieved by reaching down from above, but by igniting it from below; from within.

Balanced people unexpectedly experiencing celebrity, being in the spotlight, or having senior status thrust upon them for the first time, discover something quite surprising. Followers' expectations can have a profound effect on those 'under the gaze', whether of subordinates or the public. It can stimulate more conservative behaviours, for fear of losing the provisional esteem of others.

The subordinate nudge and power of expectation

By promoting awareness of appropriate 'coaching' behaviours over assertive dominance behaviours, the enhanced upward-awareness of team members serves to moderate outdated ways of behaving. The moderating effect on behaviour is akin to those now informing and moderating the use of language in light of growing respect for equality, diversity and inclusion (EDI).

A new generation of 'millennial' project management apprentices and graduates already show diminishing tolerance for self-indulgent command-and-control behaviours. They instinctively recognise unwarranted exhibitions of power and authority for what they are.

Holding others to account and challenging how people behave, once the domain of management, is increasingly visited upwards on management, as exemplified by the 'me-too' movement standing up for women's rights.

Look at how today's children consume media. They probably witness more of life's adult dramas, played out online and on TV, than previous generations might observe or experience in a lifetime.

The power of conditional respect and compliance on management is not to be underestimated. The digital recruitment environment is such that young professionals are far more able to identify alternative employment opportunities than previous generations ever could. As a result, their tolerance towards being treated poorly is lower than that of many generations before them.

For this reason, in seeking to influence project management behaviours, senior management should resist trying to drive change downwards. The change must, on the contrary, be based on an environment of expectation and valued behaviours, which can subtly nudge 'upwards' the disposition of those otherwise disinclined to participate.

The cultural environment organisations create can be effected from the bottom up, as well as the traditional top-down approach. Too often, projects are held up as exemplary purely on grounds of financial or technical performance. What such a focus overlooks are those where success has been achieved through the agility that comes with empowered collaborative performance; where teams are stronger at the end of delivery than the beginning, as opposed to being burnt out.

The concept of the 'Fundamental Attribution Error' in Social Science highlights the significant role the project leader can play in engineering a good delivery environment. Students learn that, while an individual's disposition is often attributed as the cause of their behaviour, more often than we suppose, it is their *environment* that triggers and drives it.

For the project manager, this applies to the relationships and culture of team interactions that they promote. Experience of emotional contagion – where a team member's, and especially the project manager's, bad mood influences the whole team, has been directly experienced by most. The relevance of this work in every walk of life, and especially in project delivery today, is that it highlights the crucial importance of the true project leader in creating environments bringing out the best, rather than the worst, in all.

In a famous experiment, psychology students were prompted to pay close attention every time their next lecturer moved to their left in class. But every time the lecturer moved to their right, they were told to gradually remove eye contact and, without being abrupt, to feign lack of interest.

The students entered the next lecture as usual – the lecturer unaware that *they*, in fact, were the 'subject' of a lesson their students would likely never forget. Each time the lecturer moved left, pens were scribbling, attention increased. Each time they moved right, it fell away.

What happened? By the end of class, the lecturer was leaning against the wall to the students' left. Asked why they had moved and why they were there, the lecturer had no idea – they were not even conscious of gravitating to the students' left, or being influenced and conditioned to stay there.

Creating a negative environment will foster a culture of inhibited and degraded performance. How often, by body language, tone and cadence, does the project manager convey the sense of trying to catch members of the team out, and even with the intention of then making examples of them? Many can recall being in a situation where the requirement for reporting is communicated so that it feels as though reasons for blame rather than praise are being actively pursued.

In organisations with such toxic cultures, individuals are blamed for performance to distract attention from more pertinent factors, just as pilot error might be attributed as the cause of an accident when the fault is later revealed to lie esewhere.

Several lessons flow from awareness of the Fundamental Attribution Error for all project management at the organisational level. First, it highlights the potential for falsely attributing blame to individuals where the environment was poor. Second, it offers insight for addressing and informing the challenge of cultural and individual change described above.

In addition, the Fundamental Attribution Error prompts recognition that promoting project leadership competence in developing Insight should not be restricted to top-down initiatives. Project teams can be educated to recognise the behaviours of true exemplars of project leadership. The moderating influence of the way they *expect* to be treated, can go a long way to counter the acceptance of forms of leadership behaviour that are no longer fit for purpose.

Organisational influence on project leadership culture through hiring standards

Hire those who evidence a desire to nurture Insight in others

In addition to measures aimed at those intent on embracing change to realise their potential, and those reluctant or unable to achieve the necessary stage of interdependent leadership, there is a final group contributing to the population of project managers.

This group may enter project management from outside the organisation, or they may be promoted or transfer in from another profession. To appreciate the challenges this offers for the function and form of project leadership, consider the following.

It is clearly the case that the HR function in many organisations is still shackled to traditional modes of assessment promoting command and control behaviours in recruitment. This includes the conscious and unconscious use of legacy language within job adverts that have the effect of dissuading applications from women and minorities. Interviews focus on skills such as assertiveness, holding others to account, or the ability to take control in a group activity such as the 'plank exercise' described earlier. This process imports novice leaders into the profession who have secured their places by exhibiting the exact opposite of what the form and function of project leadership requires today. Hiring such individuals will only perpetuate cultures where leadership style is based on demonstrably outmoded views of command and control.

The following scenario illustrates the dynamic still at work in all too many project management assessment centres, which may be set up and led by teams with little knowledge, understanding or direct experience in project management. The assumptions made by some project management capability organisations may well promote the need for traditional commmand and control leadership skills and, inevitably, 'assertiveness' as a key characteristic of such leadership.

At the same time, there is rarely any attention given to seeking entrants to the profession who show the enabling skills that underpin contemporary project leadership, such as appropriate motivation, empathy, emotional intelligence and a preference to empower, rather than diminish others.

How often do recruitment exercises target behaviours facilitating emergence and collaboration, rather than those exercising assertiveness while demanding subservience and compliance?

The counter-productive result of a traditional project management interview and assessment

You have been asked to participate in an interview, including a group exercise. One by one, the candidates are led in and interviewed, before being asked to participate in a group exercise where you and your fellow assessors observe and make notes.

Emerging literature from the human, psychological and social sciences all evidence the degree to which first impressions can establish an often unconscious observational bias seeking to confirm initial impressions made in the first minute or two.

The prejudice this fosters is further accentuated by the unexamined expectations and biases that many interviewers for project management positions hold.

As in the above group exercise example, it is not difficult to imagine members of the officer class attending, with white lab coats and clipboards at the ready, singling out the individual most assertively imposing their will on others. It is an almost unavoidable temptation to conflate or associate the idea of taking charge with that of leadership. The question never arises as to what the others in the group think.

So **Candidate A in Group A** reads the instructions for the team exercise furiously, with the apparent intent of finding a way to take charge virtually immediately, by telling the team what to do.

Among Group A, though, some presented with the 'fait accompli' of another telling them, or others, what to do, face a predicament. Do they precipitate conflict by refusing compliance? Do they fear this will be interpreted not as leadership, but indicative of an insubordinate character? Do they place the value and importance of working together above that of sowing discord and conflict and so undermining group achievement? Are they likely to be credited for this?

Meanwhile, Candidate A presses on, regardless. Eye contact is sustained just long enough to cover the issuing of a command or direction, then meved to another to remove any suggestion that conversation is encouraged. The eye contact within the group is distinctly limited and mostly only sustained for long enough to receive instruction from Candidate A.

In **Group B, Candidate B** stands out from the rest of the group not by 'telling', but by 'asking'. For the first few minutes, she is clearly writing down her own ideas and then watching and listening – eventually approaching some individuals with questions. A few minutes later, she invites members of the team to openly express their thoughts and ideas to all – continuing to make notes. Then she makes suggestions, taking the best ideas that have received group support. When she suggests steps to take, the team agrees, and self-select their actions.

Throughout, there is significant eye contact between all the members of the team as they seek assurance that all are on board.

In **interview, Candidate A** presents as highly confident, to the point where one might suspect they have been coached into what to expect, and have rehearsed the answers expected to press the right buttons. They freely express their intent from the outset to *"take charge of the team"*, and assert their authority. Asked if they knew what the answer to the exercise looked like, they admit they did not know, but knew they had to *take charge*.

They unhesitatingly assert their willingness and preparedness to hold others to account. They appear decisive and self-assured, not to be trifled with or challenged. Their eye contact is bold, and leaves no doubt that their opinion is not up for question. They are not likely to ask questions for clarification, in case this should signal uncertainty or indecisiveness. When questioned on any view or opinion they have expressed, there is in their demeanour a sense of being affronted that anyone should have the temerity to question them. Open questions are met with closed answers – there is a sense that they resent discussion, and find it unsettling.

In **interview, Candidate B** is asked the same questions. She makes clear her perception from the outset that those doing most to help the team succeed would be seen in the best light as prospective project managers.

She explains that she had initially taken the time to think of ways to progress the task, before gradually becoming concerned that the team did not seem to be working together.

In the end, she says she had realised that someone needed to *"take care of the team"*, so she had consciously sought to engage each member in turn, in order to get the best ideas out in the open so that everyone could think about them.

Questioned about this approach, Candidate 'B' clearly took the question seriously, not just focusing on the fact that her opinion was being questioned. There was a considered pause before she answered, and she was clearly not apprehensive that, by asking for clarity about the question, she might be perceived as weak.

Despite all evidence accumulating to the contrary, many human resource departments and those conducting interviews are none the wiser about assessment and interview than our Candidate 'A'. Most who are selected to conduct interviews from their respective professions are not given training in discerning the characteristics appropriate to project leadership. In the project management profession, there remains a broad lack of clarity as to the nature of the role. Nor is there clarity around how both traditional form and function have been overtaken by repercussive changes in *what* is delivered and by whom (the growth and diversity in stakeholders' relations), how it is delivered, and the VUCA environment in which it is delivered.

Organisational responsibility for appropriate project management assessment and selection

For this reason, many project managers are still interviewed, assessed and appointed like military officers. Interviewers or assessors are encouraged to draw out evidence of a willingness to exercise assertive behaviours and hold others to account. Over-confidence and low tolerance for discussion is seen as decisiveness. Rote responses are sought and rewarded. Scant evidence or emphasis is placed on actively discerning those who are in a state of interdependence and who value the role of bringing out the best in others and in the team as a whole.

Ironically, it is those seizing upon opportunities to exercise Candidate A behaviours with alacrity that do most harm when appointed. Since gaining a licence to behave in this way is what attracted them to the role, they will exercise their ability to diminish others while elevating themselves with a clear conscience.

Egotism and vaulting ambition presenting as self-confident entitlement is not a good foundation to fulfil either the form or function of contemporary project leadership. If anything, current trends in technology and project delivery complexity will only increase and multiply.

Nevertheless, so far, assessments for project management and its perceived leadership function continue to elevate and promote an emphasis on traditional stereotypes; caricatures of battlefield leadership.

This is a key factor resulting in the appointment of the project managers least inclined to, or capable of, promoting growth, motivation, insight, or the coached empowerment and delegation necessary for team members to achieve and sustain ownership.

In light of the above, organisational responsibility for appropriate project management assessment and selection must select in favour of Candidate B, and actively select against the behaviours evidenced by Candidate A.

More than half the equation necessary to promote insight in individual team members is embodied in the project manager as leader and coach. If the organisation fails to appoint those inclined towards, and capable of, such a function, and fails in setting the standard and maintaining it, nothing will change.

This concludes consideration of why and how, at the organisational level, project leadership behaviours promoting personal insight might meet some resistance, and how it might be addressed. The next section looks at what the development of insight requires of the practitioner, and how it might be acquired.

Organisational foundations enabling and supporting the project leader journey

Chapter 5 Learning outcomes

1. Organisational support is vital to the realisation of project leaderships benefits.
2. Promoting and establishing standards of appropriate project leadership behaviours will raise awareness of those that are not.
3. Evolving expectations of project leadership behaviours should include the culture and psychological delivery environment they create.
4. Hiring, selection and promotion must evolve to reflect the sought after 'soft' skills, qualities, attributes and competences required of the project leader.

6

Steps 1 to 3: Insight: informing situational awareness

The project leader is guided through the first three steps prompting insight into self, team members and stakeholders as individuals and as a collective to be engaged in delivery.

Following these steps will foster enhanced situational awareness and understanding. The significance and application of both are explored.

The First Catalyst: 'Insight'

The First Catalyst: 'Insight', encompasses, as do the other three, self, the team as individuals, and the team as a collaborative unity. As a catalyst, it prompts and triggers the project leader to actively consider and foster personal Insight and to then engender and foster it across the delivery team.

Each iteration of the Nine Steps informs and clarifies this 'Insight'. They all inform each other in an ongoing iterative process throughout delivery. For the attentive project leader, this process serves to continually enhance and evolve personal effectiveness, revealing opportunities and highlighting potential risks before they are realised. When Insight is effectively communicated and adopted, the active intelligence driving the project forwards is shared by the entire team, rather than being confined and constrained by what a project manager alone can do.

Situational awareness

Situational awareness offers an aerial 360° overview, a map or 'radar' view of where we started from in relation to where we are now, and our destination.

It is a catalyst for the project leader to gain externally informed Insight, per Figure 9, into self, team members and team respectively.

Situational awareness can be distorted by 'observational bias' – only 'seeing' in the environment, or others, what we expect to see. This can have a profoundly negative impact if the project leader is not sensitive to their own prejudices and biases.

By contrast, mature situational awareness is far less distorted or tainted by such reluctance to check assumptions for bias or reflex responses.

Well informed and enhanced, rather than limited or hindered by experience, situational awareness becomes endowed with 'Insight'. With Insight, historical learning and experience enriches understanding.

Applied to project leadership, Insight is knowing and understanding what *is*, in relation to self, team members and team functioning.

Insight Step 1. Self as leader, strengths and weaknesses now

"I am able to control only that of which I am aware. That of which I am unaware controls me. Awareness empowers me."

Coaching For Performance by John Whitmore

The awareness Insight provides can offer a paradigm shift in awareness. It can literally overturn a lifetime's habits, opening the door to previously unimagined possibilities of personal development – a step change in personal evolution and self-actualisation.

A previous example highlighted the step-change in awareness resulting from the realisation that the driver who cut in front of us was a surgeon on call.

This instantaneous shift in awareness as a new perspective on how things were previously apprehended is what experiencing a paradigm shift in awareness and consciousness *feels* like. Insight makes us conscious of that of which we were unconscious. Gaining Insight in any environment is the difference between merely describing what is observed, and being able to explain it; understanding why things are as they are.

Insight not only transforms awareness from apprehension to comprehension, it also enriches understanding of what is now, with why it is the way it is. This in turn enriches awareness of what may be, and hence brings the potential to influence outcomes.

As the light of Insight penetrates the shadows surrounding everyday awareness, it empowers every aspect of life. Such an examined life is not only

Steps 1 to 3: Insight: informing situational awareness

worth living, but it extends personal resilience and quality of life to an unimaginable extent. It offers a greater return on invested time and commitment than any other activity. Insight into self is like a personal MOT, opening the engine cover to reveal the very mechanisms enabling the emergence and realisation of maximum personal effectiveness. A new, supercharged, you.

Motivation – an energy source to light the darkest path

For the project leader, aspiring or existing, developing Insight into self begins with examining and understanding one's motivation. For the 'why' underpinning any human endeavour, or journey of self development, provides compelling reasons to persist when the going gets hard. It is the source of resilience in its most powerful form.

Nevertheless, for some, it must be acknowledged, the motivation to lead is not a source of resilience, but a liability. These individuals, on discovering that leadership in project management is no longer a licence to dominate others, may feel disinclined and lose interest. Fortunately, however, another and surprising discovery awaits, against which the attraction of, or need for, 'command and control' pales into insignificance.

As with all achievement, an initial investment is needed. Achieving Insight does require some perhaps uncomfortable honesty, in order to recognise and acknowledge what it was about traditional images of leadership that seemed so attractive. Becoming aware of that unquestioned, unexamined inner need, prompts the revelation that what was sought through command and control is more than equalled by the realisation of *true l*eadership, and the benefits it brings to all.

For the status of true leadership, as accorded by a willing followership, offers not a lesser, but a greater status than the power sought or even imagined from command and control.

By any measure of status, obedience and conformity cannot compare with empowered collaborative working in a complex, unsettled environement. Shifting one's aspirations from gaining fake leadership status characterised by compliance and resentment, to one of voluntarily conferred respect, and being willingly accorded true leadership status, represents, in fact, not a loss, but a game-changing win.

Anyone reluctant to relinquish the long-promoted stereotypes of command-and-control behaviour is encouraged to squarely face up to the comparative attractiveness of being a dominating yet resented manager, when compared with achieving the status of a trusted, respected, looked-up-to project leader.

Motivation breeds resilience. With motivation now informed by a vision of what characterises true leadership, Insight into self can offer a grounded and calibrated level of situational awareness. It is clear where we are in relation to the now informed destination: the function and appropriate form of project leadership.

Caught up in the day-to-day pressures of delivery, it is all too easy to lose perspective. Taking time out to practise Insight, remembering what led to one's ambition for leadership and what its attainment will look like, provides a firm foundation on which to build. It serves to reframe the challenges of the moment in the context of a larger picture, and restores balance.

Insight into personal effectiveness

For any individual, at any level, these are sobering challenges:

- What difference have you made this week?
- In project delivery, what has changed because of you?
- What tangible value have you added through your work *this week*?
- Cost, time, quality and scope – which of these have your interventions improved upon?

Such questions frequently expose disproportionate time, effort and cost consumed by non-value-adding activities. Generating reports, attending or chairing meetings that change nothing, can evolve, un-noticed and un-commented upon, into an administrative treadmill of routine. It can feel like work, it can feel 'busy', yet add little real value.

Are planned cost, time, quality and scope the same at the end of the week as they were on Monday morning? Is this the result of a Herculean effort to avoid change resulting from emergent complexity – holding the line against forces and changes seemingly intent on changing some or all? Or has a focus on process come at the expense of making things better?

Situational awareness: 'Where am I in relation to where I want to be?'

Leadership, done well, empowers the project manager, as reflective practitioner, to step aside from day-to-day concerns; to take stock, see the wood for the trees, and identify ways to do things better.

Steps 1 to 3: Insight: informing situational awareness

Insight is the result of an intention to invest time and effort in establishing the conditions for its emergence. In this, it parallels the same investment of the project manager as leader in order to realise the power of synergy seen in a team working collaboratively. Rather than promoting slavish adherence to process, the faculty of Insight drives and underpins the development and maintenance of situational awareness; a clear, context-informed appreciation of what is, now. But this is just the beginning.

Achieving Insight, although it is just the first of nine steps supporting the emergence of project leadership, is, in many ways, the most profound. Lack of awareness, as described in the quote from Sir John Whitmore at the start of this section, is often manifested in habitual behaviours and unconscious, reactive reflex-thinking. In much that a project manager does from day to day, there is routine; standard processes to be followed, and conversations that go over old ground.

But Insight is born of awareness, and awareness is something that daily routines do much to inhibit.

Most of the time, indeed, human actions and interactions are largely automatic, habitual and carried out on 'autopilot'. The potential to develop Insight begins with awareness of how much occurs unconsciously. Becoming aware of what generally passes unnoticed opens the door to a universe of new possibilities – opportunities one otherwise remains blind to.

Think, for instance, of driving or cycling to work. The sheer concentration and intentionality involved in learning to do what now happens almost unconsciously, is rarely recognised. Yet, just beneath the threshold of consciousness, immense brainpower is involved just to avoid collisions and navigate the journey safely.

Even cutting-edge AI still struggles to do what humans do 'without thinking'. Driving can be done while listening to the radio, engaging in conversations or thinking about anything but driving. This example hints at the myriad of decisions we can make in relation to our actions and the environment that we are almost unaware of making. The same is often true of our interactions with others and the manner of them, to which little thought is given. The phone call is made and the questions asked with no thought or consideration given to the person at the other end of the line.

What we say is largely ungoverned at a conscious level. More often than not, perhaps disconcertingly on reflection, ,we do not know in advance the words we will say before speaking or responding

Experiments show that many – or even most – decisions are arrived at instinctively. In a job interview, for instance, are decisions all made rationally, and only at the end of the interview? No. Evidence shows that such judgements are made in seconds, and observations following are skewed by confirmation bias – an intent to justify, or at least corroborate, a decision arrived at pre-consciously. Without some level of insight into, and hence control over, such predispositions, one is influenced pre-consciously even by irrelevant factors such as the hot or cold drink one is holding, or the strength and firmness of a handshake. Research really does show that a warm drink inclines one to perceive a stranger more positively than a cold one.

Evidence also shows that judges are statistically more likely to pass abrupt, harsh sentences at mealtimes, or late on a Friday Stage magicians, salesmen and countless others have similarly manipulated people's perceptions from time immemorial.

Even ancient, primate body-language techniques are still consciously and effectively deployed to manipulate perception and engineer outcomes. Body language and mirroring posture are contrived to signal absence of threat, or to present as one well-disposed and 'open' to affiliation and co-operation. By mimicking and mirroring another's body language, cadence, tone or language, they will be more inclined to drop their guard, seeing the other primate as a potential ally. Today this 'aping' of a particular group's way of presenting themselves to the world is shown, for instance, in the wearing of a particular team's football shirt, which can accord a level of acceptance to an individual that is otherwise granted only to kith and kin.

Other skills similarly merge seamlessly and unconsciously into our day-to-day activities. From our early, fumbling steps learning to use technology, from phones to computers, we soon find we need to make no conscious effort at all. Autopilot takes over, and the working day passes by in a predictable pattern of activities. Higher brain functions close down and attention becomes myopic and limited.

Suddenly, a fire alarm goes off, or something startling and untoward grabs the attention. It is as if we are woken from a trance; monochrome routine becomes technicolour, as slumbering primal survival instincts and senses burst into wakefulness. Spatial awareness flickers from mundane-mono into stereo surround-sound. Without any conscious intention, heartbeat and respiration increase, adrenaline flows and senses leap into overdrive. Such an abrupt return to awareness informs insight into the now. Being triggered unexpectedly, heightened conscious awareness informs the fight-or-flight reflex; "is it safe, am I safe?".

Considering project delivery and its environment with increased awareness and questioning our assumptions can be a powerful exercise, but in this case, the call to awareness of the 'external' environment is a metaphor for yet another level of insight: increased personal inner-awareness.

Fostering self-awareness of others' perception of us

Applied with informed intent and discipline, insight into self can trigger an evolution, or even revolution, in personal effectiveness as a person, a project manager, and leader. But to realise these undoubted benefits, gaining insight into one's own self demands what can be a formidable effort. Insight into oneself lights the path to leadership. Being unable to see ourselves as others do, to understand the effects brought about by our behaviour, our words or our silence, guarantees failure in the most basic of leadership competences, communication.

Just as engagement in much day-to-day activity is undertaken with little reflection or questioning of assumptions, our behaviours and interactions with the team can become habitual and unfocused. Unquestioned assumptions about others not only blind us, biasing our perceptions, but, by impacting our disposition towards them, will likely prejudice their perception of us.

As well as leading to misunderstanding, an inability to communicate your intentions effectively is an immense obstacle to effective stakeholder engagement.

Simply intending to appear to the team as self-confident, decisive, assertive or 'in-command', is no guarantee of being so perceived. The opposite may be the case. Is the team inspired and motivated by such behaviours? Or do they, in fact, feel intimidated, bullied and humiliated?

Domineering behaviours can act in the same detrimental way as does 'calling to account'. After all, what result is sought or expected when the subject is made to feel helpless, denied choice, completely at the mercy of someone without sympathy? Triggering the fear response is the very opposite of inspiring individuals to realise their potential.

Asserted dominance erodes self-respect, self-esteem, rapport and collaboration. The 'tunnel vision' that fear imposes cannot compare with the performance enabled by coaching.

Equally damaging, over time, are the effects on team members caused by leadership's absence or silence; the effect of what is *not* transmitted. This, paradoxically, communicates more than may be intended – it literally speaks louder than words.

If the project manager does not care about individuals in the team as human beings, what effect will this have, both on them as individuals, and on their commitment to the team? Is it reasonable simply to assume that team members, 'as adults', do not need assurance – of their importance or their contribution?

If a team member does not feel valued, impairing their motivation and hence performance, does this reflect badly on the project manager, or should the focus be on them? Should they be advised that they should 'pull themselves together' or be moved off the team, as failures?

If the way a team member is treated triggers a mental condition, or has any other impact on their health, with secondary impacts on their family, is this any concern of the project manager?

Can the project manager as leader expect those in their team to automatically extend loyalty, respect and commitment? Does the leader *need* to express any interest in the personal life or wellbeing of the team member, or should they be expected, 'as adults and professionals', to look after themselves, keeping all 'personal issues' out of the workplace?

These are searching questions. They further expose behaviours detrimental to the function of project leadership and so endorse its necessary distancing from traditional, command and control leadership.

Effective project leaders necessarily, and by definition, have an acute sense of the effect their *own* behaviours can have on others, regardless of what is said or not said. But, far more importantly, they recognise the power such Insight bestows to create productive relationships with and within their team and stakeholders. Again, the wise project leader knows it is *not* productive to treat all in the same way, since their needs, disposition and current developmental status will vary.

Scientific evidence demonstrates clear differences in learning styes, and the competent project leader will take due account of this in communications and coaching. Discovering what individuals prefer and whether their preference is conscious or not can be a powerful means to establishing rapport, for it communicates to the team member that the leader is showing respect for them by even asking.

Various models outline the way that some prefer graphic communication, while others prefer to read. Some prefer to read alone, while others prefer the classroom and interaction with others. Think about the situations that have enabled you to learn most effectively. In the next section, 'Insight into the team as individuals', the prompt offered for this conversation can help the individual on the path to realising their own potential, and in so doing deepen the bond and loyalty they feel towards the project leader.

'Insight into self', as the first of the nine steps to project leadership, is a catalyst for personal growth.

Growth can be painful, and for this reason may not at first seem attractive. But, just like taking up a musical instrument or sport for the first time, the greatest source of resilience and motivation is to 'have the end in mind'.

For those already accustomed to a form of leadership heavily coloured by traditional, command-and-control stereotypes, there may be both discomfort and reluctance. Deciding to set aside habitual or previously unquestioned behaviours, or adopting new approaches and skill-sets, can be hard. But again, to focus on the short-term investment or cost alone is only half the picture.

What seem like costs in time and effort at the outset are like the effort in opening a door on, not only a new path, but a destination otherwise unachievable. What might seem like the 'price' of putting others first, empowering the team to perform as a collaborative unity, actually unlocks a synergy of benefits greater than the sum of individual endeavour, including that of the leader.

The paradoxical power of 'we first', over 'me first', is that it results in others following; this is genuine leadership status, as only achieved when accorded to the project leader by all.

As a result, individual team members will commit more and realise their potential, and in so doing fulfil that of the leader. Project delivery effectiveness will be maximised, and organisational recognition and honour will fall upon all.

At project's end, the team as a unity, having supported each other and been supported, will be stronger and ever more resilient. And throughout delivery the project leader will have moved the team from 'forming' and 'storming' to 'norming' and 'performing', where the latter is not characterised by obedience and conformity, but by agility and empowerment, such that the leader applying 'Insight' and 'Foresight' has the latitude to navigate delivery dynamically, anticipating emergent challenges and maximising opportunities.

As a catalyst, 'Insight' prompts a conscious intent to consistently seek to raise personal self-awareness. The preceding questions and answers illustrate how far-reaching this activity can be, both in terms of its impact on project delivery and every stakeholder.

There are numerous readily available tools to inform Insight into self. Entered into with the benefits to be realised in mind rather than any short-term discomfort, '360° appraisals' and feedback offered on various leadership programmes can offer much food for thought.

Consider also the potentially profound effect on an existing relationship between an established project manager and team member when the need to inform Insight is grabbed by the horns. As always, when leadership behaviours are considered, ask 'How would I feel, or respond to being treated in this way'?

The power of signalling "I see you!"

Imagine a traditional command-and-control relationship, where answering many of the above questions would have resuted in the team member being expected to

Evolving project leadership

look out for themselves. They probably see the project manager as, in some ways, a distant figure they know little about. Communication with them has been restricted to uni-directional instructions. Any questioning is reacted to as if it were evidence of either inability or insubordination. Such relationships are reminiscent of those in traditional military settings, where any communication outside the bandwidth permitted by action are actively frowned upon. Any questioning, however pertinent, is instantly and by definition deemed insubordinate and 'out of order'.

Where these relations are firmly established, there is no true leader-follower relationship, nor the commitment, motivation and loyalty it fosters. The aspirant leader, evidencing Insight, introduces into this relationship a whole new dynamic; truly a catalyst for multi-dimensional change. For it is not simply the enlightened awareness of the leader that is altered. The team member and potential follower will find, despite any prior perception of the project manager, that all assumptions will come under fire. They will see a new side to their manager. They will discover, maybe for the first time, a sense of 'being seen' as an individual in their own right. In the next section the development of Insight into each team member fosters this dynamic for change.

Before venturing into team relationship development, however, the aspiring project leader must take concrete actions to develop a clear-eyed Insight into themselves. They must develop situational awareness of themselves in the context of the current external environment, against which they must then calibrate their current knowledge, skills and competence to ensure they are fit for purpose.

In many organisational project delivery settings, the project management office (PMO), or project management capability function, may set requirements for certain qualifications and ongoing continuing professional development (CPD). This element of Insight offers immediate scope for improvement to identify and address gaps in terms of outstanding personal training. Beyond the immediate workplace environment, for example, the project leader might pursue APM chartered status, in light of its growing recognition

These products of Insight are relatively straightforward to identify and progress. However, the single most transformative insight one can achieve, in order to evolve from project manager to project leader, is that underpinning the Performance Curve transition from 'dependence' to 'interdependence'.

Often both project managers and teams share open plan offices. Many can attest to the experience whereby senior managers pass by daily, possibly for years, but never even say hello, introduce themselves, or nod an acknowledgement of their existence, never mind contribution.

Conversely, most will attest to the positive effect of a senior manager taking the time out to say hello and express some interest in those working for them. Receiving such an acknowledgement that one is not only noticed, but one's work is valued, however tacitly or implicitly, stays with one for days, weeks, months and even years. The message is clear. Awareness of self includes acting on the Insight that communicating some level of kinship with those lower in the hierarchy has an immediate effect more tangible and visceral than any amount of printed statements of organisational values.

Insight into self requires the ability and regular practice of consciously taking time to step out of one's own perspective; to see oneself, and any given situation, through the eyes of others. The mental exercise of walking in the shoes of a team member, seeing things, especially project delivery, from their perspective, is the royal road to achieving rapport, and hence leadership.

The project leader as detective

As with any aspect of life, the development and application of Insight and Foresight can make all the difference between success and disaster. While conflict in securing stakeholder engagement may not be predictable, it is probable. Preparation in this context is about consciously entering any context where conflict may occur with intelligence in two senses. First, having acquired prior information that can inform the process of achieving rapport as a prerequisite for collaboration, and second, with an approach to the stakeholder that is emotionally intelligent – sensitive to, and rising above, any emotional triggers that are pressed either intentionally or not.

The first of these – gathering intelligence, does benefit from some preceding encounter with the stakeholder, but it can also be applied from the very first meeting. However, there is an important step in developing personal Insight the project leader must take even before that.

By nature, project management demands intense focus on detail, an ability to discern and extract significant information from vast amounts of data. Every moment of every day, the project manager is presented with invitations to 'dive into the detail'. This can soon lead to the establishment of repetitive behaviours and thinking. Habitual patterns of thought and interaction drive automatic behaviours and a degree of 'change blindness'.

In psychology, an arresting example of this phenomenon can be seen in online videos that are readily available. The observer is invited to watch a team of people wearing t-shirts of one colour bouncing a ball between each other amidst a team wearing another. The observer is invited to count how many times the ball is 'bounced'. When the video ends, they are asked for their 'count', before being asked about an additional detail. Did they see the gorilla?

"What gorilla?" most will ask. The same video is now replayed and, sure enough, mid-way through, somebody in a gorilla costume ostentatiously swaggers into centre stage, waves their arms at the screen, then wanders off again. Find it online by searching for 'change blindness gorilla'.

What this vividly illustrates, is a trait which all can fall foul of unless they are prepared. How often, before meeting someone, is there an intent to consciously take stock of the environment and the disposition of the other? If on their territory, an office or other work environment, what clues are there to their preferences? If it is a personal office, are there any works of art or personal touches such as pictures of their family? Is it a meticulously neat and tidy environment or somewhat disordered? Consciously asking oneself what this might indicate about the individual can be helpful in and of itself, but it can also, with due care, provide a helpful source of coversation. Seeing a picture in a foreign or familiar setting, one might pick up on that or use it to ask about a place never visited. Imagine saying "Oh, I have always wanted to visit . . ." What one is immediately signalling is quite literally some common ground and interest.

The individual themselves, as classically illustrated by Arthur Conan Doyle's Sherlock Holmes in *A Study in Scarlet (1891)*, by his boots, by his trouser-knees, by the callosities of his forefinger and thumb, by his expression, by his shirt-cuff – by each of these things a man's calling is plainly revealed."

Meeting someone, taking note of their posture, how they move, the clothes they are wearing, the pace, tone and cadence of their speech, all offer clues. How do they sound? In all this observation there is one end in mind, which is to deduce information about the other's emotional state, as well as their general disposition. What is sought from this observation and deduction is information that will prove key in securing stakeholder engagement.

If conversation is so informed, one can achieve and communicate something all too often neglected, perhaps revealing a potential source of conflict, or else fully collaborative stakeholder engagement.

Consider the previously described meeting where the project manager enters and gets straight down to business. The likelihood is that all attendees will perceive themselves as 'cogs in a machine' – that they are not seen as individuals in their own right. This is the opposite of leadership. In such a transactional relationship, ideas of commitment, inspiration and loyalty are quite alien.

In sharp contrast, what is needed is for those present to be in no doubt at all of their project leader's message, 'I see you'. For the project leader, consciously making a point of acknowledging all present as individuals can occur either through appropriate, meaningful eye contact or verbally.

Insight-informed stakeholder engagement and influence

In the *Body of Knowledge 7th edition*, APM highlights the change in the function and form of project management that is necessary when there is no line authority over essential contributors to delivery. That contribution can take many forms, including the power to deny access in an operational setting, or resources necessary to facilitate delivery.

This again highlights the pivotal role of the project leader in influencing each stakeholder to embrace their part in realising the project's vision. Early stakeholder engagement is crucial, and meeting in person one to one is always preferable to digital communications or relatively impersonal meetings.

Such introductory stakeholder engagement meetings can benefit from an informal setting, perhaps with coffee or tea. As with any potentially emotionally-charged situation, take a couple of mental steps backwards; avoid kicking off debate without testing for mutual false assumptions.

Do all parties have the same view and understanding of what was said, or otherwise communicated? As always, the aim is to seek shared ground. It is highly unlikely real progress towards collaboration will be achieved without rapport. Achieving that, by definition, means different sides of the debate must first be open to seeing things from the other's perspective. This *can* be a problem for some.

In the tradition of 'stakeholder management', one might assume that entering any new relationship with a stakeholder involves engaging them as might the commander an army, or captain of a ship.

Such an approach without line management authority is doomed to failure. In fact, telling or demanding has the same effect on the subject whether authority or licence to behave this way exists or not.

Those who most strongly advocate assertive behaviours, imposing the will of one on another, are, ironically, the people who are most likely to take exception to being so treated. Telling or demanding simultaneously sends the message that the subject's perspective is irrelevant; that their opinion has no currency, no value, and is not worthy of consideration.

Nevertheless, as the following diagram from the *APM Body of Knowledge 7th edition* makes clear, such attitudes and approaches promote and encourage competition, rather than collaboration.

Evolving project leadership

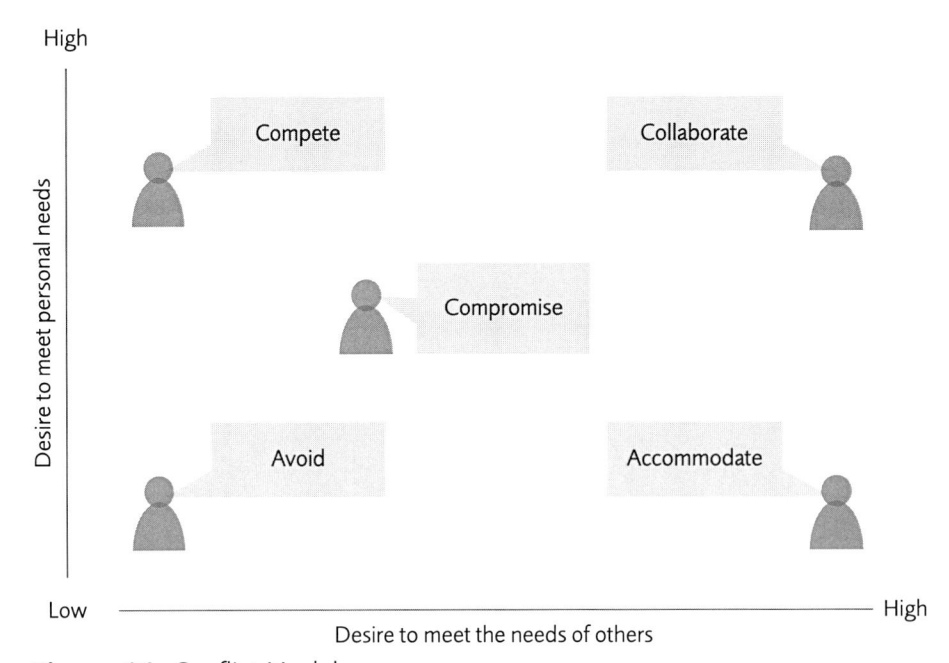

Figure 11 Conflict Model

Source: Adapted from the Thomas Kilmann Conflict Model Instrument

If one is to achieve a state of active collaboration, the needs of the other, the stakeholder, *must* be understood, appreciated and then fully taken into account. When communication becomes two-way, a conversation, then a genuine relationship between both parties becomes possible.

When only one voice or opinion is heard and all others are suppressed, collaboration is impossible by definition, since it should encourage people *"towards their agreed-upon objectives in a way that fosters participation, ownership and creativity"* (APM Body of Knowledge 7th edition page 112).

Insight into self encourages awareness of the counter-productive impact those seeking to dominate have on others, whether team members or stakeholders. The ability to engage with and influence others demands an ability to transcend any personal inclination to control them. As has been explored above, maturity and competence in project leadership requires the emotional intelligence to overcome such instincts. Rather, an informed approach to understanding stakeholder and team member needs in relation to delivery is adopted, where collaboration results in a combined focus to balance the needs of both.

Increasingly dynamic and complex project delivery environments mean the project leader cannot expect their development of personal Insight to be a one-off exercise. Projects and teams come and go, and stakeholders' interests will vary in relation to the complexities affecting the environments they operate in. The project leader must get in the habit of continually assessing the status of their competence in meeting the challenges in the here and now but, as will be shown in Step 4, they will need to continually apply foresight to anticipate future needs.

First, however, Step 2 will open the way to developing an effective, collaborative delivery team, which starts by developing the project leader's Insight into each member and coaching the development, in turn, of their own potential.

Insight Step 2. Team as individuals, strengths and weaknesses now

Step 2 requires the project manager to engage in activities that might initially seem like an overhead to achieving their primary objective of delivering the project.

This perspective and resistance reflects a fundamental misunderstanding of the project leader's function. The process of developing Insight within self as project leader, and within team members, in and of itself acts as a catalyst fostering more productive relationships and a collaborative culture.

While project delivery could once be likened to a large machine that can be operated by one person, namely the project manager, this is increasingly not the case. It is more like a complex, multi-disciplinary system requiring SMEs working to a synchronised plan to realise delivery. The role of the project manager as leader is to facilitate and co-ordinate, while managing the many interfaces between the project and its diverse stakeholders.

By developing personal Insight into individual team members, and so informing their own Insight, the prospective project leader simultaneously accomplishes a far more potent function, a subtle shift transforming team members into followers, and therefore, a project manager into a project leader.

This change in how the team functions marks a profound change in its dynamic. Instead of an attitude of 'what do you want me to do?' the team member is coached to a level of maturity and delegation where their mindset is one of 'what do I need to do?'. This latter status can only be achieved when their vision as to where they are going, and how they are to get there, is shared by the leader.

First, imagine a project where the project manager and team members' relations have, to date, been primarily transactional. The project manager's communication and interaction has been confined to setting tasks and demanding reports. The project manager knows little about, and is clearly not interested in, each team member as an individual, and this attitude effectively communicates little concern or care for any of them as a person.

Since, as has been shown, effective leadership is defined by the establishment of a relationship that inspires willing followers from the inside out, how can such treatment ever qualify or be worthy of such a relationship?

To bring home the transformative power of the catalysts, imagine that, after perhaps years of being so treated, the team member is invited to attend a one-to-one meeting with the project manager.

Setting the scene

Entering the room, the team member is greeted by the project manager, welcoming them with good, friendly, direct but not threatening eye contact. As this is the first meeting, while the traditional shaking of hands following the 'new normal' COVID Restrictions may not be practical some friendly gesture and small talk help break the ice before indicating a seat at the table. Letting the team member sit first, the project manager then sits, not opposite, but at 45 degrees to the team member. Both sit with the light behind them or to one side, rather than in their eyes.

The project manager opens the meeting by explaining they have become increasingly aware of a need to address increasing challenges in project delivery and complexity. They share their increasing appreciation and reliance; both on the team, and them. They express their appreciation for what they do.

The project manager then shares an example of what this particular team member has achieved, showing that it was noted, and is appreciated. The project manager is curious to learn how the team member is finding their role. Do they feel they have been given the opportunity to use all their existing skills and experience? Are they interested in further personal and professional development?

The project manager builds on and is informed by this opening conversation, describing how the first step in their initiative will be to provide all team members with an opportunity to develop new skills. To achieve this, the first step is to establish a baseline of current qualifications, experience and personal aspirations.

It is not difficult to envisage the effect such an experience might have on a team member who has come to believe themselves unappreciated and unseen. This time round, all the SCARF 'Reward' rather than 'Threat' buttons are being pressed! There will, inevitably be some caution or scepticism; that is entirely natural and to be expected. Nonetheless, by being consistent and authentic, the project manager will be tapping into a dynamic that is older than language.

Steps 1 to 3: Insight: informing situational awareness

How often, when taking receipt of a report generated by a team member, does the project manager seek to encourage *them* to consider or comment on what the numbers signify – what might be done to address any variance? This ancient dynamic is one of building mutual respect and rapport. It happens when the recipient feels they are seen as a person, respected and *encouraged* (literally being given the courage and right) to grow.

So, in this process of learning about the individual, their expectations and aspirations, the project manager will be acting as a catalyst by establishing precisely the conditions that facilitate the emergence of a leader/follower relationship. Walking out of the room, the team member will have an entirely new perspective as to 'who they are'; feeling part of something bigger than themselves – one of the most powerful antidotes to the disabling dynamic of feeling ostracised or cut off. The deep triggers indicating they are recognised and accepted as 'kin' is something only those with solipsistic mental disorders will be untouched by.

Being aware that one is perceived as being of value, and is indeed valued as a person, establishes yet another intensely powerful dynamic. It means the individual concerned will now feel a powerful reluctance to undermine, erode or let fall the image the other has of them. They will want to live up to the expectations the project manager has expressed that they have of them.

Coupling this 'threshold experience' with the ongoing confidences and disclosures offered by coaching will further act as a catalyst in inspiring perception of the project manager as a leader; someone the follower feels able to invest trust and loyalty in.

The intelligence and understanding of the individual gained through these conversations is to be respected and treated with all due integrity by the project manager. It will also, when brought together with Insights into the other team members, begin to inform the next step and catalyst, Insight into the team as a whole.

During the investigation stage, the project manager's Insight will be further fuelled by an appreciation of each individual, and in this way yet another evolutionary power will now begin to stir.

The APM promotes development of the faculties and skills in a project manager that are necessary to becoming a 'reflective practitioner'– the ability to review experience in a detached and emotionally intelligent way and to learn from it. This, in turn, requires the development of a disposition prepared and able to step out of any situation and see it objectively, or through the eyes of another.

Although far more easily said than done, this facilitates the emergence of a capacity to realise, in an intimate way, that one is not what one feels. This is exactly the capacity catalysed in the exercise of nurturing Insight, not just for the project manager, but also for the team member.

Mentalisation: a catalyst for Insight into self

By encouraging the team member to explore their current status and aspirations, to reflect upon, and then to articulate them, the project manager is exercising a process discovered by psychotherapy and known as 'mentalisation'. The act of articulating and putting personal feelings into words serves to objectify and in some sense externalise them, making them more readily open to personal scrutiny and validation or review. This is a powerful tool for both the project manager and team member, since it makes visible, hence assessible and controllable, internal predispositions of which either might otherwise be unaware.

An example of this is first to ask the team member what they perceive their strengths are; what aspect of their job they enjoy and if that is the same as the things others say they do well. For most, such a question is rarely consciously addressed. Starting to think about this prompts thought to be given, inviting the individual to, in a sense, step outside themselves; to observe and see themselves as others do. This process very much mirrors that of the Johari Window, whereby an individual can gain Insight into themselves through first anticipating, and then learning, how others actually see their strengths and weaknesses.

Thoughts and feelings of which one is not consciously aware, can nonetheless persist or steadily accumulate over a period of time, they can significantly influence mood and actions. If, in the midst of this, one is prompted to take stock, find words to articulate their inner state, such 'mentalisation' can lead to a genuine revelation and release of tension. It can encourage new Insights into self, and lead to the identification of influences and pressures of which one had not been consciously aware. Gaining such Insight offers a new freedom of thought and action. It opens the door to a conscious evaluation of whether what one feels is justified, and enables the addressing of otherwise un-named influences head-on.

Mentalisation: a catalyst triggering Insight into others' motives and influence

One example of how such influences are brought to bear is when a stakeholder sets out to gain leverage over others by making them feel guilty, or 'playing the victim'.

Being aware of such games, gaining Insight into the way others operate, increases situational awareness and frees one from automatic reactions and responses. Otherwise, being made to feel intimidated, obliged, guilty, indebted, etc, puts one at an immediate disadvantage. Whether project leader or team member, one does not want to be disadvantaged or put on the back foot when seeking to influence or negotiate with stakeholders.

Developing such an ability to discern the motives of others is a product of emotional intelligence and Insight. The latter empowers the faculty of understanding the disposition or outlook; it is suppored by empathy to see through the eyes of another. Insight into others not only serves to reveal stakeholder motives, priorities and needs, but simultaneously sensitises one to others' attempts to manipulate or influence. This is particularly true when seeking both to influence stakeholders and win their engagement.

Securing team engagement

The previously introduced techniques of coaching can be a powerful tool to support both the establishment and development of the faculty of Insight into self and others, by each team member in turn. The 'GROW' Model detailed above provides a ready tool for the project leader to seek engagement and followership from each team member. Goal, Reality, Options, and Will need not even be applied in a formal session. Over time, each element can be raised more or less formally, and may even be introduced, to some extent, in group sessions, as well as one-to-one.

When the project manager is seeking to obtain Insight into the disposition of team members, there are a number of characteristics that distinguish those most likely to be open to growth, inclined to strengthen existing competences, and acquire new ones. These characteristics signal an enhanced potential for development upwards on the performance curve to interdependence.

The binary and mutually interdependent path to interdependence

Perhaps ironically, only through the process of learning to facilitate the development of others to interdependence can the project leader find a route to realising their own potential. The evolution to interdependent competence in project leadership is realised through the empowerment of others to realise their potential as individuals and working in synergy together as a collaborative team.

The project leader, in practising the following 'enablers' in the context of **Step 2,** the coaching and empowering of team members, simultaneously activates mutually empowering inter-relations with and across the team that effectively realises their interdependent status. Just as the team member suddenly finds themselves relating to the project manager as leader, so to, by practising the enablers, the project leader finds themselves in interdependence.

So, this dynamic serves to evolve the project manager from the independence level on the Leadership Performance Curve towards interdependence.

How does the project leader achieve interdependence themselves? The literature is not clear on this subject, but several preconditions can be identified. They are the enablers for the project leader to gain Insight and Foresight into their team, both as individuals and collectively. This increased awareness will itself foster a heightened level of awareness for the project leader as to their dependence on the team and the sense of interdependency that emerges from that.

The Five Enablers of interdependence

1. **Motivation to learn and grow.**
2. **Ownership.**
3. **Empathy.**
4. **Emotional intelligence.**
5. **'We' before 'me'.**

1. **Motivation to learn and grow (Including CPD)**

    Motivation can take two distinct forms in project leadership. First, there are those who are motivated to become a project leader who are drawn by its form and function. They aspire to developing the necessary skills and competences needed to realise their own potential by leading the team to synergy. Delivery, for them, is a means to benefit *all* stakeholders.

    The second form of motivation is about ambition for self over others. It is attracted by and aspires to the status of position, job title and authority to control others. Delivery is a means to personal ends.

    By now, it is clear that the first of these forms of motivation is itself a necessary enabler for the personal evolution to interdependence.

    The motivation to project leadership fuels the capacity to persist despite the inevitable challenges imposed by projects, life and others.

    The motivation to persevere is always vital for those seeking growth and development. Psychological First Aid (PFA) has proven highly successful when deployed in the aftermath of disasters. This is backed by research that has shown the difference this kind of intervention can make to the resilience of those surviving traumatic events. Researchers were surprised to discover that those experiencing the maximum-recommended three interventions were more likely to recover than those undergoing long-term formal therapy.

The main reason for this is that, following a basic triage session ensuring the survivor has food, heat and shelter, the focus of the intervention moves to enabling the victim to identify their own personal source of inspiration. 'Is there a person, known to you, who inspires your respect and admiration, who sets an example of lived human qualities you deeply admire?'

Thinking of such a person in a time of difficulty can be like opening a window in a dark room, revealing some distant peak, shining in sunlight, with a future self imagined on the summit. Even their name or memory can serve to stiffen the spine or upper lip, to inspire, or stir resolve to press on.

Helping team members to identify their own sources of inspiration enables them to tap into a deep reservoir of both motivation and resilience.

Team members who are 'self-starters' do not need constant encouragement, direction or prompting. They are motivated from the inside-out. They *want* to learn and grow. They are open to change, and will readily test new ways of seeing, or adopt new perspectives, offering a richer picture and deeper Insight into themselves and their world.

The informed, competent project leader consciously and conscientiously coaches the team member to identify and then tap into the source of their own personal motivation and resilience. With this accomplished, their motivation fuels ongoing growth and development.

As with all stakeholder engagement, clarifying and substantiating personal motives and discovering those of others provides a royal road to influencing and securing others' engagement effectively.

A characteristic of those exhibiting a sense of entitlement and over-confident self-sufficiency is their presenting as being beyond the need for further training. They 'arrived' years ago, and should be exempt from ongoing professional development on the basis of exceptional skills, knowledge, and often exaggerated experience. Their CV will claim as 'project management' their years of training or apprenticeship. In stark contrast, those reluctant to claim personal credit and glory stand out, preferring instead to credit others; speaking of what 'we' delivered.

As all great scientists and people of experience discover, and are readily willing to acknowledge, the more one grows and develops in the growing project management profession, the more aware one becomes of the immense tectonic shifts defining what must be achieved to ensure delivery; its form and function.

A sincere, authentic **motivation to grow** must, by definition, reflect a recognition that growth is necessary. Such a recognition, equally, demands the underpinning of a fundamental trait – humility. This is not, however, the humility that some would immediately leap to portray as reflecting 'subservience'. For those seeking in this way to equate humility with weakness are often precisely the people who find insufferable the notion that they need any form of training, and suffer from an inability to recognise their own limitations in knowledge, ability or both.

Humility in project leadership is, rather, the *absence* of grandiosity suggesting one knows it all, is beyond question, and is incapable of error. In the willingness to listen and consider others, there is a tacit communication that one is open to new ideas, that one's ideas and views are contingent and provisional, based on what is known and so open to revision. In the true leader, it also communicates one's true and authentic humanity; that one's being and personality is not dependent on a particular view of things. Such a level of personal exposure, however, is anathema to some. They react with a fury out of all proportion to any challenge of their views, however minor. Their persona rests on the maintenance of a fragile, projected image covering deep personal insecurities. By contrast, the humility of a project leader acknowledges the impossibility of knowing everything in uncertain delivery environments, and when they are surrounded by multi-disciplinary SMEs.

2. **Ownership**

A team member may be motivated but as yet unable to run unaided. Achieving ownership brings ability in coaching to the fore. A team member may be quite comfortable sitting with the cost engineer, who builds a picture reflecting the current status of spending through earned value, and cost/schedule performance indices. They may become competent in reporting back and drawing a clear picture. The next step towards delegation and ownership is to nurture motivation towards gaining situational understanding – asking questions like: What has to happen to return spend performance or schedule adherence to the baseline?'

Achieving the competence necessary for ownership reflects a successful transition from their needing a 'directing' form of leadership to that of 'delegation'. Ownership and delegation are not the same thing, however, for while the line manager might delegate a task, it is only truly owned when the

Steps 1 to 3: Insight: informing situational awareness

individual team member shoulders the responsibility as their own, and takes the initiative to actively engage in driving delivery forwards.

For some team members in the early stages of growth, it may be they are either not motivated to move on, or they are not aware of any expectation to do so – even how they could do it. In the former case, there may be a number of reasons for this. Some project managers at the 'independent' stage on the leadership performance curve, as highlighted above, will actively 'bonsai' those in their remit. In the ancient Japanese art of bonsai, a sapling is continually cut back until a fully adult tree emerges, but in miniature form. So too, line managers being 'in-dependence' on 'esteem-from-others', reactively 'nip in the bud' any emerging team member traits intimating a desire to grow or move beyond a role of unquestioning, blind obedience.

The hidden cost of bonsai

This section is intent on promoting and encouraging the emergence of team members' individual capacity for ownership. The need for, and benefits of, this will be the more compelling when understood against the backdrop of many current working environments, where the above scenario plays out day by day. As will be shown, *to actively suppress Insight, the motivation it offers, and the ownership it leads to, is to the detriment of the organisation, its stakeholders and all whose potential for growth is smothered and suppressed*. This is explored further on page 200.

Ownership builds on a foundation of motivation, yet despite this, all too often the command-and-control mentality is fixated on obedience, such that any intimation of emergent initiative or growth is discouraged or punished.

In promoting the development of team member Insight, it would be remiss to ignore the impact of failure to do this. A long, hard look at the effects of such behaviours – traditionally accepted and even encouraged under the guise of leadership – is long overdue. That those inclined to deny others access to their own potential are more often acting in their own perceived interest than that of the organisation, only accentuates this.

While the image of a group of people obediently doing what they are told, like slaves building a pyramid, or team members earnestly generating project reports, may present an image of calm, order and discipline, it hides the immense, invisible potential so suppressed. Insight not encouraged is actively smothered. Such simple images of apparent, well-ordered ways of working, and team meetings characterised by dominant and submissive behaviours, also graphically convey the root cause of many a project failure, as attested to by leadership failures in all times and places.

In historical, stable environments, a single point and line of command-and-control was never questioned, not least because it diminished or rendered redundant the need for any but the leader to think or fret about what was to be done.

In project environments where the project manager was the expert directing the entire, relatively unskilled, delivery team, there was no need to encourage team members to develop Insight motivating growth into ownership. Never trained or encouraged to think for themselves, many a follower accepted their lot, knowing short shrift would be offered for not doing so. Inevitably such treatment and diminished expectations arising from it meant others simply persevered, never knowing what might otherwise have been, or what they might have become.

But as has been shown, today's project delivery environments are anything but stable. The moment the environment becomes unstable and uncertain, all plans and intentions are under threat and generate uncertainty. How many commanders in the field have set out their strategy under assumptions about the disposition and anticipated behaviours of the enemy, only to be thwarted by the unexpected?

In the example of the team exercise, we saw the corrosive power of one person exercising their perceived entitlement to assert authority over others and dominate them. The same dynamic applies in every project delivery setting. The unmoderated, persistent exercise of command-and-control behaviours results in diminished individual and team performance. This applies both to projects, and to every other domain of human activity where the emergence of individual and team potential and synergy is suppressed. The drive for expectations falling on the project manager to actively develop individual team member Insight addresses this shortcoming head-on.

Promoting Insight is not an occasional exercise

Exercising coaching skills, encouraging individuals' motivation to aspire to ownership and competence, is not something the project manager should engage in by exception, nor just when other perceived priorities permit. It should inform their every interaction with the team, as well as with wider circles of stakeholders. It is not a nice-to-have added extra. It is now the core responsibility of every project manager.

Maximising performance in project delivery is the responsibility of the project manager. Project leadership is the central competence necessary to achieving this. There are no exceptions. Where organisations identify the qualifications and experience in project delivery necessary, whether for appointment or ongoing assessment, there is no more telling measure than this.

The development of individual Insight as a metric of organisational health. A top priority for the organisation, the project management capability function, the project management assurance function, and the project management office.

What has the project manager, in their necessary capacity as leader, actively done to coach and develop their team members towards realisation of their individual potential? Where is the evidence of this? Any claimed exemption to this fundamental requirement in project delivery must be subjected to the most rigorous scrutiny. Because, in assessing any alleged short-term benefit claimed by those exercising commmand-and-control behaviours, it is not enough to consider the cost of suppressing individual potential for growth. There are far more insidious costs, both short and long term, too rarely acknowledged, but increasingly rising in public awareness.

Human physical wellbeing is an undisputed priority in project delivery. Little sympathy would be extended to any project manager found guilty of neglecting the physical wellbeing and safety of those under their duty of care and on whom delivery depends.

So too, increasingly and rightly, responsibility for factors impacting adversely on mental health in the workplace falls upon employers. As the above references to the David Rock's SCARF Model, and its implication for the way team members are treated, makes clear, there is ample evidence that behaviours presenting as a 'threat' both actively suppress and inhibit performance, and also upset mental and emotional wellbeing.

Now, and increasingly, a burden of responsibility is placed both on organisations and project managers to exercise zero tolerance towards behaviours such as bullying and discrimination. At the same time, organisations are understandably seeking ever greater efficiencies in pursuit of competitiveness.

But now there is another emergent factor; a growing awareness of the need for greater 'sustainability'. This applies to all resources, including human ones. In the context of project management, leadership and delivery, those who make projects happen at the workface, should also be treated in a sustainable manner.

Maximising the effectiveness of team members is clearly in the remit of the project manager. Employing them in a manner that does not encourage disaffection, alienation, or burnout is now becoming a responsibility as fundamental as ensuring physical safety.

Sustained command-and-control behaviours asserting dominance and demanding submission are self-evidently corrosive, not only to individual development but to basic mental wellbeing. Only a lucky few have not experienced or witnessed the bonsai effect and its debilitating, demotivating corrosive impact on others.

When directly experienced, rather than just being read about, or seen on screen, are there many instances where command-and-control behaviours are not actively, and actually, corrosive?

Situationally aware project leaders shun resorting to command-and-control behaviours in all but the most exceptional scenarios, and even then, adopt them for the briefest possible period. A considerate project leader will also, after the fact, make a point of closing out any incident that demanded strongly assertive behaviours by ensuring those on the receiving end understood the reasoning behind them. Doing this reinforces followers' bestowed respect for the leader. They would certainly dismiss their adoption as a normal way of working as not only ineffective but counter-productive.

Encouraging the development of Insight in team members

The challenge, then, is to build upon team members' motivation to grow – to encourage the individual team member's gradual accumulation of responsibility as competence increases. Initially, there is inevitably a degree of direction and instruction to be given, but it is vital that this is used to reinforce the relationship of coach and coachee rather than parent and child.

Encouraging Insight means the project leader is always sensitive to opportunities to prompt the team member to become more aware of what is going on. In developing this heightened level of awareness, Insight will be fostered. Before or after a shared meeting, for example, the project leader might prompt the team member to express their 'apprehension' – what they perceived, and 'comprehension' – what they understood.

Consciously bringing to awareness what is expected, preparing for it, and reflecting upon what happened and why, is the golden path to increased Insight. The project leader can then bring a further dimension to this exercise by inviting the team member to step outside their immediate involvement and reactions to what has happened; ask what they thought was in the mind of the other – how they were feeling – and their priorities.

One of the most telling Insights to foster in team members, is a keen awareness of how others perceive or respond to what they say or do. This opens the door to increasing their confidence, as they develop their ability to present themselves to the team and stakeholders in the way they mean to.

Steps 1 to 3: Insight: informing situational awareness

This series of enabling steps leads to a deeper awareness of the team member's Insight into self, as they learn to see themselves as others see them. This, in turn, can then inform a positive feedback loop, as they consciously moderate their behaviours to achieve an intended result.

There will be times when it is appropriate to communicate an exclusive intent and focus on the demands of the project, but this must not obstruct a sensitivity to situations where communicating on a human level, establishing and maintaining rapport, is critical.

Imagine, for example, chairing a meeting, being the last to turn up and immediately calling all to silence before launching into the first agenda item. What tacit message does this send to all present?. What would it feel like to be on the receiving end of such behaviours?

In sharp contrast, consider the scenario where the project leader arrives ahead of time and engages in conversation before starting the meeting. Is this a waste of time? Or consider them arriving on time and still engaging in conversation before starting the meeting. Is this a waste of time? Is the project leader being inefficient or even incompetent?

The answer to these questions is a resounding 'no'. If the chair of the meeting failed to engage with the team or meet delegates on a human level, not only would the attendees be unlikely to feel valued as individuals, but they would also probably feel disenfranchised or antagonised. The effect is as negative in some ways, as the planks exercise example, where the so-called leader effectively 'lobotomised' the team by undermining their ability to achieve rapport and a shared sense of purpose.

By talking to individuals in the team on a personal level, numerous other potential pitfalls will be avoided. By engaging in preliminary conversation, the project leader, as chair, can swiftly gauge the 'emotional temperature' of the room and levels of engagement and motivation. It may also be that someone is present who has information to share affecting the agenda as a whole, or which takes priority or supersedes an agenda item.

The start of a meeting is also a vital time to re-flag the Vision and mission of the project – contextualising the meeting rather than, as often happens, getting too involved in details and losing sight of the bigger picture.

Encouraging team members to self-assess their relations within the team

Just as a core role of the project leader is to engage with and influence stakeholders, so too every member of the team has the potential to make or break relationships critical to delivery. In addition, the project leader will take opportunities that present themselves for the individual team member to consider their relations with other team members. Some will be strong, others not so much. This may be because of the greater or lesser need to work together, but just as the project leader might use tools such as Belbin Team Member Analysis for themselves, it can be very revealing when team members are invited to report their perceptions, both of themselves and of other team members.

From this start point – this Insight into relations as they stand now, some assessment can be done to identify any areas for improvement.

These initiatives undertaken by the project leader are clearly offering real benefits in terms of their individual team members' Insight and effectiveness, but this is only half the story. The project leader is, throughout this process, gaining active intelligence into their own team, and more. For the project leader will not limit this development in awareness to the immediate project team – their line reports – it can extend to the wider, integrated project team and beyond, to stakeholders.

Understanding the immediate team, uncovering previously hidden potential and individuals' aspirations to do and become more, the project leader is empowered with Insight where before they were blind. For now the project leader is in a position to identify scope for team members to engage in challenges equal to their motivation and newly discovered potential.

The significance and advantages in project delivery effectiveness resulting from this process are undisputable. But it raises challenging questions at the organisational level. Are project managers being employed to select in favour of appropriate traits and competences? Are existing team members actually being empowered for maximum effectiveness? For the transactional project manager, or those locked in an independent rather than an interdependent mindset, this is a question hidden behind a wall of silence. It is a silence that obstructs the very function the project manager as leader is responsible for fulfilling.

Coaching a team member to the level of full ownership is clearly a salutary achievement. Eventually, though, the time will come when, in order to grow and realise their potential, they must not only be permitted but encouraged to seek ongoing development. With Foresight, the project leader can plan ahead to ensure the best path for their development is anticipated and prepared for. This falls under the third step, which focuses on exercising Foresight for the individual team members.

Steps 1 to 3: Insight: informing situational awareness

3. Empathy

Psychologists identify three kinds of empathy: cognitive, emotional and compassionate.

Cognitive empathy is simply an ability to recognise what another is feeling without actually feeling it.

Emotional empathy mirrors the emotions felt by another, like the pain a parent feels to see their child suffer.

Compassionate empathy is emotional empathy, but the intensity of feelings are moderated by the retention of perspective. Although resonating with the other's perspective, one can see the wood for the trees.

Most will readily relate to and remember instances of experiencing either emotional or compassionate empathy. A moving, immersive story can evoke emotional tears, while the news can evoke compassion.

There are those, however, who are confined to experiencing cognitive empathy. Many have directly experienced being around those who remain indifferent or even blind to the emotional states or reactions of others. This can be particularly disturbing when their behaviour causes distress or hurt to which they do not, or cannot, relate, and for which they accept no responsibility – "That's their problem", or "If they can't take the heat, they should get out of the kitchen".

The preceding section, headed 'The problem with Insight', highlighted the challenge that those without empathy, those 'unconverted' to interdependence, present for those at the organisational level of management. Why should those without emotional or compassionate empathy decide to abandon their licence to command and control? This question was answered by suggesting they might be 'nudged' to a point where the newly perceived benefits of change outweighed initial resistance.

Where this nudge is effective, and those knowing only cognitive empathy intellectually recognise the value of interdependence, they can learn to function far more effectively and realise success their dependent forbear could not have imagined. Developing Insight by observing the impact one's words or behaviour have on another, makes one aware of their effect. Although untouched by another's emotions, or even sympathy for their needs, there is still, therefore, a way to become aware of their impact and moderate their behaviour to good effect.

Empathy as the ability to see self through others' eyes

Empathy is a gateway offering Insight into others' perspectives and emotions, including how they perceive you.

Evolving project leadership

The function of successful stakeholder engagement is to secure and sustain buy-in, commitment and collaboration. The form of approach necessary relies heavily on the project leader's capacity to exercise empathy. It informs understanding of the stakeholder's particular perspective and priorities. Understanding them sheds light on the form of approach most likely to secure their engagement.

This function has nothing in common with an approach to engaging with stakeholders as one might 'engage with the enemy'.

Empathy is the catalyst enabling this evolution in perception and awareness. It is like shifting from a one-dimensional 'description' of the relationship between self and other, to a three-dimensional 'explanation'. It is the difference between looking at a stakeholder matrix identifying those of maximum power and interest, and actually understanding what that power and interest is.

In practical terms, this equates, for example, to the difference between simply knowing a stakeholder *resists* some element of project delivery, and understanding *why*. The latter knowledge and understanding, Insight, opens up the possibility of identifying what might be done to alleviate the stakeholder's concerns, so assuring delivery.

Empathy is, in fact, a superpower. It invests those capable of it with a level of Insight into others' disposition, enabling the single factor most likely to facilitate a collaborative approach: rapport.

Rapport, convincing stakeholders that they are understood and respected, and that their concerns are recognised, is a catalyst for collaboration in the same way that Insight is a catalyst for empathy.

> INSIGHT → EMPATHY → RAPPORT → COLLABORATION

Expressing an interest in a team member's aspirations, especially when it has not happened before, in and of itself encourages them to relate differently towards the project manager. Triggering ancient mechanisms such as the positive 'Reward' triggers in the SCARF Model inclines the team member to perceive both the team and leader as 'kin'.

Having established a relationship of mutual respect, the project leader can broach questions indicating the team member's aspirations, their likes, and their perceived strengths. This information has the power of a hidden password, opening the door on a multitude of opportunities benefiting both the individual and the organisation. Applied more widely within the context of stakeholders, the application of empathy can begin to undermine stakeholder resistance to change and encourage engagement in building alliances rather than lines of resistance.

Steps 1 to 3: Insight: informing situational awareness

4. Emotional intelligence (EQ).

Emotional intelligence builds on empathy, which, in turn, builds on Insight.

By getting to know and gaining Insight into individual team members as individuals, as human beings rather than job-title-holders, the project leader discovers not only their unique perspective on situations, but something of their wider personality. Observing and engaging for Insight, one draws a richer picture of their ability to deal with stressful situations and pressures of various kinds, and their current ability to handle and resolve difficult conversations or situations.

While the ability to bring EQ to bear offers clear benefit in generating Insight for both the project leader and the team member, it is equally clear that failing to apply it not only denies such benefit but can significantly harm relations, undermining the necessary conditions for collaboration and synergy.

As in the previously described example, where outrage and indignation directed at an apparently inconsiderate driver evaporates on learning that they are a surgeon on call-out, the ability to be aware of strong emotions triggered by some external input, whether a situation or person, is the first step to control. Imagine if, whenever distracted by a strong emotion, one could consciously prompt oneself, 'I am not these feelings, I am experiencing them, I am just feeling *this* because . . .' so rendering impotent those feelings that so often derail rational thought.

The 2020 film version of Jack London's 'The Call of the Wild' shows a scene where the novice sled-dog, Buck, causes the sled to crash and all tumble into a painful heap. The musher, Perrault, stands, and, for a moment emanates pain, frustration, anger and annoyance. He menacingly advances on the bemused Buck. It looks like, and feels as though young Buck is in for a painful beating.

It does not happen. Instead, Perrault stops, stoops, and staring Buck square in the eyes, explains what he just did and it's effect. *This* is the turning point for Buck, as he both forms a new bond with the musher, and discovers within himself a path to becoming something more.

This is a graphic evocation of emotional intelligence in action. The sled dog called Buck becomes a vehicle to communicate the inner growth of emotional intelligence in Perrault. It is about the remarkable ability and real power afforded one able to transcend ordinary and perfectly understandable feelings so turning what could so easily have been yet another excuse for asserting the right to dominate and punish, into a mutually beneficial learning experience.

The project leader, faced with many situations and emotive behaviours by others, must, if they are to become effective, rise above them while keeping the larger perspective in mind. The acronym STAR: Stop, Think, Act and Review, has many applications, and here it can be used as a useful prompt to pause for thought whenever powerful emotions are aroused.

Stop! Think!
- What am I feeling?
- Why am I feeling this way?
- Is someone or something (e.g. an advert) manipulating my feelings intentionally?
- Am I getting the whole story?
- What do they want?
- What outcome do I want?
- What can I do or say that will bring clarity on others' intentions?
- What can I say or do to defuse my emotional state, and that of others?

Act! Review.
- Having verified what 'all that' was about, what is the best way forwards?
- What have I learned from this situation?

The biggest challenge for most is achieving the state and presence of mind necessary to 'catch' emergent emotions before they take over, hijacking thought processes, triggering emotional responses and, more often than not, closing down rational thought.

One of the most powerful questions that a coach can ask a team member both stimulates curiosity and potentially provides a pivotal Insight into self. Consider a situation where the team member is clearly emotionally charged, perhaps, for example, with anger or frustration. The project leader engaged with them and making a point of coming to a clear understanding, as to what triggered this state, might describe how they, or someone they knew, was asked 'are you your feelings?'

To ask 'who is feeling this anger?' is to realise that the self and the experience can be, with awareness and Insight, two separate things. Objectifying feelings in this way opens the possibility of moderating and so transcending situations where one is unconsciously conditioned to feel and act in ways that are not in their own interests, and, in the case of project leadership, the interests of all stakeholders.

Establishing personal emotional intelligence is like developing and deploying a matrix of internal sensors to monitor emotional reactions. This cannot happen by simply deciding that such an ability is worthwhile.

Steps 1 to 3: Insight: informing situational awareness

Developing it is, in many ways, like learning to ride a bike. It is about establishing a habitual response to triggers that must be conditioned so that it becomes automatic. As soon as something starts to trigger anger, a mechanism kicks in that says, 'wait a minute – what is happening here – and why?'

One approch to this is, in everyday situations when levels of emotional arousal are relatively low, to make a point of observing feelings in the moment. It can also be helpful to anticipate triggers in advance as this activates those sensors. A good example of this is where one is preparing for a meeting. Any competent project leader will at least anticipate to some degree what is to be discussed and decided, and why. An additional note anticipating the likely position of others attending can serve both to forewarn and prepare for any emotional reactions or 'games' played to influence outcomes, and also to stimulate appropriate considerations, so that issues are addressed in a constructive mannner.

Modern aircraft fitted with terrain proximity-sensitive AI will emit an audible warning to the pilot: "Warning. Terrain! Warning. Terrain!" If the pilot does not pull up or alter course to avoid flying into a mountain, for example, the AI will take control and take appropriate action, including increasing engine power to climb.

Developing EQ serves a similar function. Instead of being drawn into an emotional response by others, or inadvertently carrying some level of emotional activation from one context into another, the EQ moderates arousal and, where appropriate, triggers an automatic distancing from the source.

The project leader can add significantly to the personal EQ resources of each team member by encouraging them to be aware of their own bodily state when under pressure.

An awareness of increased heart-rate and breathing can inform both EQ and Insight, but with practice, it can also serve to prompt a powerful personal response. Stressors in the immediate environment not only trigger feelings and emotional responses. They also have a very physical and biological impact on the human body that has been conditioned, and selected for, throughout all human evolution.

If a sudden, environmental trigger activates the human threat/reward or fight/flight mechanism, as outlined in the SCARF Model, the body will do what evolution has proven to be most effective, and it will usually do it without conscious influence or intervention. The human brain consumes oxygen at a rate out of all proportion to its size. When under threat, the body does what has proved to be the most successful strategy in terms of internal resource deployment; it diverts blood and hence oxygen from the brain to the body, and in particular to the muscles. The reason is binary and extreme: fight or flight, and both are primarily based on conditioned, physical reactions. Landing the first blow, or getting a head start in escape, statistically won over 'pause for thought'. Evolution in early human and even pre-human environments proved and endorsed this trait and strategy beyond any criticism or doubt.

The environment in which that evolved, bio-psychosocial organism finds itself today is vastly different from the plain, savannah or forest in many ways. In some ways, though, it does share similarities. Perceived threats may not be primarily physical, but they may present as significant and immediate, nonetheless. What this insight offers is both an awareness of what is happening, and how to respond to it effectively with EQ.

There have been many cases where people suffering from stage fright or panic attacks at the prospect of public speaking, have been able, not only to overcome this, but to reach levels of performance beyond their peers, tapping into the very sensations that previously made them anxious. They have come to an informed understanding and exploit this metabolic step-change in performance to their benefit. The key to this ability consists in first being aware of what the body is doing, and then intervening, overruling or actively exploiting these reactions in an intelligent way.

Imagine a situation where relations with a team member have been fostered to a good level of trust, so that they. feel able to confide their apprehension or nervousness about leading a meeting or standing to talk publicly. Previously, they may have been reluctant to do so, for fear of being humiliated, or in case such an admission is seized on as a sign of weakness, incompetence or lack of potential. This latter view would tend to diminish ability in performance, while the former inclines and encourages the team member towards ever greater personal insight, and in so doing, maximises the realisation of individual potential.

In order to moderate and over-ride the inhibitory biological results described in the case of public speaking, simply being made aware of what is going on in one's body and why, can serve to allay anxiety. The next step is to make a conscious decision to accept it as a healthy sign of the body going into a higher gear to facilitate, rather than hinder, performance; to ride the adrenalin.

There is yet another crucial step in realising this ability to enhance performance, however, and this takes the form of consciously moderating one's own breathing. As the above scenario made clear, the body's natural reponse is to increase the heart rate and the pace of breathing. Taking over consciously, one can compensate for the reduced blood flow to the brain response by breathing more deeply and slowly. This reduces heart rate, and means that the fight/flight mode is reset, as electro-chemical signals signifying a threat are replaced by a sense of being in charge of the situation. Whether the latter is, strictly speaking, true, is open for debate, but it is, at least, a start in maximising blood flow to the brain and overruling other 'threat/panic' effects on the body.

Emotional contagion

Developing team members' Insight into their own abilities and gaining EQ about their own internal responses to external triggers is the first step in what can turn out to be regaining, to a surprising degree, control over one's own disposition and hence the ability to interact with the rest of the team effectively. However, the ability to influence and moderate one's own effect on others is equally important.

Emotional contagion is what occurs when one's own mood, disposition or heightened level of emotional duress is communicated to others.

Suddenly, what had been confined to one's inner state is transmitted like a virus, triggering a threat status in others. In fact, without doing or saying anything, the tension across the entire team can be affected by one person.

Any stakeholder engagement is necessarily and inescapably damaged by influences adverse to establishing the rapport that is a pre-condition for clear communication. For this reason, developing team member and personal Insight into EQ is a crucial prerequisite for becoming aware of potentially corrosive signals one might be sending out.

When the project leader engages with team members, there must always be a developed sense of Insight and awareness as to the 'Zeitgeist' or EQ status of self and the team. Before or after a meeting with a stakeholder, for example, the project leader may encourage some assessment by the member – their reading of the emotional temperature of any meeting, as well as the individuals participating. Are they aware when discussions or negotiations stop being objective and measured, and move into the realm of personal comments? Are they aware of any changes that take place in relations and what prompts them?

Clearly being aware of the negative impact that emotional contagion can have on others helps the project leader become more aware of their own behaviour in the context of encouraging Insight in others. There are two sides to this ability to influence others' capacity to perform, however.

While the communication of 'Vision' drives **Steps 7 to 9** of the **Path to Integrated Project Team Leadership,** there is a very real sense in which the behaviour, body language, tone and content of communication with the team and stakeholders in Steps 1 to 6 can inspire, motivate and empower. Communicating high expectations of others sets a bar few are keen to fall below. When a competent project leader looks a team member in the eye and states they have high expectations of them and foresee them achieving excellence, it is unlikely they will seek to prove such tacit respect misguided or delusional.

EQ is a fundamental competence for the project leader, and if shared with the team and encouraged, informs stakeholder relations, helping to alleviate many obstacles devolving from unhelpful human dispositions. All too often in project delivery, and far more often in reports explaining a failure in project delivery, it is human factors and failed relationships that are responsible; the way some treat others, or personal agendas running to the detriment of the greater good.

5. 'We' before 'me'

Having an interdependent disposition is core to realising collaboration and synergy. An attitude that promotes the success of the team and looks out for colleagues is the product of a personal evolution from being independent of the team and demanding obedience and compliance from it; to being an interdependent team member fostering the emergence of collaborative synergy.

In any group of team members, just as in any group of project leaders, people will be at different stages of maturity and personal growth. In some, relatively inexperienced, team members, ambitions and motivations towards success and power can result in over-confidence and arrogance.

Mature project organisations with a capability function or PMO increasingly assess suitably qualified people for specific project roles with an additional pre-requisite: experience. Evidence of actual competence in delivery, assessed against more than metrics of cost, time, quality and scope are rightly on the increase.

It is in the interest of the organisation to assess project management behaviours against criteria that reflect and promote an interdependent disposition. This applies to all who aspire to project leadership as well as ongoing development.

There is a tradition that command-and-control behaviours are warranted where sharp-turnaround, high pressure delivery deadlines loom, or costs are to be radically cut. It is a myth. When such an approach is adopted, it causes collateral damage to ongoing capability, which is then hidden or brushed under the carpet by a short-term focus on time or cost.

Steps 1 to 3: Insight: informing situational awareness

Any assertion that this is an effective approach stands little scrutiny. The imposition of command-and-control behaviours undermines and erodes self-esteem. It is also a myth that such treatment brings out the best in people, or that those made of 'the right stuff' thrive under such circumstances. Rather, those who do manage to perform lack the very social and inter-personal sensitivities vital to achieving interdependence and collaborative working, for they are self- and ego-centric.

Triggering the SCARF Model 'Threat' responses actively inhibits and corrodes both individual performance and team synergy. Furthermore the sense of disaffection and alienation created within team members also subverts future commitment and performance.

The prospect of incurring such impacts on performance suggests that organisations seeking enhanced project delivery will benefit from the promotion and nurturing of those disposed to embrace interdependence and who strive to realise the potential of all.

Long overlooked, it is those members of the team who actively encourage others and pick up on interpersonal issues between team members who exhibit the interpersonal skills that every successful team needs. They may have been the ones who were sidelined in favour of those self-promoting and over-riding others – even putting down or suppressing good ideas or individuals who constituted a threat to their own assumed authority, These are not the behaviours that inspire or motivate full engagement and ownership. They exhibit little if any empathy or emotional intelligence, and inevitably place 'me' before 'we'.

This section has focused on why and how the project leader should seek to develop Insight in their team members. It has highlighted the importance of the Five Enablers of Interdependence.

Asked to identify a set of criteria for the measurement of leadership in project management, in light of all the above, is there *any* case to be made for ignoring or downplaying these characteristics as being fundamental to effective team performance in the short term, and excellence in the long term?

1. Motivation.
2. Ownership.
3. Empathy.
4. Emotional intelligence.
5. 'We' before 'me' (interdependence).

Evolving project leadership

The compelling case for *organisational* adoption of the 'Five Enablers'

The changed form and function of project leadership provides a compelling case for project organisations to embed processes promoting each of these Five Enablers. All are uniquely essential and build on each other, to inform Insight, underpinning situational awareness.

Those charged with developing a project management leadership capability must identify and establish effective processes and methods that encourage their adoption, application and continuing professional development in competence.

As with the promotion of project leadership at the individual level, there will be those ready, willing and able to embrace the ethos of developing and promoting the empowerment of the team and its members.

As acknowledged and addressed under the heading 'The problem with Insight' above, there will also be those who will resist. Nevertheless, since the case for tackling this formidable challenge head-on is now undeniable, it should be a priority. Not to embrace the need for change is akin to driving a faulty vehicle and studiously ignoring or putting off the need to fix it. With every passing day, the risks and costs increase.

Many organisational initiatives are promoted on the basis that they offer some efficiency. However, the cost and accumulating damage inflicted rarely makes up for any short-term gains. One of the greatest hindrances and negative influences to individual and organisational development is those who assert that the project being run under the command-and-control ethos is such that it warrants such an approach – that the ends justify the means. There is a tacit acknowledgement that when the building is on fire such dominating behaviours are warranted and justified.

Rarely is the substance of the parallel being drawn held up for scrutiny or challenged. Such exceptional events last seconds or minutes. They demand obedience without question, and there is no benefit from collaborative engagement.

Projects occupy far longer timescales than this. There is no comparison.

Imagine a high pressure meeting, either about to take place or in progress. The project leader, as described above, under the heading 'Too busy to coach' needs just seconds to engage with individuals; to consult, empower and coach them.

The behaviours exhibited by those in-dependence on others' esteem, who are driven by ego and the need to dominate, do not hold up to scrutiny, and neither does the claim that some projects are exceptions.

Projects invariably benefit from interdependent leadership, and suffer from outmoded, traditional command-and-control behaviours. The 'Five Enablers' are not a cosmetic, added extra. They are like the yeast that causes the bread to rise. It is simply no longer justifiable to accept the behaviours of those whose values, or lack of them, run counter to the ethos any respectable professional orgsanisation will wish to be seen to promote, with integrity. No more is it acceptable to ignore the demonstrable ill-effects such traditional behaviours have over time. Pandering to the ego of one comes at too high a cost of all, not least because it promotes the very opposite of engagement.

Following the Nine Steps of the Triple Catalyst inevitably generates a 'paper-trail' of evidence. Those resisting the adoption of the 'Five Enablers' can, in light of all associated benefits, be set an expectation and corresponding objectives that demonstrate unequivocally their engagement and intervention in the individual and team development of those in their care, including their own willingness to engage in reflective practice and ongoing professional development. This reference to those 'in the care' of the project leader is telling. How often do those embracing every opportunity to exercise command-and-control behaviours, or promote themselves, evidence any care for those from whom they demand obedience without question?

This is evidence that cannot readily be faked The requirement that they show in concrete terms how they are empowering others and developing themselves and their team, will soon reveal those for whom such activities are starkly at odds with their preferred behaviours. An organisation might then proceed to protect the team and all its members in the same way as it dealt with any situation where a project manager placed the team, its members, or the reputation of the company at risk.

Insight Step 3. The Integrated Project Team as a unified team: collaborativeness

The Integrated Project Team (IPT) will vary in size, and its members may or may not belong to the client organisation. The project leader will have, in '*Step 2*', begun or maintained a level of relationship with each individual, characterised by rapport and collaborative inter-relations with each.

In '*Step 3*', the project leader now has the task and responsibility for actively seeking Insight into the chemistry across the IPT, for it is only through the effectiveness of this system of inter-relations across the entire IPT, that synergy will begin to emerge, and all its benefits to the individuals, the team and all stakeholders, can be realised.

Evolving project leadership

The Nine Team Types identified by Meredith Belbin are well known:

- Resource investigator
- Teamworker
- Co-ordinator
- Plant
- Monitor evaluator
- Specialist
- Shaper
- Implementer
- Completer finisher

Beyond the model or type

Consciously observing the interactions between team members, the project leader will endeavour to develop Insight into where strengths and weaknesses lie. As with the application of any tool or model, however, it is important to remember that its focus is to reveal a particular facet or characteristic. So, while the 'team types' help cast light on various ways individuals are disposed to operate, their prime focus is not on how they operate together; how they interact as a team.

Becoming aware of this, the project leader must then go a step further for the way individuals are interacting need not, as wth the Belbin Team Types, be a permanent characteristic of a given individual. Has their manner of relating changed, and if so, is there any apparent reason for it? These questions can be especially powerful in the early stages of team formation, or when a new member joins or else someone leaves.

As individuals grow and mature, they may be surprised to discover that they have abilities that catch them unawares. Someone who is normally quiet and retiring, quite prepared for others to be the centre of attention, may, when some subject arises in a conversation or meeting, suddenly become animated and take on an entirely new and unexpected role in the group. This has offered storytellers down the generations an opportunity to portray the dramatic emergence of, if not leadership, then a powerful inner source of energy that propels an individual to some novel personal role or insight.

During meetings, for example, it is tempting always to focus on the speaker, but it can be valuable to note how other members of the team respond to each other. There are always complex dynamics at play and rarely is all that is said – or not said – purely about the subject matter or agenda. Just as Bruce Tuckman noted the progression in team formation from 'Forming and Storming to Norming and Performing', so too there are numerous dynamics at play that reflect individual perceptions and strategies, whether conscious or not, in relation to their power and status within the group.

For example, when someone who is usually quiet suddenly speaks up and voices an opinion, the response of others may simply be to react as to some perceived challenge, regardless of the content of their contribution. An effective and interdependent project leader will actively encourage the participation of all, and proactively seek, rather than being reluctant to hear, alternative opinions on issues.

Is the whole team in rapport? Are they collaborating effectively? Do they show awareness beyond their own sphere of interest, and do they take appropriate action in looking out for, or alerting others to, issues, or feeding back information another team member might otherwise be unaware of?

If they are, it will mean that any individual member of the team, attending a meeting on behalf of the project or visiting a workface, will be alert, not only to any issues concerning them personally, but which may be of note or interest to other team members. Suddenly, one person at the workface is literally 'looking out' for all. It is as though each team member suddenly has eyes and ears in multiple meetings and locations, like remote sensors.

In meetings, do any team members contribute only to be negative about others' ideas or suggestions? Are they doing this consciously? Is there an opportunity to help grow Insight by engaging with team members individually and encouraging them to offer their perspective?

The project leader is of course part of the meeting dynamic. Is there a significant change in the atmosphere when they enter a team meeting, or when an individual turns from speaking with another member of the team? Do they make eye contact? Do they seem animated or reserved?

Awareness is the first step to becoming a conscious agent of change, where it is needed. In addition to using the Belbin team member typology described above to gain Insight into individuals, there is also an opportunity to learn how the individuals interact with each other. In any case, as must be remembered in applying all such models, dispositions will not remain constant – relationships can be quite dynamic.

This dynamism is especially apparent as a team evolves through the Bruce Tuckman Team Development Stages of 'Forming, Storming, Norming and Performing'. As project leader, it is important to recognise and accept that the unconscious rituals played out by primates and other higher-order mammals are the result of bio-psycho-social stimuli. They apply equally to humans. Fortunately, with practice and the moderation afforded by emotional intelligence and awareness of contexts in which such reponses are triggered, much can be done to avert their worst effects.

Referring back to the Threat responses reflected in the 'SCARF Model', it is not difficult to see that, when ostracism or exclusion from a group is threatened, every one of these buttons is pressed. Status, certainty, autonomy, relatedness and fairness are all compromised, and this is true whether one is inside a social grouping or outside and trying to gain entry.

Forming: new team member inductions

In the forming stage of team development, the project leader should be the single most significant determinant of the team's values, culture and vision. The style of leadership adopted by the project leader in the forming stage should be exemplary in the literal sense of the word. Leadership cannot be commanded or demanded, it is conferred, and the single most compelling thing the aspiring project leader can do to be seen as a leader is not to act as one, but to be one. Meeting team members for the first time, what will elicit respect and a commitment from them to do their best? Is it likely that treating them with respect and conveying the sense that the project manager has high expectations of them will win more kudos and goodwill than simply setting them targets in a mono-directional, transactional manner?

Being told by a manager that they wll do all they can to help those who work for them to do their job better is far more likely to press those SCARF buttons in a way that signifies 'Reward', rather than 'Threat'. Meeting a team or individuals within it for the first time is a rite of passage.

The alert and informed project leader must make a conscious point of engaging directly in these rites of passage. One-on-one introductory communication with a new team member is a critical milestone on many levels.

First impressions can, if not carefully managed, set in train a form of observational bias that results in the perceiver ignoring anything that does not fit with that impresssion. Such prejudice is widespread and its most obvious forms are triggered by skin colour, gender, sexual orientation and even accent. Other triggers can include clothes, the way one walks or moves, and how one responds to particular conversational triggers or prompts.

Having avoided these pitfalls and made a new member feel welcome by pressing as many of the 'Reward' SCARF buttons as is practicable, the project

Steps 1 to 3: Insight: informing situational awareness

leader should then seek to orchestrate their introduction to the team in such a way as to pre-empt and avert instinctive responses to a newcomer. By discovering, in exploratory conversation, some common ground between the new team member and the existing team a good platform for acceptance can be identified.

In introducing the new team member, this can be brought to the fore. Of course, an obvious example if all else fails, is some indication as to how the new team member will be instrumental in supporting the team to reach its mutual objectives in delivery. Stories are very powerful in this regard, and being able to refer to some prior connections or successes can also pave the way for acceptance.

In making such introductions, the project leader, mindful of the existing status quo, can more or less overtly indicate to everyone there the 'reporting or deference lines' already established and where the newcomer fits in. This simultaneously serves to reassure existing team members that the new arrival does not themselves constitute a threat, and signals to the newcomer that they are welcome.

Storming: conflict

Inevitably, however, conflicts arise, and this tends to happen especially frequently in the initial or subsequent 'Storming' phases, as members leave or join, so changing the team dynamic. In each case, there is a vying for status and control, a sounding out of the depth and team-perceived value conferred on each member. For the project leader, there should be no illusion that this is an easy process. The team will be assessing and gauging their own response to, and form of relationship with, the leader, which can profoundly alter the dynamic of the team.

The style of leadership most suited to the Storming stage is to a measured extent achieved by 'retiring' from the front line.

Ironically, when a team has reached the Performing stage, the appearance of a new member can be expected to trigger some level of challenge; a mini-storming, however tacit. Are 'they' good enough to join 'us'? The project leader, anticipating this, might, in introducing them in a meeting, make a point of establishing some common ground or pedigree that establishes their worthiness to belong.

Expecting and anticipating changes in the team dynamic, recognising that it is happening, can, in and of itself, help remove the stress or anxiety that might otherwise occur – for instance, understanding why a simple conversation suddenly spirals out of control, and emotional triggers turn conversations 'personal'.

Predicting the occurrence of conflict, the project leader can choose either to let things follow a natural curve or actively engage and intervene at appropriate moments in order to avoid lines being crossed, potentially avoiding long-term resentments that can be hard to resolve.

Conflict can, of course, also offer opportunities to gain valuable Insight into the team, both as individuals and as a unit. Are there particular subjects that cause an increase in emotional contagion? Why? Do any members of the team exhibit greater awareness than others or any apparent desire to moderate any conflict that arises? Do any of the team demonstrate that core attribute native to potential leaders – a desire to intervene not for the sake of self-promotion, but to arbitrate and moderate conflict for the greater and emergent good?

While the project leader is gaining Insight into the team, they should appreciate and take note of the fact that, interaction-by-interaction, the team, whether consciously or not, is gaining insights into them.

As in the world beyond project delivery, a prime cause of failure is failed communications and simple misunderstandings. When this happens, preference must always be given to face-to-face communication.

Where this takes place can also be more significant than is generally acknowledged or consciously considered. In sport there is no doubt that playing on one's home ground is advantageous. In a similar way, sitting in another's office, one is more guarded. One is immediately in SCARF territory: Status, Certainty, Autonomy, Relatedness and Fairness; all sources of threat are on early-warning.

Removing such triggers is about removing negative influences while at the same time introducing things that will work positively to foster the development of rapport. To this end, achieving Insight into the other party will greatly help in discerning what will work for *them*. This is where the project leader will benefit from adopting something of the skillset of Sherlock Holmes: observing and incisively inferring a wealth of information from small clues most would not even notice, as shown in **Step 1**. Driving team maturity from Forming to Performing, It is inevitable that resistance will be enountered. In fact, it should even be encouraged, for it can be literally 'constructive' when conducted well.

'Storming conflicts' can be avoided or defused, as described previously, by bringing to bear all the tools of emotional intelligence, and adopting strategies that pre-empt and avoid conflict.

Entering any 'conflict zone' personal awareness and the avoidance of emotional contagion benefits from breath control and informed body language. Developing insight into the other's disposition, uncovering what *they* value may reveal common ground upon which rapport and mutual interest can be identified and realised.

Despite the best of intentions however, sometimes initially building rapport directly with a new team member may be problematic, especially if, for example,

Steps 1 to 3: Insight: informing situational awareness

the other is already negatively prejudiced towards you. In these cases, affiliation and rapport with others who *do* have positive rapport with them may offer an indirect route to secure postive influence.

Where a new team member is finding their feet in the team it may also be more effective to identify who they readily relate to and then encouraging *them* to mediate: build bridges with the rest of the team. This can serve to reduce potential and actual conflict by establishing the necessary norms of mutual understanding and respect.

In other situations stakeholders may provoke conflict by demeanour, tone or content in a way that drives the delivery team into victim mode or provokes responses enabling them to claim they are the victims. But the same people may well moderate all these behaviours in the presence of someone they defer to, for whatever reason – personal or operational. Making an alliance with such a network of influencers can be an immensely powerful way to achieve influence and stakeholder engagement by proxy. The project leader should not let their own ego and outmoded narratives of leadership beguile them into seeking win/lose interventions.

In short, in managing and leading through conflict, the project leader must be capable and competent in transcending personal emotional triggers other stakeholders may press, whether inadvertently or intentionally. They must avoid being lured into habitual patterns of interaction that disadvantage delivery. All this moves the focus from introspection and an awareness of the now, forwards through situational awareness into the realm of Foresight and **Steps 4 to 6**.

Norming: moving the dialogue from 'me' to 'we'

Just as there is a fundamental inner transformation required of the project manager from 'independent to interdependent', so the very function and form of stakeholder engagement has changed. Its objective: the recruitment and enlisting of stakeholders' commitment; their engagement with the project. When this happens, their focus shifts from being exclusively self-oriented to identifying with the delivery team's objective, and feeling themselves to be part of the team.

Norming is something that will happen by itself, without any intervention by the project manager as leader at all. What normal looks like in terms of the ethos and dynamics of the team may, however, be something quite at odds with team synergy.

As in Forming and Storming, the insightful project leader has a powerful role to play in both directing the team towards the Norming process, and in determining the form it takes in underpinning the vital benefits of 'Performing'.

Evolving project leadership

On every occasion that the project leader interfaces with the team, digitally or in person, they should be an exemplar, embodying, in their every word and behaviour, what '*good* looks like'. This is crucial, because presenting as short-tempered, for example, undermines credibility in encouraging emotional maturity and intelligence in others. The project leader must be consistent and act with integrity at all times.

Remembering the core lessons of the SCARF Model, rather than focusing on negative behaviours, it is most productive to pick up and hold as exemplars any behaviour or contribution by the team that is *positive*. It does not need to be ostentatious or pretentious; it could be a simple nod or subtle affirmation – enough to register in all that *this* is going in the right direction.

Moving from a directive form of leadership to one that is more focused on empowerment, there are subtle triggers the project leader can employ to signal, promote and support a change in orientation within and between the team members. In a very real sense, the project leader is attempting to do what those who have successfully led families and tribes have done from time immemorial. The liberal use of the word 'we', in referring to the team, encourages the development of a sense of team identity.

Another contributing factor in team formation is proximity. Obviously, in an ideal world, the team benefits from being located together. But even if team members are located remotely, the team can have an identity captured traditionally by name and associated 'branding' in letterheads or digital signatures. It is also as important for the team members, as for the world outside, to be provided with narratives of which the team can feel proud, and will wish to be associated with. This serves, step-by-step, to encourage the team to feel they have an element of identity associated with the team and in which their own self-esteeem is willingly invested.

As in all spheres of life, learning from experience (LFE) is a defining characteristic, not only of individuals, but of groups and teams on the sports field and those most successful in project delivery. Taking opportunities in meetings to pause and consider as a team what has been learned adds a level of Insight with immediacy for all.

Evidence of emerging desirable norms can be encouraged as individual members start to take it on themselves to both look out for, and be sensitive to, information that others in the team need to know. The norming process can be nurtured by actively encouraging and engaging the team to think about and report back on what has been learned or noted in the periods between meetings. When what is presented is acknowledged positively, this reinforces

Steps 1 to 3: Insight: informing situational awareness

the desire to do it again or to do it in return – a virtuous spiral towards 'performing'.

These interventions by the project leader have as their focus the intent of igniting team synergy – where each team member sees and feels themselves as a valued part of the whole. As this happens, the team moves from 'norming' to 'performing'.

Performing leaders eat last

Sir Ernest Shackleton famously made a point of being last to eat during the long journey to safety after the *Discovery* sank in Antarctica. Performing project leaders in interactions with the team must often subordinate their own perceived immediate needs to that of nurturing and empowering the team and its performance.

As the project leader succeeds in engaging stakeholders within the team, the characteristic form and function of leadership that is needed changes again. While interventions through the early stages of team development can, in certain situations, require an element of guidance from direct direction through mentoring then coaching, this will now fall away as team members move into greater delegation and personal ownership.

The engagement of stakeholders outside the immediate project team is sought and secured by a combination of team members and the project leader. It is, however, the project leader who must recognise and take ownership of the task of setting the standard for all. If the team member tasked with engaging someone outside the team does not have a clear appreciation of the importance of establishing rapport and a good relationship, they may take a very shortsighted approach, and in so doing will not only fail to bring them on board, but may even have a negative effect on the project.

Traditional leadership models such as Hersey Blanchard Situational Leadership® would have characterised this period within the team as one of moving from 'direction' to 'delegation', via 'coaching' and 'supporting'. However, the word 'guidance' is used here to differentiate this as the appropriate style of leadership and set it in strong contrast to traditional, command-and-control 'directing' behaviours.

In the section titled, 'Modelling stakeholder engagements', reference was made to the following illustrations:

These serve to illustrate the difference between the two styles. Most will readily recall the experience of being on the receiving end, of both kinds of

Evolving project leadership

behaviour. The 'adult' or 'coaching' style of leadership serves as 'guidance', though this does of course presuppose a willing audience as described by McGregor's theory Y.

This seems a reasonable assumption, given the above-described shift from non-expert to multiple SMEs in today's delivery environments. While McGregor's Theory X assumed a workforce of little motivation or professional training, the very nature of project delivery has, as discussed above, now changed significantly to consist of motivated SMEs.

There will, however, always be individuals who show no sign of, or apparent intention to, 'norm'. What then?

Where this occurs, it is all too easy to leap to judgement, adopting a 'parental' form of leadership. As with traditional leadership behaviours, those who adopt this style are not well disposed to understanding 'why', since their immediate response is to 'tell'. However, there is inevitably a reason behind any failure to connect with the team and engage, and here again, traditional styles are severely handicapped in any attempt to rectify the situation. Not only are they disinclined to understand, but they do not accept any responsibility for addressing the problem: "It's not my problem – fix it".

The coaching style has no such impediment, for the coach sees and understands their key role in helping the individual find their way to engagement. Perhaps, for example, through respectful enquiry, they discover that the one apparently not engaging actually perceives the blame for this lies with others – because they feel they are not accepted or even ostracised? Imagine this were the case. The traditional leadership style would not even have asked the question. The so-called leader would have, without even being aware of it, sided with the person in the team who, for whatever reason, obstructed this individual from being a part of it.

Figure 12 From 'Parent' to 'Adult'

The focus of the coach as leader, by contrast, is to uncover such obstacles and pave the way to acceptance, inclusion and engagement. Whenever an enquiry reveals that people's attitudes to others are emotionally loaded and irrational, there is invariably some underlying issue – often one that has nothing at all to do with the recipient of such negative prejudice.

This example illustrates a core responsibility of the project leader as coach. It reveals where the true power of project leadership resides. Securing the engagement of all, then engineering and maintaining their inter-relations for maximum transparency and reciprocal commitment releases a power for delivery that no individual can match, or that any group of individuals acting as individuals can achieve either.

Insight into the team, as a unit, is central to this core task of igniting synergy in project leadership.

Whether the team is forming, storming, norming or performing, the focus of the project leader in each team interaction, formal agenda aside, is to discern what might be done to nurture the team, however embryonic. At the outset, the project leader must in a real sense embody by word and deed the mores and values of the team. They must establish the boundary of what is acceptable, and the team through storming can offer more opportunities for the project leader to illustrate 'what good looks like' than any verbal or written mission statement.

Chapter 6 Learning outcomes

The necessity of wider strategic and organisation support in structures and processes highlights the fact that the project manager will not achieve the full benefits of project leadership alone. Account is taken of guidance offered by the *APM Body of Knowledge 7th edition* in relation to teams, diversity and inclusion, and workplace stress, its assessment and intervention.

1. 'Insight into self' precedes all other steps, because the project leader must know themselves, their strengths and weaknesses and the effect of their behaviours on others.
2. In order to foster team engagement, the project leader must have empathy sufficient to gain engagement from team members and the team across each stage of Forming, Storming, Norming and Performing.
3. The project leader must anticipate resistance from those unwilling to face up to their own weaknesses.
4. Subjugation of the ego seeking esteem from others precedes the evolution to project leadership based on acknowledged interdependency with the team. The move from 'me' to 'we'.
5. Maturation from behaviours intended to control and exert power over others to those intended to realise and release the power of *their* potential is at the heart of project leadership.

7
Steps 4 to 6: Foresight

The project leader is guided through Steps 4 to 6 developing Foresight into the challenges ahead. Following these steps fosters enhanced situational understanding, so how best to prepare and develop both self and team as needed to surmount them.

Again, the necessity of wider strategic and organisational support in structures and processes highlights the fact that the project manager will not achieve the full benefits of project leadership alone.

Specific guidance is also drawn from the *APM Body of Knowledge 7th edition* in relation to 'People and Behaviours' and team development'.

The second catalyst: 'Foresight'

The second catalyst, 'Foresight', encompasses, as does the first, self, the team as individuals, and the team as a collaborative unity. As a catalyst it prompts and triggers the project leader to actively consider and foster personal Foresight and to engender and foster it across the delivery team.

Each iteration of the Nine Steps informs and clarifies this 'Foresight'. For the attentive project leader, this process serves to continually enhance and evolve personal effectiveness, revealing opportunities and highlighting potential risks before they are realised. When Foresight is effectively communicated and adopted, the active intelligence driving the project forwards is shared by the entire team, rather than being confined and constrained by what a project manager alone can do.

Situational understanding with Foresight: developing the delivery team (Steps 4 to 6)

'Situational understanding' adds the project leader's dynamic 'intelligence of intention', to the 'static overview' of situational awareness. It is the difference between having a satellite view of the land between here and the destination from height, and in understanding what will be involved in getting from 'A' to 'B'.

Situational understanding emerges when Foresight and Vision merge. It articulates both the desired end and what is necessary to achieve it.

The difference between situational awareness and situational understanding is the difference between apprehension and comprehension.

An engineer or architect would 'comprehend' a drawing, while a layman merely apprehends it. Much that the layman apprehends would have little significance, but the expert would abstract from the image and text a deeper understanding of what is involved in construction, and the underlying forces at play within the designed structure. The expert has an immediate appreciation and comprehension built on experience of what the drawing represents, and what would be involved in constructing it.

Foresight: anticipating what could be – self and team member potential

So, the focus now shifts from consideration of the current status and potential of individuals, and the delivery team as a unit, to one which consciously and proactively anticipates and takes stock of what the project or business may require in delivery looking ahead; actively seeking to ensure the delivery team will be ready, as a whole, and as individuals, to meet the anticipated challenges.

The original concept of 'situational understanding' was developed for the aviation industry, and in particular the US military. For the leader in the field, it offers full cognizance of the way ahead; anticipation of obstacles, any emergent challenges, and a strategy to deal with each. It must necessarily also include a cogent appraisal of team and individual maturity, any needed development, and how it might be nurtured and facilitated.

Situational understanding within a military context can be described as having situational awareness, combined with understanding of context, with insight and foresight required for effective decision making.

Having assessed themselves and individual team members, the project leader should consider the characteristics of the team as a whole; what will be needed and demanded by the delivery journey ahead? What will help in proactively leading or managing the progress of individuals, including themselves, to realise their maximum effectiveness within a team?

All the measures and models described above inform the project leader in meeting these demands of leadership, as encompassed and endorsed by the APM definition.

Conversely, a failure to employ these behaviours will adversely impact the performance of project managers as leaders, resulting in sub-optimal performance by themselves, their team members and the team as a whole.

Foresight Step 4. Developing personal leadership behaviours

Effective project leadership behaviours foster productive relationships in the wider delivery team and beyond. As the team begins to perform in collaborative unity, they, in turn, go on to engage with the wider stakeholder environment and with each other in a manner that ignites a new and powerful dynamic.

Having considered 'Insight' into self and the team as individuals, the next three steps identify, anticipate and rise to meet the varied challenges situational understanding with foresight uncovers. This situational understanding, is, in turn, informed by the over-arching Vision. As awareness of what the journey involves is made clearer through Insight and Foresight, so too is the Vision. It is the difference between apprehending what the project deliverables will look like when in place, and having a clear understanding of what getting from here to there involves.

As each component of the Triple Catalyst is activated and developed, it informs all the others. It is not a linear process. Developing Insight informs Foresight, Vision, situational awareness and situational understanding. Activate one catalyst, and all benefit.

Here, at Step 4, looking forwards to anticipate what future delivery will demand of self and the team, the project leader must begin by turning inwards.

Self-reflection helps avoid the trap of rumination, focusing on what one thinks one knows and must be informed by active interaction to build up a picture that is balanced. In this case, Foresight looks to discern what demands the project in prospect is likely to throw up as challenges in delivery. The project life cycle will offer distinct challenges at each stage, as well as the need to navigate governance and assurance milestones and gateways.

At Step 1, Insight into self, the project leader has taken time out to assess their current status; how up-to-date their training and development is. Now the time has come to understand what will be required of them going forwards. In the early stages of project delivery, a specific focus is given to identifying who the key stakeholders are; their influence, interest and power. This is not a once-only exercise, for unanticipated changes in scope and the environment during delivery

Evolving project leadership

are virtually inevitable. For the project leader, this again raises the need to keep a watching brief where not only any change to scope, but changes in the environment may herald the need to account for new stakeholders with their own interests in delivery.

Anticipating the need to identify and maintain currency with project stakeholders raises a subject highlighted by the *APM Body of Knowledge 7th edition* – for all stakeholders must be 'engaged' rather than 'managed'. This engagement is not merely something the project leader and their team do; there is also the need to influence stakeholders such that they willingly engage with the project.

Foresight on the part of the project leader must therefore take cognizance as to the part they and their team must increasingly and unavoidably play in securing and influencing stakeholder engagement.

The disposition of the project leader, in their demeanour and ability to engage and influence stakeholders in an effective manner, now comes under increasing scrutiny. Whether interacting with the immediate or integrated project team or wider stakeholders, the project leader is increasingly in the position of being literally unable to 'command' respect. As described in the underpinning case for a change in the function and form of project leadership above, the project leader now stands or falls depending on their ability to secure the buy-in and commitment of them all.

Where competence was once determined by the ability to tell others what to do, now the role of the project leader turns on their ability to elicit the right thing to do and their commitment to do it. For the project manager, their every interaction must now be informed and moderated to achieve an end. Whether verbal or body language, the effect on the other must come first. Foresight as to what effect is sought from each communication, and what is appropriate for a given audience, is not a feel-good, 'nice-to-have' but one of the most powerful things a project leader can achieve.

If the project leader successfully engages a team member, the way is open to their conferring the status of leader and the commitment, motivation and loyalty that goes with it. The project leader has literally ignited a dynamic that repays their investment and commitment many, times over.

Similarly, when seeking to elicit commitment and motivation from others, there is real value in the leader, from the outset, communicating and inviting the establishment of an appropriate level of mutual trust and respect. Every encounter must, however tacitly, include this communication of respect and the message, "I *see* you" as an individual. This applies at first meeting, and throughout the relationship.

Some of the best individual and team achievements are realised when a need or desire is triggered for us to feel we do not wish to 'let down' those we deem to have placed trust in us.

Those project leaders bestowing a raised level of self-respect and esteem set the bar at a higher level. Others will strive to fulfil that expectation precisely and understandably to avoid losing such trust and respect.

But it is important for the project leader to present themselves as part of the team – supporting it. When asking something of a team, such as their embracing new values, culture, or ways of working, it is more compelling to couch it as an invitation, to "join me there", rather than being 'told' where to go, as it were, from afar. The latter approach presents the leader as 'remote'; immune to harm, while commanding others to 'charge the guns'.

The effectiveness of a project leader is defined by their ability to coach. Sir John Whitmore tellingly observes: "In essence, coaching is about partnership, collaboration, and believing in potential" (Op Cit p.21). Communicating such a belief and trust is fundamental. It is further endorsed by Stephen M R Covey's *At The Speed of Trust* (2008).

Many change initiatives are heralded with banners proclaiming 'The New Vision', or vividly portraying a coming 'Transformation' in organisation and culture. But while 'visions' and 'mission statements' have their place, as in Steps 7 to 9, focusing on 'destinations' at the expense of the journey must be guarded against. The project leader must also show Insight, manifested as situational understanding, to win the confidence of the team in their competence and integrity. The team and stakeholders must have confidence that the project leader really has thought through what delivery will entail, and has the foresight to anticipate the challenges that delivery will inevitably throw up.

To secure commitment and motivation, it is therefore a prerequisite to earn the trust and respect of the team. A fundamental component of this is the ability to communicate personal integrity.

It has often been said that 'managers do things right, and leaders do the right thing'. Even the most fleeting of spoken comments and observations, or just a look given to another on greeting or parting, as observed by either the recipient or another, can communicate a thousand words.

'Active listening' to another includes the ability to communicate to them that they have the listener's full attention. This includes establishing, and also being able to hold, eye contact. Averting one's eyes, whether speaking or listening, signals some level of deception; of not being fully aligned, that other agendas are in play, and that the spoken words avert some other 'truth'.

Evolving project leadership

Respect and disdain, trust and distrust: all these can be communicated with just a glance. Intonation and body language, tone and cadence in speaking – all are potent signifiers that can pre-empt or bias receptivity to the spoken word. Behind all human reactions, ancient, inarticulate and emotion-ridden instincts operate, largely below the level of conscious thought – our 'gut instinct'.

Such instincts are potentially a problem for the project leader who remains ignorant of their effect on others, their ability to incline others towards unconscious and even unjustified reactions. In *The Strange Order of Things* (2019) neurologist Antonio Damasio draws attention to the enteric nervous system. Within the stomach, 500 million neurones constitute a 'brain' that in evolutionary terms preceded the one we are all familiar with.

Nobel Prize winning Daniel Kahneman's *Thinking Fast and Slow* (2012), also highlights how the intuition offered by gut instinct is a super-power, but one that is vulnerable and susceptible to error. These errors manifest when our 'buttons are pressed', whether inadvertently or in ways contrived to manipulate or set us at a disadvantage. When something is said or done that triggers an instinctive emotional response, rational thought is impeded. What makes this even more invidious is that when it occurs, information reaching the rational brain has already been filtered and limited by 'observational bias'. In other words, we are not aware of what has been filtered out. At the same time, anything that supports the initial impression is seized upon to confirm the bias.

First impressions profoundly affect the way a relationship develops. Meeting a stakeholder for the first time, one might be reminded of someone else who had a significant impact on one's life, for ill or good. If they then utter some turn of phrase or throwaway comment that resonates with that memory, there is a real danger that a die is cast from which it is difficult, even with emotional intelligence, to escape. This can also be understood in neurological terms, for what is happening is rooted in hard science. When we learn about anything, it is necessary that certain patterns and pathways are established, linking neurones in a defined pattern. When we see a face we recognise, it is literally the case that the incoming optical signal is run through a pattern-matching algorithm, such that we remember faces we have not seen for years or decades.

But along with these optical memories comes so much potential baggage that it can be a real obstacle to unfettered, unbiased perception. Knowing someone well as a child, but then meeting rarely, one can find oneself responding to an adult as if to that child once known – especially where most of the memories of that person are from their youth. Appreciating that neural pathways and the memories they offer can adversely influence initial perceptions and value judgements about people is a valuable asset in the ongoing quest for emotional intelligence.

With this in mind, one can more readily appreciate the mechanisms set in play in meeting a stakeholder for the first time when such neural pathways are activated.

Within seconds of meeting someone, an initial remembrance can cause perceptions of them to veer from a vague memory being triggered, to full-on suspicion that some emotional experience is being relived. This is not a new experience for those suffering from Post-Traumatic Stress Disorder (PTSD). But these phenomena are not hugely different from what those enjoying mental wellbeing experience every day. What is different is the magnitude of the response, and its ability to drown out the moderating voice of higher reason and perspective.

Meeting a stakeholder who reminds one of someone else, one is automatically and often unconsciously 'on guard'.

Perhaps they make a remark or look at you with a familiar expression, tilt of the head or eyebrow raised – perhaps a smile, or was it a smirk? Perhaps they say something ambiguous – what did they mean by that? Suddenly the gut instinct triggers the SCARF Threat/Reward response; a ferocious focus kicks in, intent on confirming what is suspected. Such is its single-minded intensity that anything not confirming suspicions is discounted or ignored; drowned out as irrelevant. What really matters is whether that suspicion was justified. Unfortunately, this discounting process, this 'observational confirmation bias' includes things that might moderate opinion. The individual may, for example, be saying things quite at odds with the judgement or 'prejudice' now in full flight. Perception is polarised, and balance is lost. Like seeing in monochrome or with tunnel vision, the mid-range perspective is lost – everything is polarised.

This same dynamic plays out whenever someone makes a political statement on an emotive subject. Instantly they are subliminally cast as being 'one of them' or 'not one of us'. It is a tribal or pack response and it is as powerful today as it ever was. The raw, emotional power of this plays out on the sports field as well as in political discourse. All humans experience it and none are exempt.

To be human is to have opinions and beliefs. They are what confers and constitutes our identity and sense of self. When someone appears to hold an outlook starkly at odds with ours, they inevitably constitute a threat. What sets the competent project leader apart from the majority is the degree to which they have set a course for themselves to transcend these immoderate instincts and avoid being the pawn in emotional games others all too often exploit for their own ends.

Evolving project leadership

A particularly insidious form of this adverse impact on rational thought occurs when some small trigger causes observational bias that we are *unaware* of; that we do not 'feel' because *no* strong emotional response was triggered. This often takes the form of prejudice, whether reflecting racist or sexist attitudes or homophobia.

A focus on developing personal 'Foresight' will set a course that includes achieving ever greater maturity in becoming aware of innate prejudices and instinctive reactions that may be misleading and counter-productive. This is especially true when the task at hand is to communicate to a stakeholder that one is bringing a disposition to the table that is mature, rational and, above all, reasonable.

Daniel Goleman's *Emotional Intelligence* addresses many of these tasks, as discussed under Step 2 above. This, the fourth 'Enabler of Interdependence' really is a key enabler in fostering stakeholder engagement.

Emotional intelligence is a form of mindfulness. It informs decisions and judgements based on a more conscious awareness of otherwise unconscious, instinctive processes and hence, informed reflection. In its absence, unacknowledged and unaddressed, such primal, uninformed reactions and the behaviours that follow, constitute what Carl Sagan called 'evolutionary baggage'; they actively impede and hamper productive performance.

Achieving collaboration: fostering rapport

Collaboration is a core characteristic of a successful project delivery team that shows full stakeholder engagement. But collaboration, in turn, depends on the nurturing, establishment and maintenance of mutual rapport, within and between

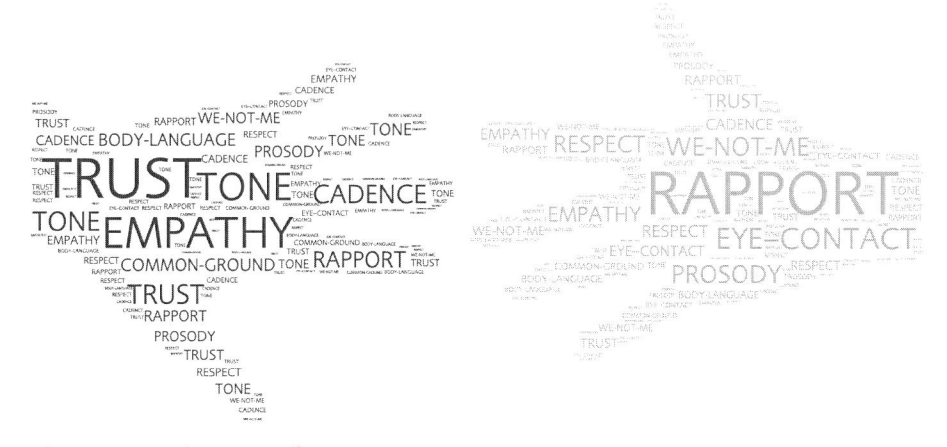

Figure 13 Elements of rapport

all team members. It is also a fundamental characterisitic of high-performing teams.

What is rapport? It is described as "A close and harmonious relationship in which the people or groups concerned understand each other's feelings or ideas and communicate well". *Oxford English Dictionary*

The ability to establish rapport is central to leadership in all domains of life, and its achievement is a central responsibility and competence of an effective project leader.

There are a number of approaches to achieving rapport that benefit from tried and tested standard counselling skills.

Reflective/active listening

One is the practice of 'reflective listening' – sometimes called 'active listening'. It is a powerful technique facilitating the empathy necessary as a prerequisite to establishing rapport.

This activity achieves effectiveness by communicating, however subliminally, to the other that they are actually understood and acknowledged; in other words, "I see you". What is sought is a mutual recognition of some element or degree of shared kinship.

So what can the project leader proactively do to facilitate such acceptance?

The great 20th century physician Henry Murray once said: "There is nothing so powerful as a well-phrased question."

- Why should that be so?
    - What does a well-phrased question really get you?
    - It gets you Insight into the person.
    - It gets you Insight into their needs.
- It demonstrates and communicates respect for them, that you are attentive, not pre-occupied with 'telling them what to do'.
- It communicates, "You are valuable, I'm here to help, but need your assistance to help you."
- It demonstrates curiosity.

This last point is a telling one, for it communicates that one is not simply 'asserting'; reiterating one's own point of view. It is worth noting here the fundamental difference between entering a room where a group of people are earnestly collaborating, and one where the dominant mode of communication is assertion.

Curiosity is the catalyst for rapport

Collaboration demands rapport, which demands curiosity. It is fundamental. Collaboration rides on the power of multiple inputs focused to achieve aligned ends. Curiosity and assertiveness do not sit well together.

Similarly, those focused on collaboration have a primary focus on what 'we' can deliver together. By contrast, those asserting their will over others often promote themselves and their authority even ahead of their declared interests. Here again, the distinction between those in the 'in-dependent' stage of leadership development and those who are 'inter-dependent' is highlighted. Immaturity in leadership is all the more apparent where in a meeting of differing views one side will put their not 'losing face' ahead of finding common ground, lest they be seen as weak.

Curiosity fosters a collaborative approach, for it is focused on understanding and seeing the merits of another's point of view or contribution. Assertiveness is about pushing self-interest, even if it is at the cost of discounting another view, whatever its merits. It is like a courtroom where the prosecution and defence mount and stage their case with no quarter given to their opponent. If that were the end of the story, of course there would be no outcome, only a war of sorts, and a hardening of polarised views.

What is to be found in a court of law, of course, is the next part of the process, which is not readily established within the context of project delivery and relations between stakeholders. The jury and judge arbitrate and moderate to abstract an outcome where, in the majority of cases, one side wins, and the other loses and bears the expenses.

This, then, is another reason that traditional assertiveness offers little by way of benefit in the interactions characteristic of contemporary project delivery. The task of the project leader is to develop their own disposition and demeanour to facilitate the stakeholder in exploring and finding the benefits in prospect for which engagement with the project is justified and necessary.

Only when the other believes you 'understand' them – their point of view, their stake in the game – will the path to trust, and hence collaboration, be open. Only when I believe you 'understand and can relate to where I am coming from' – that you understand on a personal level, 'see' my point of view – am I likely to begin to trust you.

So the first and most important step in achieving rapport is to drop the traditional, assertive approach and habit of thinking about what *you* want to say, what you want to achieve. It is about actively *listening* to the other – putting yourself in their shoes. Be curious.

Steps 4 to 6: Foresight

The tremendous power of this approach, coming to genuinely appreciate the stakeholder's 'stake', what the 'win' is for them, is that from this new perspective our map of the situation is hugely enriched. Now the territory to be navigated is understood; we are in the position of situational understanding. Shared goals and potential benefits can be identified; bridges can be built and, just as importantly, their use, size and position can turn out to be far less onerous than might have been supposed. When all parties understand this territory, the ability to identify a path based on intelligence from all is far more likely than the altogether riskier approach of trying to dictate a path across unfamiliar terrain.

When a project manager is charged with delivering a project in an operational context of which they have little knowledge or experience, the advisability and necessity of bringing all operational stakeholders on board from the outset is immediately obvious – yet many a project manager has presented their intention to operational stakeholders who have not been consulted. The approach assumes the role of the project manager is to get the operational stakeholders to stand well back while the expert project delivery team delivers. Such an approach is not only susceptible to failure through ignorance of constraints in access or context-specific risks in delivery, but it conveys an arrogance likely to antagonise and alienate the very agencies who are best placed to facilitate successful delivery.

In the absence of achieving the 'common ground' of collaboration and rapport, any attempt at stakeholder 'management' is likely to turn into a game of 'telling', asserting without listening, resulting in mutual misunderstanding and a negative, spiralling polarisation of attitudes and behaviours; the exact opposite of collaboration!

Only in establishing rapport as basis for collaboration and good stakeholder engagement on any project will the benefits of success through working together be realised.

Foresight for the project leader necessitates not simply identifying, prioritising and planning to foster stakeholder engagement but also developing a personal capacity and appetite for it. If anyone aspires to successful project leadership, and by definition the role of project manager, they must be more than willing to take ownership of their own development and increasing maturity in the core skills necessary.

Any project leader exercising Foresight will also take the time to understand the power of nurturing a wider circle of influence, including organisational peers and others, who share Insight into the specific project delivery and operational environment. These others may offer the opportunity for alliances and intelligence

Evolving project leadership

that will inform procurement or delivery. Others may have a successful or at least informative take on what works, and what doesn't, with a given stakeholder.

Barriers to rapport

The number one barrier to rapport is having a project manager in the 'independent' stage of leadership development. They demand, and actually need, 'esteem from others' to support ego-centric self-construal. They do not want, or seek, rapport. They are preoccupied at all times with obtaining power and control over others.

As an immature leader, low on the leadership performance curve, this very real psychological need compels them to seek out and contrive relationships offering them control over others as a source of identity. They often present a persona apparently brimming with self-confidence and impervious to self-doubt, but behind this bravado there is a real fear that without title they are nothing.

Adopting behaviours contrived to suggest their entitlement and pre-eminence over others, they are not disposed to collaborative endeavour. They recoil from activities such as collaborative dialogue, where voices other than theirs carry weight. Curiosity is alien, and is even seen to represent weakness or failure in assertiveness. Curiosity suggests an acknowledgement of ignorance, and to those in-dependence this is anathema.

Any attempt to initiate an open and honest discussion is swiftly over-ridden as they monopolise discussion and assert their view, which is not open to debate. Again, they recoil from acknowledging or acceding to another's point of view. Even where previously unknown information is brought to the table, it is likely co-opted, reframed and presented as their own.

What is to be done where the path to rapport and hence collaboration is constantly subverted and disrupted by those lacking the inclination or ability to engage in the influencing of relationships with stakeholders to secure their engagement?

Under the preceding heading, 'Key challenges in developing Insight' a variety of approaches to this very real problem were highlighted, including the 'nudge', to develop a culture where all take exception to and discourage such behaviours. They are coupled, critically, with the explicit promotion of more appropriate measures and training to create a compelling culture where the function and form of project leadership are openly rewarded, while the support for counter-productive behaviours is removed.

There will always be those who see themselves as exceptions to the rule; those who do not believe rules applying to other project managers should apply to them – they need not meet the same educational standards or requirements for continuing professional development. Equally, there are those who rush to complete all required training courses and assume this automatically entitles them to promotion and the authority and responsibilities that go with it.

The call to organisational leadership

Here, finally, it falls to senior management to recognise the fundamental changes in project leadership behaviours required today compared with traditional project management. Training and assessment should be established to demonstrate competence against all Nine Steps to Deliver Team Project Leadership. Such an explicit standard will be self-selecting. Those aspiring to command and control others will be actively discouraged and disinclined to follow such a path. At the same time, those who are in, or aspire to, interdependence will readily embrace the training, disciplines and demands for ongoing personal growth it imposes.

The second barrier to rapport is the stakeholders with an active agenda to disrupt.

Such individuals consider conflict as a means to their own ends and reflecting their own preferred modus operandi. This is actually their comfort zone. They have a clear understanding of where their power and ability to have maximum effect lies. During the 'game' of delivery, there will be moments when they 'hold all the cards'. Rather than welcome or invite early engagement, such stakeholders will remain distant and hard to get hold of. For them, early engagement, and addressing early on the questions they have the power to demand answers to, diminishes their impact.

It serves them to postpone getting involved until the moment when their ability to say 'no' will have maximum impact and put all on the back foot; in-dependence on them.

They relish a platform and audience for this exercise of their power. For this reason, they will finally attend a key meeting where their failing to appear would 'publicly' reflect badly on them.

Here, they suddenly announce that contact should have been made with them weeks or months ago, and draw attention to actions that should already have occurred. They should have been consulted. This will be said with an air of disappointment. Immediately, the delivery team is on the back foot, and the stakeholder

Evolving project leadership

benefits from declaring themselves the 'victim' and entirely justified in pushing back.

Many seasoned project managers will have experienced first-hand this pattern of behaviour. It can be avoided by early engagement, even if it means contriving ways to intercept the stakeholder in person, rather than leaving ignored voice or written messages, or wasting time in email 'ping pong' or other digital pursuit and evasion games. Where the earlier advice is adopted, the project leader may succeed in obtaining learning from others' experiences, and might use alliances or senior management to secure timely access to and engagement by the stakeholder in question.

All of the above are prompts to stimulate the development of personal Foresight, building on Insight, and this includes, not just that acquired by Step 1, but what Insight has been gained in Steps 2 and 3 about the team as it is now.

The development of personal Foresight through Step 4 includes the need to anticipate, nurture and foster stakeholder engagement. But Foresight for self should not just take into account the immediate and foreseeable demands of project delivery. Personal development should be a project in and of itself for the project leader, irrespective of the project they find themselves allocated to.

This is of benefit for several reasons. From time to time, project delivery, or the project of life itself, may present prospects and experiences that are less than welcome or fulfilling. When this occurs, the availability of activities offering opportunities to persist in growth and become stronger, offers a tremendous source of personal resilience.

Those finding themselves, out of the blue, locked down due to the COVID-19 coronavirus in 2020 were faced with such a dilemma. Presented with this enforced absence from work, the conscientious project leader might actively plan to divert their time and energy to other personal development projects. Continuing professional development (CPD), is key to the attainment of an APM Chartered Project Professional (ChPP) qualification, but with applied Foresight it offers an avenue for professional development in its own right. In other words, Foresight should not be confined to current project delivery, but extended to encompass longer term objectives, a career path and personal aspirations.

Insight into individual and collective team performance triggered by steps 2 and 3 also informs Foresight. An individual struggling now may require additional support and training to achieve the necessary competence and ownership to meet future delivery requirements.

Insight into team performance as a whole also serves to illustrate and substantiate any intervention required in terms of necessary training, as well as encouraging team evolution from Forming to Performing. Also, what have the investigations informing Insight taught the project leader about their own strengths and weaknesses?

The level of necessary intervention varies with individual and team maturity. But whatever the project leader determines will be of individual and team benefit, there will be a corresponding question for them as to their own ability and competence to act on that Insight.

By consciously activating, and then acting on, the catalysts of Insight and Foresight, the situational awareness and situational understanding afforded the project leader means they have a significant advantage over the traditional project manager. The focus and measure of delivery in traditional project management is based on 'what' is to be done as defined by the schedule and discrete work packages. Equally, the functional ability of the traditional project manager is assessed in relation to hard metrics of what has been delivered, at what cost and by when, and using earned value to determine adherence to the plan reflecting cost and schedule against time. This clearly reflects progress, but it can also be highly misleading in terms of reflecting project leadership.

Assessing project leadership effectiveness

As shown, the function of the project manager has been significantly superseded by that of the project leader. The significance of this becomes especially clear when seeking to assess effectiveness. Contemporary metrics serve to show that, measured against cost, time, quality and scope, something has gone wrong; but they cannot say anything about why. It is similar to medicine, where all too often a symptom is confused or conflated with a cause. It is like saying someone had a heart attack because they were overweight. The two are connected, but correlation is not causation.

Judging that a project manager has failed because a project is behind schedule reflects the same error in reasoning; it fails to identify or address the reason why. It is the equivalent of claiming that, if an aircraft crashes, it is necessarily and automatically a reflection on the pilot. Any airline attempting to lay blame like this today would be roundly and rightly condemned, and exposed as grossly unfair, unreasonable and un-professional. The reasons for project failure are more often than not multi-variate and complex.

Evolving project leadership

It is therefore unreasonable to automatically equate failure in project delivery with a failure in project leadership.

Success in project delivery is not a matter of simplistic, linear cause-and-effect. Just as someone successful in sports must eat the right food *and* exercise *and* practise, to an even greater degree, the factors contributing to project delivery success or failure are many and varied, and, in increasingly VUCA delivery environments, critical factors can be outside the control of the project manager.

Measuring successful project leadership against delivery to cost, time, scope and quality is like assessing the competence of a pilot by their ability to arrive 'on time', regardless of weather or refuelling delays – or expecting a delivery driver to arrive on time regardless of road conditions. Such metrics miss the point, and are often simply adopted as a lazy way to apportion blame.

Is it possible a project manager has done all anyone could do, but the project is still over-cost, or behind schedule? Of course. Therefore, any metric used to assess project leadership must identify what they *should* be doing, whether they *are* doing it, and how well. What happens in delivery to impede progress can often come down to dependencies, inter-dependencies and imposed constraints entirely outside their remit or ability to control.

As an example of this, many projects are delivered in operational environments where business as usual must continue as far as practicable, and may in fact be demanded by economic or public safety considerations. In a nuclear environment, for example, it is simply not possible to stop day-to-day work maintaining safety, and in large manufacturing plants, project work on a given production line may be constrained, such that access is entirely subject to factors over which the project manager has no direct control.

Such examples make abundantly clear the extent to which the assessment of project leadership cannot reasonably be measured against the constraints of cost, time and scope.

Moving forwards, it is also clear that any measure of project leadership competence must reflect the significant change in function and form of project leadership. Fortunately, the Triple Catalysts and Nine Steps specifically focus on the core activities at the heart of project leadership. They establish the conditions necessary to realise the emergent benefits of synergy and collaborative working. As a direct consequence, organisations now have a source of concrete evidence demonstrating project leadership activity and competence.

Completing the table and questions in the **Appendix** will reveal the extent to which the project leader has engaged in and structured activities intended to activate the Triple Catalyst, and progress through the Nine Steps. Having assessed the need for, then planned and undertaken, self and team development, the next stage is to assess effectiveness of these measures.

Is there evidence that team members are taking ownership and progressing their own development? The uptake and progress in training is a good indicator, and there should also be evidence in the form of logs and outputs from coaching sessions. How is the status of team collaboration assessed and nurtured?

Because these areas may, in many cases never have been considered at the organisational level, their unfamiliarity will inevitably make the task of project leadership assessment appear to be quite difficult and hard to pin down. In reality, though, as the **Appendix** shows, there are numerous activities prompted by the Nine Steps that any project leader should be able, as a matter of course, to show evidence for.

As with all record keeping, it is likely that those reluctant to engage will object that following the Nine Steps is an unnecessary overhead on getting the project delivered. Where this occurs, the question senior management needs to ask has already been answered. Either the individual concerned does not understand, or else they are reluctant to relinquish traditional command-and-control behaviours, and averse to empowering others.

Any such response, or any objections to The Triple Catalyst and Nine Steps to project leadership, based on the time taken, or effort involved, fails to account for the inescapable fact that the returns outweigh the investment by orders of magnitude – it is a 'gift that just keeps on giving'. The benefits within project delivery are transformative, as all are empowered to realise their individual potential, and the agility and resilience of both individuals and the team result in an ability to meet the challenges of emergent complexity in a way that traditional management cannot begin to equal.

But this is only the beginning. Every member and stakeholder within such a delivery team walks away from the project with a network of relationships, alliances, competences and personal maturity, such that the time to reach full productivity in future projects will be reduced, and their effectiveness increased, many times over. What the project leader will have achieved in their empowerment of team members is to have nurtured the Five Enablers of interdependence within them too. And this will also have repercussive benefits.

A further interesting, if challenging, question is how these various benefits might be reflected in the business case.

Once a team member has experienced delivering with a project leader who coaches, respects and empowers, they will have seen and experienced for themselves how liberating and rewarding it is to be a part of a mutually supportive team. They will realise, too, the extent to which their own ability had been hidden from them as permission and encouragement to grow was witheld or actively inhibited by those more concerned with their own, egotistical need to dominate.

Ego is in many ways the single greatest obstacle to the realisation of the power of project leadership. It is paradoxical that the individual obsessed with acquiring personal power *over* others actually subverts and disables the very dynamic that releases their combined potential.

The activity, or even the thought, of developing Foresight as project leader is unattractive to those limited by the myopic perspective their own ego imposes. It constrains perception, disabling an ability to empathise – to see through the eyes of another, or to appreciate their point of view. This 'single-mindedness' can result in stratospheric levels of self-confidence and self-promotion, precisely because they recoil from entertaining any view on things but their own.

Clearly, there are situations where such unwavering self-belief and focus is necessary but, as outlined above, the costs placed on others are high, and in anything but the short term – of the order of getting everyone out of a burning building – it is a liability.

Fostering personal Foresight informed by Insight into what is, now, within the context of project delivery is significantly informed through scope definition. And from that scope, a clear sense of direction is provided and available to all in delivery. But for the project leader, something more is needed; a Vision that goes beyond 'why' and 'what' is to be delivered to embrace 'how'.

While the catalyst of Vision is activated in steps 7 to 9, it is clear that, from day one, the project leader will be constantly seeking to clarify and detail both what is to be delivered and how it will be achieved, in a way that goes far beyond what resources, or mechanical plant or expertise is needed. The 'how' of project delivery goes to the heart of what makes the project happen day by day – the 'culture' that exists within and defines the delivery team.

Developing self, the individuals and relationships with stakeholders, as well as the integrated and extended project delivery team, the culture that is established is often markedly different within the same organisation. The prime mover in setting the culture is the project leader who, from day one, will be closely observed by all involved. How they interact, how they deal with difficult situations and people, as well as their persona and disposition in everyday situations – all inform the team, however tacitly and even subconsciously, about the kind of behaviour and attitude towards others that is expected and acceptable.

During a meeting, a tray is brought into the room with mugs, and coffee or tea.

- Does the project leader wait for someone to pour them a cup, or pour just their own and leave others to help themselves?
- Or, if someone arrives late for the meeting, are they openly reprimanded, asked to explain themselves in front of everyone, or ignored?
- Someone says or does something untoward during a meeting that is noticed by all. Does the project leader call them out there and then, or ask them to remain at the end of the meeting?

Situations vary, and what is appropriate in one situation or context will not be in another. What *is* constant, however, is the need for the project leader to embody and communicate in all they say and do how they want the team to deal with each other. Implicit within all communcations will be a key ingredient that will determine whether the project leader is seen as a manager or a leader. Do they communicate respect for others, or do they succeed only in so asserting themselves and their importance that everyone else feels they are merely an extension of the manager's ego?

Foresight, then, will be informed and enriched as Insight and Vision are developed, and grow siuational awareness and understanding. Here in Step 4, Foresight is so enriched, that it offers the compelling potential both for personal transformation, and for evolution towards the project leadership maturity of interdependence.

For those willing and able to embrace the process of setting aside assumptions and personal preconceptions, the process of informing Vision will expose the project leader to many new dimensions and perspectives within which the project is to be delivered. The first dimension includes priorities and drivers encompassing the scope to be delivered from the perspective of the project team, but the project leader must go beyond this if they are to obtain the intelligence necessary to influence stakeholders in a manner favouring and eliciting their willing engagement.

There is no other way to achieve successful stakeholder engagement consistently. Attempting to influence others without real understanding or Insight into *their* perspective, *their* priorities, and their longer term objectives represents a level of uninformed speculation completely at odds with the professional status of project management.

Just as any competent project manager would not even contemplate any form of construction without establishing the underpinning foundations or supporting structures, so, too, the competent project leader is obliged to plan and approach their role in securing stakeholder engagement in a structured way.

At this point, from the point of view of the aspiring project leader, it is clear that Triple Catalyst steps 1, 4, and 7 prompt project leadership self-reflection for Insight, Foresight and Vision. But they also invite the aspiring leader to take personal responsibility for, and ownership of, a personal jouney of self-discovery that may lead to a paradigm shift in their outlook and maturity.

It is not a journey everyone will be inclined to take, but making this clear, while discouraging some, *will* provide the impetus for those long overlooked, because not self-promoting, but who yet harbour both the desire and ability to become the 'living catalyst' capable of transforming a group of diverse individuals into a collaborative project delivery team.

Having brought Insight and Vision to bear with situational awareness and understanding, the project leader's Foresight maps the route and personal development necessary to meet the challenges of project delivery. This includes a structured approach to garnering intelligence; securing stakeholder identification and tailored, informed interventions such as will positively influence stakeholder engagement.

Among these stakeholders are the individuals in the integrated project team, and to these we now turn.

Foresight Step 5. Team members

From developing Foresight in themselves, the next step requires the project leader to take into account the views, needs and aspirations of the delivery team, so informing and enriching an effective vision that will influence all to engage.

There are specific sources informing this wider Foresight that the project leader will need to systematically explore as follows:

1. The project leader developing Foresight into their line reports develops understanding of their respective individual aspirations in both the short and longer term. This provides the project leader with an opportunity to evidence their commitment by integrating these aspirations, where practicable, into delivery. An individual may, for example, be looking for increased experience or skill in some aspect of delivery across the life cycle. This can be a win in its own right for the project leader themselves, since they now have additional Insight into what motivates this particular individual. Furthermore, such

exploratory dialogues, by communicating both intent and respect, are a tremendously powerful catalyst fostering rapport, mutual commitment and collaborative working.

2. The project leader, while developing their own Foresight, must also foster it within each member of their delivery team. It should reflect the project leader's Vision for how the wider project is to be delivered in terms of culture, as well as work packages and delivery responsibilities. **Step 6 Team to synergy** covers this aspect. Informing collective Foresight by fostering the desired culture ensures the delivery team is clear about the expectations of the project leader in terms of behaviours, both within the team and in their interactions with all in delivery. This can even be explicitly incorporated into a 'charter' during the team's 'Forming' stage, where all contribute so that it is owned by each team member, and it can also be used during on-boarding of new team members. Setting behavioural expectations, it is important to focus on the benefit to all of working collaboratively, knowing all members of the team are looking out for each other. To avoid the trap of appearing to impose culture from the top down as an expression of the project leader's will, it can be productive to have a collective, facilitated event, where all are invited to contribute to a set of agreed values and behaviours.

3. This wider, inclusive vision then informs and contextualises specific roles envisioned for each team member, and will need to include discrete deliverables and milestones. These objectives provide the team members with Foresight into their own role, and expectations for delivery against which their success can be demonstrated. In achieving this level of Foresight it will also become apparent what, if any, measures fall to the project leader to arrange. For example, a deficit in a team member's formal technical knowledge or training may need to be addressed and supported through ongoing coaching in delivery, or as agreed for continuing professional development (CPD).

One thing to take into account in fostering and nurturing Foresight across all members of the integrated project team is that some will be direct line reports, but many will not. The former group will expect organisational support and development, especially in progressive and larger organisations where there may be formal requirements surrounding the appointment and development of suitably qualified, experienced persons for particular roles, as often set by a project management office (PMO) or project management capability (PMC) function. The project leader will need to anticipate and allow for such commitments with Foresight in relation to their project schedule.

Evolving project leadership

Those who are *not* within the immediate reporting line of the project manager are, nonetheless, part of the delivery team, and as such, clear stakeholders in the success of the project. They still also fall within the ambit of the project leader, who carries responsibility for securing and nurturing their engagement, commitment and ownership. Whether reporting directly to the project manager or not, the integrated project team and extended network of stakeholders must engage with each other collaboratively for successful project delivery.

Just as leadership operates from within the follower, so too, collaboration cannot be commanded; it requires willing participants. The difference is that between having a disparate group of people who have a myopic focus on their own remit with no care, concern or interest in the others, and having an integrated team who consistently engage with each other.

Many a project manager has been frustrated when designers from different disciplines, and possibly different buildings or organisations, produce discipline-specific drawings, for example showing electrical or piped services, with little or no account for the route the other is taking. In such cultures, 'telling' people to collaborate is likely to result in one discipline 'telling' others what they are doing in the expectation that everyone else must work around them. Collaboration is something that is to be elicited from the team, and this requires leadership.

To those unaccustomed to having no authority to 'tell' or 'command', this situation is in fact doubly difficult, because not only is there no line authority, but increasingly the team member is an SME in their own right. The project leader will be in a position to know 'what' is to be delivered, but again, in many cases, they will have to rely on the expert to do what needs to be done effectively and competently.

This dynamic reflects the earlier discussion of how both the form and function of traditional project management no longer carries the power to command and control. Paradoxically, however, the potential power of collaborative synergy that an effective project leader ignites and draws from the team is far greater than the power they might exert *over* the team, or any individual within it.

For the project leader, developing Foresight around individual team members is closely coupled with the task of fostering and nurturing Foresight within the team members themselves. A key part of this process is that, for the team member, their experience is deeply enriched by a mature appreciation of their part, place, and contribution, in the grand scheme of delivery.

Generating Foresight for team members will draw out individuals' personal future development needs from a business point of view, short, medium, and

Steps 4 to 6: Foresight

long term, but also from the perspective of meeting *their* personal and future career aspirations.

Individuals may be in a role which, in the foreseeable future, will carry them through a governance gate or transition to some new area of delivery where they have relatively little prior experience. Their own career aspirations may, at the same time, be drawing them forward to seek a greater degree of responsibility and accountability. Alternatively, driven by wider business needs, the individual may find themselves transferred to a role outside their comfort zone. In each of these cases, the benefit of generating Foresight is that gaps can be identified between competences and skills as they are now, and what will be needed. Again, engaging in such dialogues is a potent vehicle to securing rapport and commitment.

The project leader developing Foresight around team members will also seek to understand and take account of each individual's personal needs and aspirations. For the project leader, as coach, will realise that competence and efficiency in delivery will be vastly facilitated by ensuring each individual is encouraged and supported to realise their personal potential.

Maslow's 'Hierarchy of Needs' places self-actualisation at the apex. For the project leader, if it could be measured, the touchstone of competence would be the extent to which they realise the potential of their individual team members, and that of the team working collaboratively.

What achieving this level of Foresight demands from the project leader is profoundly different from the day to day activities of the traditional project manager. Now the project leader must be capable of assessing each individual's potential, as a sports coach sees the future potential within a student or player, or like the artist who sees a potential sculpture within a rough-hewn rock.

Within contemporary project management, those who recoil or shrink from developing both self- and team-focused Foresight soon come to the fore in leadership competency assessments such as that outlined in the Appendix.

Asked about their own leadership, they are likely to major on their ability to be assertive; calling and holding others to account. They will, with practised confidence, look the questioner in the eye, while affirming their ability and willingness to command and control by reference to ready examples.

Where the same project manager is invited to outline, for any given team member, what they have learned about them as individuals, and how this provides insights informing their development, a far less practised response is likely.

Asked such questions, where a moment before, they confidently and enthusiastically portrayed or asserted themselves as 'natural born leaders' they suddenly stumble. From exuding confidence and certainty, their face may freeze and their eyes shift uneasily. Feeling under threat, they may well fall back on that well-tried strategy in rhetoric: going on the attack as the best form of defence.

Such a response might take the form of a brusque dismissal. They might aver that such information is spurious, and surplus to the far more important task of 'getting on with the project'. Spending time in developing team member Foresight might be reframed as not only of little or no value, but a 'frivolous' activity, distracting attention from the delivery work at hand.

Those of a traditional or military bent might take this example further, by averring that any such social interest or interaction is actually likely to be seen as a sign of weakness in leadership, likely eroding their ability to command unquestioning obedience in delivery.

However, such rebuttals, in whatever terms they are couched, all fall flat in light of the simple, undeniable fact, all too often overlooked, that *any* claim to leadership is most aptly proven, *not* by reference to any kind or number of assertive behaviours, but by how they are perceived by those whom they claim as their followers; whether *they* willingly bestow on them the honour and title of 'leader'.

Foresight in project leadership of necessity demands both a willingness and ability to get to know team members as human beings. Rapport, collaboration and leadership all demand, as a basic necessity, a rapport founded in mutually supportive, respectful communication of the kind that simply cannot occur in command-and-control, transactional relationships.

One of the most rewarding experiences in project leadership is coaching; acting as catalyst, then seeing an individual discover their ability to take ownership in some aspect of delivery, for the first time. Encouraging the normally retiring to step forward with growing confidence, and to speak up with conviction and authenticity, will more than reward the project leader's invested effort, Foresight and Vision in coaching them to delegation.

Foresight in relation to the team is informed by and informs the Vision for delivery. It is a dialogue, and it is the unique role of the project leader to initiate and sustain it throughout delivery. This means that the insights afforded in the process of achieving Foresight, about who can do what, now, and who can do what with coaching, enable both the leader and the team to achieve maximum delegation and empowerment.

We can draw an analogy with Information Technology (IT), where distributed processing utilises and brings together the power of multiple, networked computers to share the workload and increase both the rate of information processing and resilience by orders of magnitude.

In a similar way, the ability to distribute ownership for aspects of delivery through empowerment means that the project as a whole is far more resilient than those where the project manager retains centralised command and control. Many projects now operate on multiple workfaces and, unlike traditional engineering or civils projects, they may now include workfaces that are essentially 'virtual'. This means that, while design, for example, could once be observed taking place in three dimensions on a physical drawing board, today it is likely to be the result of computer modelling.

Today, IT suffuses and infuses every stage and aspect of project delivery, and its influence is exemplified in the growing adoption of Building Information Modelling (BIM). Here, in a virtual environment, the entire project, both in execution and in terms of deliverables, can be modelled to unprecedented levels of detail and accuracy.

This technology alone establishes a virtual 'workface' potentially populated by multiple, geographically distant SMEs, representing numerous disciplines, as well as stakeholders influencing design all the way from the studies phase, through to commissioning and close-out.

Where once the project manager could largely observe, monitor and oversee delivery activity around a single design and construction workface, today this can be, and largely is, physically impossible. For this reason alone, empowerment is essential but, given that delivery environments are themselves more unpredictable and complex, delivery is immersed in greater degrees of dependency and inter-dependency, while subject to imposed constraints over which the manager has no direct control.

This means that resilience and efficiency in responding to change is now more important than ever. Those at the workface need to be, wherever practicable, empowered to make decisions within constraints established with the project leader. This is equivalent to the situation at sea where the captain delegates steering and command over the bridge to the officer of the watch. They may make course alterations to account for navigation, accounting for wind and currents or other traffic, but if a flag carrying a skull and crossbones appears on the horizon, then they must summon the captain.

For a member of the project team involved in or running a meeting in the absence of the project leader, it is acceptable and even needful that they make such decisions as they are qualified to by virtue of their disciplinary expertise, so long as the implications do not exceed an agreed level of impact on factors such as cost, time, scope, quality, environment, or Health and Safety considerations.

Evolving project leadership

The project leader's accumulated Insight and Foresight across the team necessarily implies a process through which a relationship of reciprocal and mutual respect and understanding has been achieved, and is sustained through ongoing commitment and communication.

Coaching, aligned with the 'Goal–Reality–Options–Will', 'GROW Model' focus, as discussed above, serves to both establish a productive relationship and to encourage the team member to take a journey in which their own self-insight is prompted and teased out. This process, in turn, serves to offer the project leader potentially deep insights into the team member's strengths, weaknesses and aspirations. All are key factors that the project leader will be keen to abstract and contemplate, for they inform the ongoing evolution of their own Vision for the project throughout delivery.

Where the individual's personal aspirations turn out to be congruent with the needs of the project leader in delivery, then a powerful and mutually beneficial alliance is indicated. But even in the absence of specific future aspirations, the project leader's shared vision for the individual will be to help support them to maximise their potential. The individual will be left in no doubt that their part in delivery will be valued and recognised, and that they will in a real sense be far better placed for whatever future opportunities or aspirations arise. After all, in project management so many of the core competences are readily transferable to a wide variety of professions and careers.

With developed Foresight, built through engagement with the delivery team, the project leader is in a position to articulate a Vision for delivery far more informed than the traditional command-and-control approach that treats both individuals and the team simply as a resource to be directed from beginning to end.

The project leader, having completed Steps 1 to 5, will have established the foundations for a dynamic to be triggered in Step 6 that realises the emergence of collaborative synergy. This represents the central function of project leadership then embodied in Steps 7 to 9 through the Vision as applicable for the project leader, the team members and the team as a collaborative unit.

Foresight Step 6. Team to synergy

By this point, the project leader has become informed about the delivery team as individuals and as a group. Their strengths and weaknesses will be better understood, along with their aspirations and their 'fit' with the project to be delivered.

The idea of synergy in this context is that the sum of all team members in delivery, working together collaboratively, far exceeds what the same individuals could achieve working either individually or under the constraints and limitations of traditional command and control. There are many examples of synergy that illustrate this powerful dynamic. Taking all the individual components that are brought together in a car, an aircraft, a computer or a human body, each exhibits its individual characteristics and qualities until put together in a particular way, such that the sum of all exceeds their individual qualities and characteristics.

In a similar way, a project leader might present a problem for 10 members of the team to work on and then report back on individually. They then bring them all together and facilitate a meeting where all the ideas raised are shared, compared and contrasted. Some ideas, in light of emergent inputs, will falter and fail. Well led, the discussion may then lead to other ideas evolving through debate and discussion and completely new solutions may even be prompted and emerge. The combined outputs from the group session, compared with individuals working separately, is likely to be substantially greater. This is synergy.

This synergy has many other features that make it particularly attractive in project delivery. As discussed above, the instability of delivery environments and emergent complexity that constrain and change the trajectory of delivery is constantly increasing, often driven by new technologies and levels of interconnectivity and interdependency.

What synergy brings to the delivery team, unconstrained by command and control, is a level of resilience that capitalises on delivery teams characterised by the presence of multi-discipline SMEs. Emerging new tools already bridge previously disparate areas of expertise. This is exemplified by BIM, where architects, civil engineers and IT experts *all* share the same virtual space.

Synergy fosters the resilience necessary to manage emergent complexity, that is, to manage multiple, unplanned changes simultaneously. Its effectiveness is realised when those with the level of relevant expertise are empowered to engage and act.

Wars have been lost because some distant leader was not inclined to devolve decision making to those in the field who were best able to assess threats and opportunities first hand. In today's project delivery environment, the effective project leader supports and facilitates those best placed and qualified to decide and act.

There is also a key function for the project leader in sustaining synergy by maintaining networks through which relevant information and communication reaches those on the frontline so they can operate and make decisions based on up-to-date information.

Reporting

As with all data-rich environments, it is vital that the project leader proactively drives the establishment of reporting by exception. The project leader needs to establish the reporting principles early and embed them within the IPT charter and project/programme governance; report progress by exception, escalate out-of-tolerance risks and issues that the team cannot resolve by themselves, and anticipate critical future engagements. They must identify aspects of delivery that are particularly sensitive to change, ensuring any hint of it should be signalled with urgency. LFE is potentially invaluable in this context. Did previous projects of this type, or in this place or phase, face unexpected challenges from which the current project might take learning?

Team meetings

In any team meeting, the project leader will pay close attention to the way the team interact. But, in addition, they will actively seek to influence the team towards fully engaged, collaborative working. To achieve this, they must kindle a sense of shared Foresight that will become a shared Vision. The APM website offers a wealth of material to support the project leader in preparing for and running effective meetings.

Chapter 7 Learning outcomes

The project leader is guided through the first three steps, gaining Insight into self, team members and the team as a whole. They are made aware of challenges that can arise, resistance that may well be met, and how it might be addressed. Following these steps will foster enhanced situational awareness and understanding and the significance and application of both are explored.

1. Situational awareness of what is now and how it came to be must be built upon, using informed 'Foresight' to map the journey ahead and anticipate its challenges.
2. With such situational understanding fostered, the project leader anticipating what is required can develop and prepare themselves and the team for what lies ahead.
3. The power of rapport is necessary as a foundation for all effective engagement of others.
4. Organisations have a responsibility to stop selecting in favour of counter-productive behaviours that exhibit an egotistical need and desire to dominate others.

Assessing project leader effectiveness is facilitated by the Triple Catalyst and Nine Steps, which each generate evidence of their engagement. Project leadership behaviours can be assessed and measured.

8
Steps 7 to 9: Vision: informing and communicating situational understanding

The project leader is guided through steps 7 to 9, developing Foresight into the challenges ahead. Following these steps fosters enhanced situational understanding so how best to prepare and develop both self and team to surmount them.

Again, the necessity of wider strategic and organisational support in structures and processes highlights the fact that the project manager will not achieve the full benefits of project leadership alone.

Specific guidance is also drawn from the *APM Body of Knowledge 7th edition* in relation to 'people and behaviours' and team development'.

The Third Catalyst: 'Vision'

The Third Catalyst, 'Vision', encompasses, as do the first and second, self, the team as individuals and the team as a whole. As a catalyst, it prompts and triggers a personal Vision, and acts as a source for a compelling Vision of delivery that the project leader can then cascade to inspire and motivate the entire delivery team.

Each iteration of the Nine Steps informs and clarifies this 'Vision'. For the attentive project leader, this process serves to continually enhance and evolve personal effectiveness, revealing opportunities and highlighting potential risks. When this Vision is effectively communicated and adopted, the active intelligence driving the project forwards is no longer confined to the project manager and constrained by their personal capabilities.

The project manager has one pair of eyes and ears. They can process only a finite volume of information. During any one day in delivery, for example, many decisions must be made based on information from reports affecting who does what, where and when. The project manager is not qualified to make many of these decisions, which must be devolved to SMEs. The SME, like a commander in the field of battle, must make tactical decisions, while the project leader operates at a more strategic level. There will always be exceptions, of course, and on occasion the project leader may intervene in tactical decisions, although there is a danger of alienating those who may, in reality, be better placed and more qualified to decide.

The project manager's awareness of what is actually happening aross physical and virtual workfaces of delivery is limited. Even with tools aiding 'telepresence', the sense of being present in remote conversations via phone or videoconference, they can only be in one place at a time. Assuming they knew what was happening elsewhere based on a 'schedule' has caught out many a project manager. In many projects, the delivery team may be separated geographically and, no matter how alert or inquisitive the project manager is, they simply cannot be aware of all that is happening or all the decisions that are or need to be made at any one time.

Leadership is by definition a catalyst, inspiring and aligning others with a common vision. The project leader is that catalyst embodied. Traditional delivery depended on and was limited by the project manager's personal awareness, knowledge and intelligence. Today, their single intelligence and will to delivery must, to be effective, be multiplied by the added intelligence of each delivery team member, both as individuals and working in collaboration.

Instead of the limited intelligence the project manager's eyes and ears can offer, it is now as though the individual agency of the project leader is extended by every pair of eyes and ears in the delivery team. And together they can process information and make decisions informed by extended intelligence in a way no one person can ever equal.

This is the equivalent of the exponential increase in computing power offered by distributed and parallel processing. The eyes and ears of the project leader, informed by the shared Vision of leader and team, are wherever the team are, and they are sensitised to maintain alignment with the Vision, while being aware of any threat to its realisation. This is the single most compelling argument favouring the function of project leadership over the traditional form of command and control.

Steps 7 to 9: Vision: informing and communicating situational understanding

Vision Step 7. A vision for personal transformation and delivery

The path to project leadership begins with a personally compelling Vision of a future self, informed by Insight, Foresight, and a clear situational understanding of what is, what is to be, and the personal evolution necessary to close the gap between the two.

The 'Triple Catalyst' and 'Nine Steps to Project Leadership' nurture the emergence of relationships fulfilling the function of project leadership: to align and inspire.

Paradoxically, this personal Vision is, in some ways, the primary component and catalyst. The only reason it is not presented as the 'First Step', is that effective Vision, although underpinning the ability to inspire and align others, itself demands the deep foundation of authentic Insight into the self as it is now. Coupling Insight with Foresight generates situational understanding of what is aspired to, and the development, evolution, or transformation necessary to achieve it.

As explored above, *not* working collaboratively represents – literally re-presents, time and again – a formidable cost both in terms of lost human potential, and repercussive economic impacts on project cost, time, quality and scope. Recognising this and, conversely, the power of a team working as a collaborative collective is, in and of itself, prompting a transformation to new ways of thinking about what project leadership is, and what is necessary to realise it.

When challenges and difficulties arise in all human endeavours, the resilient persevere. Research suggests individuals having a personal, clear Vision and a goal aspired-to persevere beyond the 'here and now' crisis.

For the aspiring project leader facing the challenges of engaging a dysfunctional or new team, this knowledge offers a potent resource and source of resilience. The project leader's personal time and energy in securing team member engagement, then releasing the power of their collective focus on aligned goals with shared values triggers a return on investment far greater than any individual could equal.

The journey to effective project leadership can be personally challenging for, as this book shows, it fundamentally challenges traditional ideas about what project leadership is.

Throughout history, individuals have achieved positions of leadership based on perceived charisma. However, time and again, the record shows that, however superficially charming they might be, those attracted to positions in order to secure power and control over others, often leave behind a trail of destruction and disillusionment.

Evolving project leadership

By contrast, true leadership leaves a legacy of lasting, positive effect – leaving those led the better for their invested trust.

With this in mind, anyone aspiring to project leadership faces a very personal decision: 'Am I prepared to, and in what specific ways do *I need* to change, in order to grow?'

The implicit dichotomy here is that however confident someone may be in their ability to project a persona that they *believe* represents leadership, growth may demand, not the inflation of what *is*, but, potentially, a shedding of such assumptions and preconceptions. For some, Insight and Foresight into self may inform a radically new Vision. It may transpire that they signal a need to shed some preconceptions about project leadership and its function in order to embrace and realise the benefits of new concepts and behaviours.

It is as well to recognise and acknowledge here that often the arch-enemy in this endeavour, as with all forms of personal growth, is ego. Egotism will fiercely resist any suggestion that an aspect or attribute of a developed persona is even up for debate. Their identity is so tied up with the persona they have contrived that it is out of and beyond questioning.

The following list of questions highlights the necessary disposition required of those who want to evolve to project leadership.

1. Do you want to be a project leader?
2. Do you want to be a leader?
3. Do you want others in your team to see and accept you as their leader?
1) requires **2),**
2) requires **3).**

As we have seen, leadership is not asserted, but bestowed.

For those who construe leadership as dominance over others, rather than the ability to inspire their commitment and loyalty, this responsibility of the leader to engage their followers is deeply uncomfortable.

Another example focuses on the actual function of the project leader in empowering others, rather than behaviours that elevate self over others.

1. Do you want success in project delivery as an outcome?
2. Do you want success in the process of delivering projects?
3. Do you want your team to be as effective as they can be as a team?
4. Do you want your team to be as effective as they can be as individuals?
1) requires **2),**

Steps 7 to 9: Vision: informing and communicating situational understanding

2) requires **3)**,
3) requires **4).**

The project leader is likely to chair meetings every day. For those intent on securing the engagement of all involved, encountering a circle of grim faces, as opposed to welcoming ones, signals a clear deficit to be addressed. For those primarily concerned with maintaining their position and assuming authority, it may well seem like business as usual. Similarly, the former may perceive any questions that arise as healthy – indicative of commitment and engagement – and will respond accordingly, while the latter is more likely to react to questions as signs of insolence or insubordination.

A choice must be made to adopt and promote a vision of empowered collaboration. For those able to embrace it, the case is overwhelmingly in favour of ongoing coaching and empowerment, at both the individual and team level. In an increasingly volatile delivery environment, the case for unquestioning obedience is increasingly redundant. Command and control leadership is by definition an oxymoron.

Failure to engage and inspire the team through coaching and empowerment to delegation and ownership, is not project leadership. Favouring asserted authority and 'telling' others what to do actually eviscerates the very basis on which personal motivation and ownership is built: trust and respect.

For those at the organisational level charged with developing project leaders, fundamental questions must be raised and addressed about the cultural changes necessary to accommodate the effective function and form of project leadership.

Given the emergent challenges many contemporary organisations now face in project delivery, nothing short of decisive organisational intervention will be sufficient.

The evident value of project leadership behaviours supporting collaboration and engagement by all stakeholders, including the delivery team, de-legitimises command-and-control behaviours in leadership development.

If a collaborative approach to delivery is sought, why would behaviours putting others on the defensive be promoted or adopted? Again, if they undermine the very ability to perform as highlighted above in relation to the SCARF Model, why should they be defended?

The evidence is clear, unmistakable, and undeniable – any intent or desire to dominate, 'catch-out', blame or humiliate is to be studiously avoided.

Communication, whether through body language, tone, cadence or the spoken word, must not compromise the fragile, 'collective' identity arising when all believe themselves to be on the 'same side'.

Evolving project leadership

Any project is a story. It has a beginning, a middle, and an end. The project leader can choose to create a vision for the project in delivery and completion. The vision can take the form of a narrative and may focus on means or ends. It may depict the journey as a 'treasure map', or a 'war zone'. The way situations are couched, the 'vision' influences the way others perceive, and so approach them. This applies to both the integrated project team and wider stakeholders. It can profoundly influence their disposition, which in turn influences others, for better or worse.

So, if the project leader presents in a brusque manner, appearing inconsiderate or even dismissive of others, they immediately establish a tone for the team's culture. Legitimising such negative behaviours effectively sets a dynamic in motion that extends far beyond that room and that meeting. Those in the team who are inclined to collaborative working are now marginalised; those more nuanced and emotionally mature, then, may ironically be portrayed as 'weak'. The Vision the manager so promotes might therefore, in and of itself, set the tone for, a dysfunctional team.

The above examples all serve to illustrate and highlight the role of the project leader in embodying the Vision for delivery. For some, the ability to achieve this will require a personal transformation that may be more or less challenging, depending on their disposition and the underlying motivation for project leadership.

Articulating the Vision

The project leader's Vision for personal improvement and transformation will take into account all they have learned in Steps 1 to 6. The plan will incorporate, as with any project, the steps to be taken, any milestones and goals and a schedule. Through Insight gained into the 'hidden self' using the Johari Window or other 360 degree feedback, it will be possible to engage in activities designed to address negative behaviours and in this, as in all personal development, the identification of a personal coach or mentor will be of real value.

Acitivites fostering Foresight will have served the purpose of populating the 'radar' with demands anticipated in delivery for additional training, or other personal preparation, as well as those that can be expected in order to meet longer-term career aspirations.

The intelligence obtained about the team members as individuals, and their maturity towards performing collaboratively, should also provide a rich source of material informing plans to secure their engagement.

Steps 7 to 9: Vision: informing and communicating situational understanding

The project leader asked to set out these plans should be able to say what they are, what prompted them, and what progress has been made towards their completion. This is an ongoing process and can also actively inform content for CPD. The value of establishing such plans, goals, milestones and progress will be realised as reflected directly in relation to the Nine Steps. For this reason, when the organisation, through the project management capability function, or its equivalent, seeks evidence in periodic Project Management Suitably Qualified Experienced Person (SQEP) or development review, there is no significant overhead placed on the project manager as leader, since these tools already inform and enhance their day-to-day activity.

There is, too, an expectation that project managers understand the underpinning reason behind progression and iterative return to the Nine Steps – for this will fundamentally inform their Vision of 'what good looks like'. For, while there is no final milestone or 'arrival' as a project leader, they will find over time that, as each step informs the others, their success in achieving engagement and collaboration will necessarily result in a diminished need for their own input. This is the same as the progression from direction to delegation promoted by the Hersey Blanchard Model of Team Development.

The project leader's personal Vision, then, will lay out a destination in project delivery for themselves and the team, and what characterises the journey. So far, though, this is all in the project leader's head, and as such does nothing to support congruence and collaboration. It is for this that steps 8 and 9 are required.

Vision Step 8. A Vision empowering team members

As with the preceding steps, the project leader will need to plan and undertake a series of regular, one-to-one meetings with each member of the team, which will in turn be informed by – and inform – ongoing Insight and Foresight, upon which this Third Catalyst can be activated.

Communicating the Vision for delivery to each team member will be informed by accumulated awareness and Insight into their own aspirations and abilities, coupled with the scheduled demands of delivery to which they are expected to contribute. Beyond this, with Foresight, the project leader will make due links between immediate project delivery demands, and the support of individual developmental and career aspirations that are congruent with organisational strategic objectives.

The project leader must aspire to move significantly beyond simply communicating some abstract notion or lofty vision to which the team member can vaguely nod assent, since it has little direct impact on their day-to-day activity. Many lofty and well-intentioned initiatives founder on the lack of connection between abstract, organisational values and the individual's day-to-day decisions, priorities and activities. The individual nods in blithe assent to noble mission statements, but never really relates them to or sees how they might or should apply in their day-to-day work.

The role of the project leader in involving IPT members in generating and communicating the project Vision is to make it relevant and personal to them, and this both necessitates and capitalises on the investment made in securing Insight and Foresight.

The intent is that the team member should come to a new level of awareness of where and how the project in delivery offers them an opportunity to engage which they welcome and can 'relate to'. This notion of relationship, and being able to relate to the project and others in the team is crucial. This activity is the equivalent of inviting an outsider to join a pack or tribe. The reservations and caution behind any reticence or reluctance are entirely natural and understandable. For this reason, the project leader's role is critical as they, in their demeanour, behaviours and language, are effectively communicating to the team member 'this is who we are – this is our culture'.

Any individual, in any context, whether social or work-related, encounters these situations as pivotal moments. Meeting a new manager or potential leader, especially the first time they meet or in *any* form of performance review, these questions are inevitably and actively seeking answers:

- 'Will I, or do I feel welcome?'
- 'Do I feel accepted and respected?'
- 'Do I feel my role or position is under threat?'
- 'Do I relate in one way to the manager/leader, and differently to other members of the team?'
- 'Do I feel my role and contribution is visible, valued, appreciated or recognised'?
- 'Am I being set up to fail?'
- 'Am I seen as competent, capable and able'?
- 'Am I liked?'

Steps 7 to 9: Vision: informing and communicating situational understanding

The project leader, through their words and actions, whether tacitly or explicitly, will answer all of these questions – and if they have not set out to approach them in a positive and self-aware way, there is a real danger that they will communicate the wrong message.

The '360 degree' inputs are an invaluable tool in this endeavour. Intending to come across as decisive and confident, the project leader may succeed with one team member while appearing to others to be arrogant and closed-minded. For this reason, the mature project leader will seek to avoid, where possible, meeting new team members for the first time in a meeting context. The formal persona required when chairing a meeting might be very different from the one a leader projects in a one-to-one interaction.

Meeting one-to-one, for one thing, offers a very good opportunity to convey an authentic interest in the individual, which is not possible in a public forum. It is precisely this level of 'relating' that is necessary to the essential establishment of rapport, as discussed above.

"I see you", "I respect you", and "I have positive expectations of you"; these messages, however tacit, will go a long way to avoiding the counter-productive triggers threatening SCARF's Status, Certainty, Autonomy, Relatedness and Fairness. Anyone aspiring to project leadership but flouting these basic guidelines does themselves, the team members, the team, the project and the organisation no favours.

These three messages, in and of themselves, represent significant positive catalysts for the team member, inclining and encouraging them to see their manager as something more, a leader. Being thus prompted to feel inclined-towards, and encouraged, takes the erstwhile manager a long way towards the inspired and aligned followership which is the prerequisite and fundamental condition for the attribution of leadership.

Integral to establishing the Vision with individual team members, the project leader will establish a graduated approach to empowerment, and this will include interventions designed to secure team members' buy-in to increasing ownership of work assigned, and also in developing their own personal Insight and Foresight capabilities.

In concrete terms, this means that in day-to-day delivery of tasks, the team member takes ownership, actively developing their own Insight and Foresight; reflecting on events and others' activities in relation to both their own concerns and others', as well as the project leader.

In this endeavour the project leader seeks to develop each team member in turn so they come to embody the vision and collaborative spirit of the team as a

Evolving project leadership

whole. By encouraging and communicating support for team members in achieving competence and increased delegation, the project leader simultaneously encourages them to build relationships of mutual respect and interdependence with *other* members of the team. This benefits them in turn, as others reciprocate.

This virtuous cycle of reinforcement evolves the team from a collection of individuals to a collective with a resilient, mutually supportive dynamic. Less empowering forms of management cannot hope to match their effectiveness.

Vision Step 9. Measured informed ongoing intervention

Now at step 9, as in steps 3 and 6, the project leader turns from the team members as individuals to focus on their role and function in effecting the transition to collective collaboration.

The focus now shifts to take cognizance of Insight and Foresight in the relations between team members. There is a need to understand what stage of maturity the team is at in terms of Tuckman's transition from Forming through Storming and Norming to Performing. It will not happen for all simultaneously, and steps may even be bypassed. Equally, what is appropriate and effective for one delivery team will not necessarily suit all.

In any meeting, who listens to whom, and who disregards or even discounts what another contributes? Are the comments of some listened to attentively, while others are ignored or summarily dismissed?

At the group level, initially, the sharing of the Vision can be less personal and compelling, for there is less shared experience to draw upon. But, in time, stories reflecting a collaborative, team-oriented mindset will emerge from day-to-day events. Held aloft as exemplary, they can come to define the group's identity and culture. The project leader must notice when someone goes the extra mile, and the benefits arising, or when someone looks out for, and so shows concern for, another, with repercussive positive effects. What might have happened had not 'X' done 'Y', or spoken out?

It is important to be sensitive, and to draw the team's attention to such behaviours; to 'seize upon the good', bear witness to, and hold it up for all to see. For, in such moments, the project leader communicates directly and with more immediacy than at almost any other time.

Consider, such an individual has almost certainly been perfectly conscious of doing more than strictly mandated or necessary. It is a gesture with ancient primal

Steps 7 to 9: Vision: informing and communicating situational understanding

origins. It is as though that individual, eyes lowered with respect, extends a tentative hand of friendship, offering an alliance. It is a contingent and provisional gesture for, if it is rejected or ignored, it effectively signals rejection and with that, threat. It can be seen to signal ostracism, denying access to the collective. So it is vital that such gestures should not go unnoticed.

Most can relate to scenarios where, having made some personal gesture in good faith, it is ignored or, even worse, the other appears to treat such goodwill as an entitlement to which they are due and under no obligation whatever to reciprocate.

Failing this test – failing to make eye contact to communicate recognition and mutual respect for the other's good faith – not only misses a truly golden opportunity, but likely alienates and disenfranchises, even antagonising the one who went out on a limb.

The project leader encouraging and developing a collaborative team cannot afford to bypass these signals that offer alliance. They bring the aspirant project leader to the very threshold of achieving rapport: the key pre-condition to the reciprocal commitment that characterises leader-follower relationships.

In humans in general, there is a powerful dynamic at work that makes the possibility of membership in a group offering acceptance, support and the safety of numbers, highly attractive. This dynamic can be seen within all social groupings, including sport, politics and religion. If the project leader can establish an identity based on the project and team in delivery, and some kudos associated with membership, this is a powerful incentive for others to join and, conversely, a disincentive to being excluded from membership.

Igniting the synergy that emerges from a team working collaboratively, as a collective, aligned with a common goal and mutually supportive culture, the project leader fulfils a fundamentally different function from that of the manager. The manager may view meetings as primarily a platform from which they can judge and direct. The project leader will utilise them as an opportunity to observe how the team operates and to incline it to ever-greater levels of effectiveness and empowerment, where inter-dependency is not a weakness but a source of opportunity to do more through the distributed processing power of collaborative working.

In meetings especially, the project leader will keenly observe who does and does not talk, and how team members interact with each other. Who ignores whom, and who defers to whom? There will also be an ongoing concern to ensure participation by all, and due acknowledgement of the value each brings. The quiet one may be of the opinion that they and their work is insignificant and may remain silent because of their age or lesser qualifications. The project leader might take an appropriate moment to draw attention to this individual's contribution and some critical impact that any failure to deliver might have occasioned.

Empowering growth: self-actualisation

Another significant role of the project leader in facilitating the emergence of a collaborative collective is that of engaging every member of the delivery team in a clear Vision of why and how their role is different from traditional management and what this means for them.

The project leader must actively engage themselves in the task of communicating how their function is different from that of traditional project management. They must explain the importance of all team members and stakeholders being actively engaged in the collective process of delivery.

Achieving such ownership through empowerment and delegation necessitates the explicit buy-in to agreed levels of trust and responsibility. The attraction of autonomy comes at the price of agreed levels of delegated authority. Changing the relationship from one that exists between manager and those managed, to that found between project leader and delegate, requires clear agreement and understanding about what lies within or beyond the delegate's authority.

In a meeting, the contractor announces some variation or change to what has been previously planned and agreed – at what level of change is the delegate obliged to 'escalate' to the project leader?

These fundamental changes in the role of the team member must form part of the shared Vision for the team culture that is understood and shared by all. The expectation of team members must be overtly and explicitly moved from that of delivering as directed, to their taking responsibility and ownership for defined-scope delivery.

Expectations must be set by the project leader to make perfectly clear the reciprocal responsibility for being accorded increased levels of autonomy and authority. There is, too, significant mileage for the project leader in doing this, in that it provides an opportunity for the leader to reach out with the offer of 'alliance', with all its potent attraction for those seeking the affirmation of being invited to join those who honour *them*.

For generations, those carrying out delivery in project management were effectively impeded and inhibited from progression through Maslow's Hierarchy of Needs to achieve 'Self Actualisation'. If the topic was raised or discussed, it

Steps 7 to 9: Vision: informing and communicating situational understanding

was in order to encourage the aspirant 'leader' to grow, in order to realise their personal potential, while more or less avoiding any consideration of the detrimental effect of these behaviours on subordinates' ability to perform or grow, being essentially extensions of the leader's will, rather than empowered participants in the realisation of a shared Vision.

Similarly, literature promoting assertive behaviours studiously avoided acknowledging any such hidden cost on its subjects. Assertive, 'command-and-control' behaviours trigger threat responses, and so result in impaired performance capability.

By contrast, the Vision the project leader promotes can both expose and remove that major obstacle to individual and team effectiveness, while actively communicating and establishing a relationship with the team that invites trust and commitment.

Introducing the team to what is, for most, a very different manner of working than they will have been used to, the project leader will communicate and demonstrate previously unheard-of levels of respect. For the team, the inspirational effect of being so treated triggers the SCARF Reward effects and so encourages their reciprocal engagement and commitment.

The power of this Vision, as adopted and embraced by team members, and the delivery team as an integrated collective, cannot be over-stated. Individuals realising external esteem and striving to live up to respectful and raised expectations far outperform those working under direction. The evolution from subject to intelligent agent mirrors that which the child undergoes in moving from dependence on parents to mature independence.

With rights come responsibilities, and this certainly holds true for those the project leader sets out to empower. Along with increased autonomy and ability to exercise personal initiative, the project leader will set each team member's limits to their accountability and the authority under which they deliver. For most, this will be a welcome exchange, but for the project leader, as coach, there will be a need to focus on the needs of each individual in order to nurture and encourage their growth.

> **You don't get the best out of your team by telling them what to do.**
> **The best you can do is help them do the best they can do, together.**
> **Help them be the best they can be, to do the best they can do together.**

Evolving project leadership

The cost of bonsai

The bonsai tree is an art form that requires its artisan to continually prune back new growth until, over time, a miniature version, Image 1, of the full-grown species emerges, as shown in Image 2. This is a graphic metaphor depicting the difference between individuals and teams who are hindered and impeded or denied personal growth, and those who are nurtured to achieve their full potential.

Image 1

Image 2

Imagine a team performing under traditional C&C leadership to deliver a project, while another operates, in parallel, under project leadership as described. Which would be likely to perform best?

Any team encouraged to maximise the potential contribution of each individual, combined with mutually supportive, collaborative working, will of course be far more effective.

Taken to the next level of realism, consider the relative performance where each delivery environment is characterised by 'emergent complexity'. For example, an environment where delivery is highly dependent on other agencies, or is inter-dependent, such that activities or project work packages depend on operational access or others, be they projects or operations rendering progress possible. For most who are delivering in non-greenfield delivery environments permeated by inter-connected, inter-dependent technology, this is increasingly the norm.

Steps 7 to 9: Vision: informing and communicating situational understanding

This dynamic, often unpredictable environment, where new technologies combine in previously untested configurations, offers yet another practical test for the two kinds of team and leadership outlined. Here, to an even greater degree, it seems highly probable that the empowered team will have the ability and mandate to respond with both agility and resilience. Such examples draw out the cost of any form of team delivery where deference is required to specific roles, rather than being inclined to those most qualified, well placed or competent to decide and act.

The shared Vision the project leader sets out to inspire in all must therefore include the establishment of a clear understanding of their own role, as well as that of other individual team members, and how they should relate to each other.

Situational understanding

Situational awareness offers the agent in the field, the pilot in the aircraft or the project leader in delivery, a clear picture of where they have come from, where they are, and where they want to get to. It also offers further, deeper levels and dimensions of understanding. Situational understanding adds to situational awareness, because instead of just being aware of what is, the observer appreciates its significance.

With situational awareness, the project leader possesses a deep understanding, not only of the route to the destination, but what it takes to get there. This is like the commander in the field with situational understanding taking into account the resources needed to overcome the terrain ahead. Seeing a river to cross, they will be aware of what that might entail in terms of resources and time. To develop this capacity, informed by the Triple Catalysts of Insight, Foresight and Vision, the project leader will plan their strategy as a project in its own right. With a clear and incrementally improving vision of what needs to be done – how individuals and the team dynamic can be enhanced – they will plan, then intervene to engage and foster ever greater collaboration and reciprocal rapport and commitment.

In parallel with the schedule for project delivery, the project leader will develop their own schedule for the development of that vital chemistry within and between both members of the delivery team and stakeholders to reduce or remove friction, then add fuel to the oxygen of inspiration fed by a shared vision of delivery and deliverables.

Another dimension of project delivery effectiveness is realised through fostering situational understanding within all team members. For it promotes systems rather than linear thinking. An SME going about their business in project delivery, concerned single-mindedly with the task at hand, effectively blinds themselves to anything not affecting them directly. By contrast, the team member with situational understanding finds generalised situational awareness is enhanced, because they are sensitised to the significance of specific changes around them. Walking into or working within any given working environment, situational understanding means the member of one discipline is more likely to notice something that affects delivery from another.

Reporting this anomaly back to the team, seeing it held up and exemplified by the project leader, will result in all becoming aware of the mutual and personal benefit of others literally looking out for them and effectively saving them work and effort.

Chapter 8 Learning outcomes

1. 'Vision' informed by Insight and Foresight into self and the team facilitates not only a clear view and situational understanding of what is to be done, but clarifies how it is to be achieved, including how to 'lead as they would be led'. This facilitates all stakeholder engagement.
2. The Vision informs culture and, properly conceived and communicated, will touch and inspire its audience. The message and how it is conveyed will be matched to the audience and context.
3. The Vision, whether communicated at the individual or group level, will secure a major advantage through its promotion of empowerment and commitment to realise individual potential.
4. The cost of bonsai and limiting individual self-expression and self-actualisation is raised as an indictment against all project management behaviours that ride roughshod over others or actively hamper, inhibit or impede personal development.

9

Organisational transformation

The project leader's journey to realised interdependence; a conversion from self to team promotion, 'me to we'.

Following personal transformation, the broader perspective is explored. How is change to be achieved at scale, e.g. organisational 'transformation'.

Guidance is drawn from *APM Body of Knowledge 7th edition* in relation to 'organisation and culture', 'collaboration' and 'virtual teams'.

We see how authentic project leadership promotes the ever more crucial centrality of professionalism, ethics and the wider environment while informing all the above.

Within organisations delivering projects, the benefits of project leadership over project management realised through the Triple Catalyst and Nine Steps will achieve most in an environment supported by senior management.

If any organisation is to establish a transformed culture characterised by collaborative teams benefiting from the empowering function of project leadership, there is no alternative but to embrace the need for a transformation; an organisation-wide re-alignment supporting the new function and necessary form of project leadership. This book promotes and underpins both. It offers a process all aspiring project leaders can follow.

However, such a deep cultural transformation means that both senior management and those leading the project must, with one voice, educate all as to the new form and function of project leadership and their part in it. Leadership is an empowering relationship and as such, it will not suffice for only one side of the relationship to understand its purpose.

All who are to be team members must be made aware of the profound sense in which their role has altered; how it is enriched and its potential to bring greater fulfilment for them as individuals. They should also be clear that the change will require not merely their assent, but their commitment. An expectation that respect shown will be duly reciprocated. Above all, there must be a clear message that, in a fundamental sense, they are not in the position of 'followers' but 'team members'.

Each member of the team should be informed how the function of project leader differs from project manager. While team members can initially expect some form of 'directive' support, the vision communicated must find each team member playing their part, through commitment, to progressive ownership and full delegation. The team should be aware that the function of the project leader is to facilitate and support collaborative working; *all* are expected to grow, and to keep growing.

Selecting, assessing and developing project leaders

As has been shown, traditional forms of both management and leadership are still promoted, and pervade organisations and organisational theory, despite the growing body of evidence that they are not fit for purpose.

For this reason, at the level of senior management, there must be clarity of understanding and intent in determining the criteria against which those to be appointed as project leaders are selected.

As with the case made above, showing how project leadership differs from traditional portrayals of management and leadership, so too the selection and appointment of project leadership candidates must reflect both the function they are to fulfil, and their competence in the correspondingly appropriate form of leadership and project delivery.

In summary, the function of project leadership outlined above, to be fit-for-purpose, must address the following: **More complex and challenging delivery in environments** characterised by:

- Deliverables are increasingly defined by their interdependence, constraining delivery.
- Systemic dependencies and inter-dependencies, especially technological, increase emergent complexity: one small change cascades across disciplines and boundaries.
- Integrated project team SMEs diminish the project manager's authority-by-qualification.
- Severely diminished line management authority demands sophisticated stakeholder engagement competences.

- Brownfield, and to some extent greenfield, sites are increasingly regulated, imposing constraints in delivery.
- Delivery environments increasingly impose non-negotiable constraints in both access and delivery.

In addition to the above, the 2020 worldwide paradigm shift precipitated by the emergence of the COVID-19 pandemic, has prompted more remote working than ever before. Suddenly, line and project management has experienced an unprecedented drop and loss of *visibility* of their line reports. Millions have found themselves having to adapt, if able, to 'remote working'.

Digital forms of communication now predominate. In such situations, subordinates or team members must be trusted to work without direct supervision. It is therefore more vital than ever for project leadership relations to be of a quality that inspires conscientious commitment.

The motivation to work with diligence operates from the inside out, rather than being imposed from the outside in. When the phone, video call or other digital connection ends, *that* is when the efficacy of the leadership connection is tested.

In addition to taking account of the above delivery context, due account must now also be taken of the most effective form of project leadership behaviours.

Evidence continues to emerge from neurology, psychology and social psychology, as exemplified by the SCARF Model: personal characteristics that were long hailed as characterising leadership, such as *ambition* and *self-confidence*, suppress and inhibit growth rather than *inspiring* others.

Project leadership behaviours, what good does and does not look like

Considering the necessary steps to realise the benefits of a competent project leadership function, it is inevitable and right that consideration should be given to the characteristics, qualities and behaviours to be promoted and those to be demoted or actively discouraged. In light of all the preceding, it will be immediately clear that command-and-control behaviours are not favoured. But other, less obvious or apparent characteristics and behaviours must also now be held up to scrutiny.

Ambition has long been promoted as a salutary quality in leadership. It certainly characterises all leaders, great and small, good and bad. No motivation

Evolving project leadership

– no leadership. It is the fuel enabling individuals to transcend obstacles and realise their potential. But, like leadership, ambition can be for better or worse, productive or toxic, right or wrong. After all, which dictators, tyrants or those seeking to dominate, repress and subordinate others for their own benefit were not ambitious?

Defined as a 'strong desire to do or achieve something', ambition is therefore but a *means* to some 'end'. But, as with any tool, only when the intent behind its application is known, can it be judged good or bad.

There is a world of difference between those who are ambitious to 'push' – to promote and elevate themselves, their self-promotion, self-aggrandisement, or projected sense of entitlement – and those 'drawn' by some purpose beyond themselves. They reflect the distinction discussed previously, between those 'in-dependence' on 'esteem from others' (it's all about 'me'), and the 'interdependent' (it's all about 'us').

Self-confidence is a similarly ambiguous quality. It can be passive, inwardly assured without need of display, or it can be projected. The latter often signals a posed superiority. One person's projected self-confidence presents to another as arrogance. Again, it characterises all leaders, great and small. No self-confidence, no leadership.

Those employing counter-productive behaviours that alienate, disenfranchise and antagonise those who should be inspired and influenced to 'engagement', project self-confidence and entitlement.

Self-confidence of *that* kind manifests itself through assertiveness over others and subordination of others. It is driven by an insecure ego; it needs and feeds on control.

The assured self-confidence of the interdependent has no need to maintain the artifice of any such externally projected self-construal.

For the project leader intent on securing stakeholder engagement, self-confidence arises from a far deeper place than where those driven by an insecure ego operate from. Their self-construal is not tied to a contrived or projected self-image. It is not manifested by what the leader says or does, but by what they *are*.

The mature, interdependent project leader's self-confidence does not need to be 'projected', because it is deeply self-assured – it needs, seeks and demands nothing, of or from others, to *be*. It is not dependent on others' esteem.

Manifesting as authority without domination, this form of self-confidence is observed when, entering a room or meeting, they do not actively assert themselves, but exude an aura of self-sufficiency, self-possession, being self-assured that is independent of others' approval or subordination.

Assertiveness. The effect of assertiveness and '***holding others to account'*** is equally ambiguous. As discussed above, dominating, self-promoting behaviours counter the very function project leadership exists to fulfil.

Why is it that assertive behaviours have come to be associated with leadership, when they trigger, not inspiration and willing followers, but their toxic opposite – the threat response, and fear?

Movies and stories still depict leaders commanding and controlling their willing or admiring subjects. The audience is still encouraged and subtly conditioned to relate to the leader, rather than question what it would really feel like to be subject to their will. Followers defer and comply without question or complaint. Challengers are presented as rogues, while a certain nobility is conferred on unquestioning loyalty. Stories and myths have served the agenda of the storyteller; "Once upon a time" still glazes the eyes of the listener and suspends their critical judgement.

The power of stories endures, but for project leadership to be realised, it must be exposed for what it is, and the purpose of those conflating leadership with assertiveness exposed.

It is effective only in extremis and conditional upon the subject's faith and established trust, rooted in experience, that the leader's imposition will subsequently be justified as needful.

Another reason self-confidence and assertiveness are not unconditionally justified is that, again, they undermine rather than support the primary function of project leadership. If the project leader is to adopt, promote, develop and realise the vision of a collaborative team of SMEs and external stakeholders, over whom they have no direct line authority, then they must have and exercise the quality of humility.

Humility. Where traditional command-and-control behaviours are promoted, and deemed to rest upon self-confidence, ambition and assertiveness, humility is treated with peremptory disdain and disparaged as weakness.

Yet humility – modesty and a lack of vanity or hubris – is a fundamental requirement of the project leader bringing together and forming a team from diverse individuals, from multiple disciplines and backgrounds. The project leader must be capable and self-assured enough to invite, entertain and discuss the insights and ideas of others, without any bias or ego-centric unwillingness to recognise or acknowledge *others'* expertise or reasoning. All knowledge is contingent and provisional. The mature project leader knows and respects this.

Humility, like soft skills, empathy and emotional intelligence, is often dismissed as signalling weakness by those it discomfits. Humility is framed as indicating the indecisiveness of the weak-willed. From their perspective, leadership is inseparable from the contrived and projected self-image they will defend at all costs. That necessarily means not inviting or welcoming, but pre-emptively and actively discouraging, any suggestion that one might be influenced by, and hence appear to defer, to others. This inability to learn from or listen to others, is, in fact, the self-defeating fatal weakness of command and control.

A Vision, if it is to be adopted by others, requires a capacity and willingness to embrace, absorb and appreciate others' ideas, perspectives and priorities – their worldview, even if it is not entirely congruent with one's own. The point is to find what *is* aligned. If the project leader is to articulate a Vision that resonates, this is essential. Otherwise the project leader expresses what they see as important for *them* and why, with little or no consideration as to whether stakeholder or line reports can relate to or engage with what is said. This function and project leadership behaviour is at the very heart of the art of engaging stakeholders.

Humility is therefore a necessary precondition that must be met if the project leader is to avoid engaging with the team, stakeholders or customers from a position of assumed or pretended superiority. The appropriate form that project leadership must present to all is one that is assured and committed, but always open to two-way communication rather than telling and directing.

Rather than signalling dominance, superiority or any form of entitlement, the project leader engaging others with humility immediately communicates respect. Since mutual respect is essential to rapport, and rapport is essential to collaboration, to dismiss humility is to close the door on this crucial project leadership dynamic and all that flows from it.

Facilitation skills

The form project leadership must adopt to realise its function of establishing and maintaining a collaborative team in delivery, requires facilitation skills that, by definition, cannot be averse to open discussion marked by aligned curiosity and the humility enabling consideration of others' ideas.

Project management has long accorded itself credit for delivering projects. Like 'leadership', this is an idea that convention has put beyond question or scrutiny. It appears obviously true. The job advertisement and role description likely state that the project leader will be personally accountable or responsible for delivering a project to the defined cost, time, quality and scope.

Yet, being responsible for delivery does not change the fact or the significance of the project leader's dependence on their team to deliver. The function of project leadership is to deliver the team that delivers the project – to facilitate the emergence of a collaborative team. The project leader is the catalyst, inspiring and facilitating a common Vision within, and across all, in delivery. What awareness and acknowledgement of this dependency should foster is due humility in recognising and respecting dependency on others to deliver the project, and that the focus of one's efforts is not on promoting and self-aggrandisement, but on empowering, facilitating and nurturing growth in the team.

The Triple Catalyst and Nine Steps fostering project leadership have laid out the function of the project leader and highlighted behaviours and tasks in which the aspirant project leader must achieve competence. Underpinning the very ability to do this is the absolute requirement for the aspirant project leader to understand and embrace *their* role, and to be *able* to ensure all in delivery understand and accept the new freedoms, rights and responsibilities that come with their roles in delivery. These include:

Coaching. This is central to the role of the project leader in developing the team and central to Steps 2, 5 and 8.

Soft skills: Emotional intelligence and empathy. These are key attributes and skills for the project leader and their fundamental role in facilitating stakeholder engagement.

Interdependent leadership. This is at the heart of project leadership, and represents an attitude and mindset motivated to facilitate and realise the collective power of others.

There will be resistance to the establishment of the project leadership function as described and underpinned. Those who have not achieved and do not aspire to the level of leadership maturity described as 'interdependent' are not likely to find transition to the role of project leadership attractive or desirable. The transition to a culture supporting project leadership will not occur overnight, and with increasing awareness of others, those in-dependence on traditional command and control will be inclined to self-select for other environments.

Many reading this book will have been challenged for the first time to consider what leadership is, and what the function of a project manager is as project leader. It is not an easy thing to have one's fundamental, long-standing and unquestioned assumptions so exposed.

Organisational transformation does not happen overnight. The most visionary of leaders needs time to bring others to the point where their previously unquestioned frame of reference is apprehended as conditional and contingent, rather than a given.

Someone supporting a particular team in sports does not readily switch their affiliations, and within organisations, even at senior levels – in some cases especially at senior levels – there will be those with decades of experience in 'telling' for whom the very concept of facilitating is alien.

It can be extremely difficult to relinquish stereotypes of leadership and expectations of what is required of leaders. In a project manager assessment group exercise for example, the quiet, unassuming candidate that is more focused on 'taking care of the team', rather than 'taking charge' of it, is still discounted as lacking assertiveness. HR and training departments are often still besieged by companies and consultancies extolling and promoting assertiveness training, often underpinned by entirely misguided reference to military traditions that fly in the face of scientific, peer-reviewed evidence as discussed.

Senior management discussing the development of leadership skills still dismiss the one who suggests that command-and-control behaviours are often counter-productive, or that assertiveness and holding others to account is over-rated. They will likely be peremptorily closed-down by clichéd ripostes that stand little scrutiny.

What this means is that a pre-requisite for organisational transformation is for senior managers to undergo the transition to interdependence. In long-established, entrenched cultures and large organisations bound by convention and bureaucracy, the necessary transitions to transformation will undoubtedly provoke a level of cultural and personal trauma for some.

But, as with all evolution, if some new faculty or emergent capability works, it will be copied and replicated. Project leadership can emerge within larger organisations, and the attention drawn by its success can inspire the majority to emulate it.

> The argument for project leadership turns on one inescapable fact.
> The power, resilience and agility of an empowered delivery team working in collaboration far exceeds that of a team hobbled and impeded by one claiming leadership, who insists on commanding and controlling every team member and for whom delegation and empowerment represents a diminution of their personal power.
> Any project manager failing to evidence individual and team development is failing in their key role and therefore in project leadership.

Just as there are forces at work encouraging growth in project leadership, there will be corresponding forces arising from the increasing scrutiny of conventional project management by command and control when set against successful project leadership.

A new generation of ever-more highly educated project managers and qualified SMEs in delivery all play their part in populating a project delivery culture that increasingly looks askance at overt, alpha-male dominance behaviours. Those exercising behaviours associated with traditional leadership more generally are also being viewed with increasing scepticism.

The increasing need for skilled, technologically competent project delivery also means that project delivery organisations are in a market competing for resources. Demand for skilled resources in project delivery is already outstripping supply, such that employers offering the individual growth and realisation of the potential that project leadership offers are at a clear advantage.

Informed Vision, whether driving the individual or senior management, has always been, and will always be, the fundamental driving force for change, and inspiring and engaging it will help form pockets and communities of like-minded individuals. In today's world, the formation of such communities is vastly facilitated by the emergence of a virtual platform that transcends organisations and conventional boundaries, within which suppressed awareness of other perspectives and the potential for change and growth are brought to life.

While social media can form self-reinforcing, self-referential 'bubbles', excluding other perspectives, the ability to remain within them is increasingly under challenge by local repercussions of global events like COVID-19 or the climate crisis that provoke and demand second thoughts.

As with all great endeavours it is as well, as Stephen Covey noted, to "Start with the End in Mind". If the organisation can communicate a compelling Vision of project leadership, its over-arching perspective affords *all* a source of ongoing resilience whatever the challenges ahead.

In other words, the transformation of the organisation follows the transformation of individuals within it and the way they work and interact within and beyond its boundaries. What motivates and inspires individuals to go through the uncertainty that change, as with all projects, gives rise to, is some sense that it will be worth it in the end.

The starkly contrasting images that effective project leadership gives rise to offer a rich resource of scenarios on which to offer the tag-line 'which would you prefer?'.

Imagine the familiar scene when you are immersed in a meeting as the question being discussed is co-opted as a vehicle for some to promote themselves at the expense of others. The subject in hand and the rights and wrongs of it are secondary to the promotion and protection of egos. Someone voices a question. It is seized on as representing a challenge to be repulsed, regardless of its merits. The individual raising the question is seen as insubordinate, with no right to any say in the matter.

Or again, a similar scene, where the answer to the question raised is less important than the preservation of the authority of the one proposing an answer. As each contributor makes their contribution, it is from a position isolated and separate from the others. There is no attempt to acknowledge or accommodate the needs, priorities or views of others. The atmosphere is tense and all seem intent on preserving and promoting their own agenda.

Compare this with how it feels to walk into a room where all are accorded respect and 'air-time'. If any seem particularly reticent or quiet, they will be encouraged and given space to contribute. Clearly aware that some are uncomfortable with sharing in a larger group, break-out sessions are arranged where in a less intense setting their ideas can be drawn out. When an individual rises to speak, all others offer respectful silence and attention. The primary concern of the listener is 'did I understand?' rather than 'does it threaten my own point of view?'

The project leader seeks to draw out all points of view and sources of expert observation. The dominant mood is one of curiosity and exploration, not only an openness to, but a hunger for, the richer picture and ideas that are stimulated as one idea bounces off another to produce some fresh perspective, insight or possible solution.

As ideas are mooted, the overwhelming response is characterised by 'yes, and..' rather than 'no, but..'

A team member enters a one-to-one meeting with the project manager. After a curt nod or brusque 'hello' they get down to the business of directing and telling the team member what they are to do, and what is expected of them.

Most have experience of being treated in this way. Or again, there are those instances where the manager makes clear they are not satisfied with performance. Sometimes it may even feel as though there is a wilful intent to discount significant, positive progress in favour of highlighting some minor issue. On the receiving end of command and control, it can sometimes feel that managers are intent on holding the team member to account; expectations and goals were set, and the individual has failed, maybe implying that they *are* therefore, a failure. In other words, all too often, a licence to exercise command-and-control behaviours is seized upon as an excuse to assert position power.

Organisational transformation

Now another scenario is presented. The team member, long accustomed to being treated as a resource to be directed and told what to do, arrives for their first meeting with the one, they are told, who will be the new project leader.

Entering the room, they are greeted with a smile and friendly eye contact. They are invited to sit down, and the project leader explains that they have read the CV of the team member, and draws out some accomplishment or role that resonates with the project in prospect. They explain the role of the team member, including priorities and goals, but they regularly invite comment and conversation. They are keen to know if the team member has any concerns about delivery, or their own part in it. The project leader also expresses an interest in the team member's aspirations and ambitions beyond the immediate project. How well does the project and their part in it fit in with these? They draw out any aspect of immediate delivery that might offer opportunities for further development, or any aspect where the team member recognises they might benefit from further training.

The team member very quickly begins to realise that this project leader is genuinely and authentically concerned to support their development and potential, and they are particularly impressed by the way the project leader picks up on their own strengths and what inspires them. They feel respected, and that the project leader sees them as an individual rather than a job title or resource to be directed. The way they are treated inspires trust, and the respect received triggers an inclination to offer respect in turn.

The project leader then draws the larger picture, reflecting the way they see the project being delivered and how the team will look out for and support each other. They draw out, too, how by the end of the project the team member will be stronger, and their part will be acknowledged; they will feel proud to have played a part in supporting delivery of a project they now see as worthwhile and important in the context of the organisation and its mission.

All these examples seek to embody the sharp contrast readily observed between project leadership and more traditional forms of command-and-control project management. For senior management, whether seeking organisational or individual transformation, they evoke compelling images, not simply of what project leadership does, or how, and how it contrasts with traditional forms; they offer a vision. The power of a vision is that it is a vehicle others will readily board, because they relate to the direction and journey, or its destination; preferably all three.

Unfortunate though it is that the characteristics of project leadership exemplified here are not more widely adopted and practised, there is a paradoxical benefit to be drawn from the sharp contrast it affords between the common experiences of many in project delivery now, and this vision of how it might be, and feel, to be part of a collaborative, mutually supportive delivery team.

Chapter 9 Learning outcomes

1. Organisational support for the selection, assessment and development of project leadership requires a change in culture and focus.
2. Tired stereotypes must be exposed as a liability and cost to be actively managed.
3. There is a need for active awareness and discouragement by senior management of behaviours exhibiting a preoccupation with self-promotion.
4. There is a need for organisational recognition and reward for those exhibiting interdependence and a team orientation.
5. The need for organisational promotion of soft-skill development is clear, as is the need to facilitate an organisational transformation favouring those realising self-actualisation through the satisfaction of releasing team synergy.

10

The power of project leadership

Having laid out the path and catalysts that support the transition from project manager to leader, with insight and foresight, the book brings its journey full circle with its own Vision.

It reflects on the paradox that the loss of power exercised in traditional command-and-control behaviours fades into insignificance when compared with that released in project leadership.

It closes with a new vision for success through embedding a culture of multi-lateral engagement and collaboration reflecting effective project leadership.

The power of project leadership emerges through collective ownership in collaborative delivery. It does not lie with the project manager nor with the project leader – for leadership is something that is 'done', and is realised in a tapestry of relationships extending across and beyond the integrated project team.

In order to establish project leadership, it is not enough to communicate what needs to be done and by whom.

In order to prepare the delivery team to support project leadership, the first step must be to systematically challenge and expose, as much of this book has, the outdated and ineffective stereotypes of leadership, including the changed function of the project manager and the implications of that for all.

The promotion of project leadership must include awareness and understanding among those whose roles it enhances, the roles of *all* in delivery, and why. For the benefits offered all, all must be actively engaged.

All become stakeholders and team members rather than followers. Just as an orchestra has a conductor and players of equal status, so to the multi-disciplinary team, subject matter experts are all recognised as equal contributors in a collaborative enterprise.

Evolving project leadership

Despite all its benefits, project leadership will encounter resistance, and it will come from those whose habitual ways of working its establishment threatens. This can best be addressed by ensuring all others in delivery are informed, sensitised, and alert to what has changed, how, and why.

Change is a fact of life, and lies at the heart of project delivery. Just as that change must be anticipated, so too project leadership anticipates obstacles to its adoption. Shifting focus to the part those in delivery must play in the relationship, due account must be taken of the fact that they too have their own perceptions and expectations about leadership, including behaviours and their own attitudes associated with command and control. Certainly, many still accept portrayals of leadership on screen that they would be far from happy to be subjected to personally. For this reason, there can be a clear mis-match between followers' unexamined expectations of leadership in projects and its true nature, in the same way that project leadership can be conflated with its traditional forms.

To address this, a concerted effort must be made to ensure that, just as project managers must be brought to a new awareness of their function in project leadership, equally, the team must learn the benefits of casting aside traditional expectations around both their perceptions and their role in the relationship.

Team perceptions and role: how empowering followers fosters engagement

Traditional training and books on leadership seek to inform the character and behaviours of the leader. They assume the function of leadership achieves desired ends by directing and controlling those obliged to follow through position-power, or by virtue of the leader's 'charismatic' personality. The limits of such a one-dimensional approach remain unacknowledged, and the humanity of those who follow is disregarded. Where in traditional environments followers were treated homogenously, being relatively uneducated and forced to look to their leader for direction, today, as outlined above, team members are often SMEs and, in their own discipline, more educated than the leader.

The relatively recent emergence of Situational Leadership® has to a small extent recognised this incongruity by acknowledging that one-size-fits-all leadership behaviour is ineffective. Yet it too glosses over the irony – when the project manager finds themselves following their SME followers' guidance or even instruction!

With its focus on the leader's actions and style, Situational Leadership® suggests some degree of agility is necessary to adapt to followers at varying stages of development. But, in reality, while acknowledging that different leadership styles suit different people and situations, its focus remains on how to *tell* and direct from a position of informed and (tacitly) more highly educated authority.

This disregards the profound truth that increasingly, the function of stakeholder management is replaced by the task of securing engagement. 'Telling' is simply not an option!

It's the subtle difference between a focus on what the leader does: directing and controlling, and what they enable, coach and facilitate *the team* to do. Furthermore, it is this very act of empowerment that fosters ownership and full engagement by the team members, with the added bonus of establishing mutual, positive regard and a mutually supportive and collaborative relationship.

So far, the approach of utilising the Triple Catalyst, following the Nine Steps to Project Leadership, has largely focused on the function and part played by the aspirant or practising project manager. The paradigm shift in roles and responsibilities of the project manager as leader must, however, be matched and mirrored, complemented and empowered, by an investment of trust and empowerment across the entire Integrated project delivery team.

Clearly, when the entire team comes to recognise the benefits offered them through the Triple Catalyst, their own full engagement, and hence effectiveness and resilience, is fostered and encouraged and this is far more likely to come about than it would through traditional stereotypes of leader/follower relations.

Both the organisation and the project leader must play their part in facilitating coaching and empowering every individual in delivery to understand these new relations, and the benefits they offer all.

At the organisational level, particularly, for those in a position to recognise and address the *costs* of traditional project management behaviours, it is therefore not enough to delegate responsibility purely to project managers or leaders. The function of project leadership necessitates an organisation-wide vision promoted at and supported from the highest levels. It will require a greater degree of understanding, engagement and ownership right across the delivery function, than ever before.

The roles and responsibilities of *all* engaged in project delivery now require review, negotiation and communication. There will rightly be interest from many stakeholders, including trade unions, but it is clear: the benefits to *all* stakeholders, from customers, through management to those in delivery, now wait to be realised in a genuine win-win solution.

Evolving project leadership

Embedding the Vision

Implementing project leadership to full effect requires, at the highest level of the organisation, a public commitment to supporting and encouraging the empowered roles project leadership fosters. This requires behavioural standards to be established across the integrated project team through a collective vision that all can relate to and will readily buy into.

The organisation – all project management capability functions, PMOs, operations and the delivery supply chain – *all* must be made aware of role changes and resulting expectations in delivery, balanced with clarity as to the benefits and opportunity these changes offer.

Project leadership is bestowed, not imposed. The follower conferring the status of leader must, by definition, hold the leader in respect. But such respect cannot be 'demanded'. It should not be confused or conflated, as has too long been the case, with the 'apprehension' and even 'fear', that those dependent on command and control too often invoke in imposing subservience.

Successfully implemented, the new regime will marginalise behaviours exhibiting an excess of ego and self-promotion. On the contrary, stories should be told and examples made of those embracing the opportunities for growth empowered teams offer.

Organisations realising the benefits of enhanced performance, while simultaneously casting off the costs associated with its absence, will foster that essential culture of mutual respect central to collaborative working.

Those treading the path to project leadership, whether aspiring practitioner, the organisation promoting its adoption, or the delivery team – all will encounter resistance in a variety of forms. But, whatever the guise or pretence, the most corrosive influence impeding the realisation of both individual and team potential is 'egotism'.

The COVID-19 pandemic has imposed working practices such that even the project manager's immediate team – those they depend on most are rarely in the same room. Whether using digital platforms for teleconferences or videoconferences, the visibility the project manager has of the team, is now severely diminished.

When a meeting ends, team members drop 'under the radar'. Previously, when all were in the office or workspace, knowing where everyone was, and what they were doing, was far simpler. More significantly, line reports were *aware* of that visibility.

This sense and influence of 'being observed' has been a source of control since long before Jeremy Bentham created the 'panopticon', his famous prison design. From a central tower, one guard could 'see' every inmate from a single viewpoint. Science has since repeatedly shown that this sense of 'being visible' or 'seen' is an incredibly powerful moderating influence on behaviour. For the inmates, the sense of being under the guard's gaze was, more often than not, enough to moderate their behaviours and encourage obedience.

Examples of this effect are to be found everywhere; a picture of a face, or even just 'eyes', reduces the occurrence of individuals stealing milk from a shared fridge. A lifesize, cardboard-backed photograph of a policeman at the entrance to a store, or ceiling-mounted cameras that may or may not be working – all have the desired effect.

The evidence from these findings suggest that it would be naïve for any manager to think the reverse effect of remote working on an *invisible* workforce makes no difference.

Here again, though, the effective project leader has an immense advantage over traditional managers who 'impose' or 'assert' compliance and obedience through command and control, position power, or other intimidating behaviour.

Project leadership, by its very nature and function, focuses from the outset on establishing a mutually respectful relationship; gaining rapport with all stakeholders. Communicating that respect and empowerment evokes a reciprocal commitment. The willing follower feels a powerful sense of commitment to their leader, inclining a commitment not to let them down. The follower is motivated; wanting to do, and taking ownership of, what is needful. Such reciprocal respect and empowerment will actually encourage and foster this sense of ownership, the strongest motivator of all.

In each moment of invisibility, of dropping off the radar, the quality of the relationship the project manager as leader has fostered is being tested. Do they turn away, content with whatever bare minimum of activity they need to engage in, or are they invested with this driving sense of personal responsibility; keen not to let their leader down?

One counter-productive effect of egotistical leadership, evidenced by the findings of neuroscience and discussed above, is assertiveness. Another, often fuelled by the same fire, is an equally damaging characteristic, similarly and mistakenly confused, and misrepresented as central to leadership: charisma.

Where resistance to project leadership emerges, it is likely to include those long accustomed to, and hence reluctant to question or relinquish, traditional representations of leadership – this includes the high regard and esteem with which an elusive (sic) quality associated with traditional leadership is venerated: charisma.

How and why charisma diminishes performance and has no place in project leadership

Charismatic leaders are often lionised for having the 'x-factor', some ineffable quality that cannot be measured; a 'super-power', influencing and drawing all into willing subservience.

In stories and representations, charismatic leaders exhibit magnetic charm, radiate a self-assured 'presence' encouraging confidence and trust. They radiate self-confidence, even though within them uncertainty reigns, especially when they have engineered it.

For countless generations, charisma has been extolled as the quality distinguishing those 'marked with greatness', and for some it is inseparable from 'true leadership'.

The ever-expanding genre of self-help 'leadership' books and training providers recognise the power of charisma and even make the mistake of promising to make their customers 'charismatic'. They offer techniques to achieve greater assertiveness through exercises in speaking and body language; ways to engineer charisma. There is good reason for this. Those vulnerable and susceptible to the entrancing appeal and mechanisms of charisma become willing, obedient subjects inclined to do just as they are told, without question. This is overwhelmingly attractive to those whose identity and self-construal is dependent on 'esteem from others'.

As we grow into adulthood, many stereotypical examples of role models are promoted that conspire to encourage this dynamic of dependency camouflaged under the promoted attraction of following a 'great leader'. There is a powerful, ancient and seductive appeal to this, abrogating personal responsibility and uncertainties and the insecurity flowing from them. One's own responsibilities are given up in favour of faith in another's self-assurance and confidence, which seductively offers relief from personal anxiety, or the need to make hard decisions.

Those stereotypes have two effects. They promote the attractiveness of setting aside all doubt and uncertainty in favour of following a 'great leader'; of being associated with them, and deriving their kudos by proxy and association. Second, admiration and idolisation also encourage emulation – the aspiration to become such a one, able to beguile and entrance others while being held in such high regard.

The appealing veneer of charisma, like the fable of the *Emperor's New Clothes*, swiftly becomes transparent to those sensitised to its exercise.

The traditional promotion of charisma as a defining quality of leadership disregards or plays down the cost of those intentionally seeking to beguile compliant and adoring followers. By definition this relationship is one that science has shown to induce in the followers a trance-like state in which critical faculties are suspended. It is, in many ways, akin to what happens when a speaker utters the timeless words: "Once upon a time . . .". Eyes glaze over and the listener, conditioned from childhood, automatically enters a suggestible state of mind. Charisma is, after all, a mechanism of control, and however readily benevolent examples can be cited, more often than not the followership, sooner or later, is betrayed by those exercising such control for their own benefit with little care or empathy for their followers.

In project leadership, such a quality has little to commend it. After all that has been demonstrated in terms of the actual function of project leadership, the last thing needed is compliant, unquestioning followers whose executive function enters a state of suspended animation.

Charisma as a so-called quality of leadership has echoes with, and is powerfully illustrated by, yet another ancient instrument of control with which it holds much in common: the quality of courage.

One story of Socrates told by Plato describes his encounter with Laches, a young man extolling the virtues of courage. Stories and movies extol the courage of warriors, mountaineers, rock climbers, explorers and others venturing into extreme environments: places where a single false move may result in severe injury or death.

Like charisma, courage is presented as reflecting the presence of some additional, transcendent quality, making those who have it great exemplars, to be admired and looked up to.

What makes both qualities so alluring is their deep roots in the apparent self-assurance and self-confidence of those who project them.

However, the charisma and courage of those 'in-dependence' on esteem from others, comes not from their being endowed with a *surplus* of some ethereal quality, but because of a *deficit*!

Consider the extreme rock climber, seemingly unfazed by the imminent threat of death accompanying their every move. For those rightly terrified by the prospect, they seem to have something *extra*; something readily labelled as 'courage'. Similarly, charismatic individuals exhibit a similar surplus of self-confidence – an ability to fend off, or keep at bay, the fears and anxieties experienced by others.

Evolving project leadership

'Courage' and 'charisma' can also derive credence and become attractive when presented as qualities others might aspire to. They can then be used to captivate the imagination. Ordinary mortals are encouraged to admire those presented as having that something extra. In this way, these attributes become mechanisms to suppress awareness of the fact that these people are masking underlying deficits in personality.

This example has been drawn out to demonstrate that, like leadership, and assertiveness, many unexamined stereotypes of leadership behaviours, such as charisma and courage, are ill informed and redundant.

Some stereotypes, like command-and-control leadership, *were* fit for purpose in their day, and in very limited situations, but if they are to survive and be fit-for-purpose, they must now evolve and adapt to fulfil new functions, in new forms.

The same applies to the status held by charisma in relation to leadership. In a modern project context and elsewhere, the costs associated with it are increasingly exposed, not least by a media that, while having a tendency to polarise, does, nonetheless, excel at exposing vulnerabilities, foibles and weaknesses; getting past the projected image.

It is in fact the unarticulated, unrecognised deficit underpinning charisma that accounts for its ability to charm. Just as exceptional performers in other sports tend to be hindered significantly less than most people by self-preservation instincts, so, too, the ego of the charismatic persona suppresses self-doubt and the neural overhead of worrying about others' opinions or feelings. They are often as immune to doubt, as they are to humility.

The uncanny attraction of someone convincingly saying, 'everything is under control' is formidable. But taking stock, equally forbidding is the high cost of those who conflate and confuse confidence with competence.

This same mechanism accounts for the charm and attraction of courage when one naïvely believes that it represents a quality in surplus, rather than a deficit in objective judgement. Portrayals of courage often disguise or glorify the actions of those shackled by an ego deeming itself impervious to harm; an exception to statistical probability to which others are subject. This projected sense of invulnerability impedes any objective assessment of odds.

The self-confidence such egotism promotes can be overwhelmingly attractive, and contagious to those weighed down by uncertainty. Sadly, history rarely, if ever, returns to count or account for the people who sacrificed their own wellbeing or even lives in the name of a charismatic leader. Abandoning good judgement, charmed by charisma, they never asked the hard question, was it worth it?

So, followers falling for charisma are diminished. There is a sense in which they are entranced or hypnotised; beguiled by those to whom they willingly surrender their will and judgement. Despite this diminution, those promoting traditional forms of leadership continue to see charisma as its highest manifestation.

In any career or lifetime's experience, most have had the experience of encountering, or even falling under the spell of someone's charisma. With hindsight, it may be uncomfortable to acknowledge how one was 'gulled' by the other's self-confidence and charm, and were taken advantage of, often without realising it at the time.

This superficial, charismatic projection is almost invariably draped over an egotistical, self-promoting individual whose sense of entitlement is evidenced in their willingness to both expect and take far more than they give.

History and contemporary society, politics and the workplace all offer ready examples of the perils that befall those who promote charismatic self-confidence over competence.

To establish project leadership within delivery now requires these historical illusions surrounding what constitutes good leadership in project delivery to be fully exposed and recognised by all; not just by those promoting or practising it. The superficial attractiveness of charisma must be set aside in the same way that science now empowers customers to see past any immediate attraction of fast foods and sugar. The cost outweighs (sic) the benefits.

In practice, then, for project leadership to become established across project delivery, it will be necessary to extend awareness, understanding and acceptance of the reasons driving and underpinning the new function of project leadership. These stereotypes must be brought out into the open and understood for what they are: remnants of a function in projects that, like stakeholder management, is no longer relevant.

The form this initiative must take, its significance for how work is conducted, and the inherent opportunities for individual development must all be planned. As with all projects, preparation and planning are key. Every organisation where project leadership is to be adopted will be different and face its own unique challenges, not least culturally.

Setting the standard

A structured approach to raising awareness of the need for change is primary. The necessity of obtaining buy-in by all stakeholders, so that they understand

and embrace the need for change, is crucial. From those selected to lead the way, a core cadre of 'exemplars' should be chosen.

It may be viable to select a specific project and team to run as a pilot. The team may be one that already delivers, or is drawn from, an existing capability. In light of what project leadership necessitates, the willingness to take ownership by all should drive selection.

This may be greatly supported where the disposition of those taking part reflects the characteristics that support collaborative working, embracing empowerment, ownership and a clear commitment to the envisioned form of delivery.

Redefining roles

For the simple reason that the terms 'project manager' or 'leader' carry such baggage, it might be of value to establish the distinction in roles from what went previously, by adopting new job titles.

One way to introduce this change is through a facilitated group session. All are invited to consider the evolving roles of those traditionally labelled as manager, leader and follower or team member.

Facilitating this discussion, the participants are invited to consider a 'day in the life of a project manager' and a 'day in the life of a project delivery team member', both 'then', and 'now'.

This can be a tremendously powerful mechanism to bring all involved to a new level of awareness and insight into the fundamental ways in which project delivery roles have changed.

Starting perhaps with Isambard Kingdom Brunel, or some other major 'project manager' from history, the applicability and relevance of traditional roles can be vividly portrayed as the skilled, qualified SME 'leader' oversaw delivery at the workface, 'directing, commanding and controlling' relatively unskilled labour forces under direct line control.

How this form of delivery worked on the ground can be explored – what the project manager actually 'did' and the decisions they made from day to day affecting delivery. In this way, the 'form' of this kind of project management can be exemplified.

Examples and parallels might also be drawn between the management of projects and forms of leadership adopted and deployed in military operations. Some consideration might be given to the strengths and weaknesses inherent in this function and form of management and leadership.

Turning to contemporary manifestations and 'days in the life of' will, in and of itself, offer opportunities for considerable reflection and promote perspective-shifting insight. Few project managers stop to consider, even periodically, what exactly they 'did' to make a substantive difference in delivery. Immersed in day-to-day priorities involving meetings, emails, compiling or examining reports, or dealing with other unexpected challenges to delivery, few stop to really reflect on or question the relative value of their activities.

Asked to reflect on their role and leadership in project delivery, most readily resort to those largely prevalent stereotypes of 'directing', 'assertiveness', and 'calling to account'. But further questioning, digging a little deeper than these superficial and even clichéd responses, exploring how much time was *actually* taken up in these specific, apparently 'characteristic' management and leadership activities, can be surprising.

Suddenly, a whole new perspective begins to emerge. A useful exercise to this end is the 'thought experiment' suggesting the deployment of a time and motion study; the observer, in a white coat, with clipboard, stopwatch and notebook shadows the project manager, day in and day out for a month.

How much of that time is actually spent *telling others what to do*? How many actions from meetings consist of interventions by the project manager setting tasks for SMEs? By contrast, how often are the inputs to meetings and outputs arising driven by attendees advising, seeking support from or consulting others?

It is likely to become clear that in these meetings the project manager is now more 'chair' than 'leader'. They facilitate and moderate discussion to secure collaborative outputs. The questions raised will necessarily draw forth answers from a multitude of highly qualified SMEs or those with direct workface experience.

Entering a meeting with Operations, where a project is planned, or with contractors from an extended project delivery team, the project manager is, it will transpire, rarely in a position to, or even called upon to, make some significant strategic decision, or to assert command and control over all.

Where a project manager's instruction (PMI) is on the cards, the project manager will be keenly aware that such reversion to 'transactional', contractual relationships can trigger and provoke unintelligent literal interpretations of orders, undermining the very ends they intend to promote.

Under such scrutiny and analysis, the real contemporary role of the project manager will likely emerge through their ability and competence in their leading role and function – in securing stakeholder engagement.

Drawing out these examples will soon lead to the emergence of a vivid contrast, and sharp contradictions between traditional portrayal of the project manager's role and associated behaviours, and those that effective modern delivery actually demands.

As the new function and effective form of project leadership emerges, so too the redundancy and counter-productiveness of traditional forms can be drawn out. Clear reference can be made to the findings from neurology associated with the SCARF Model. Key to this will be the communicated intent to facilitate individual growth and the realisation of potential rather than its being inhibited. It will be important, at this point, to draw out lessons supporting the quality and nature of expected and mutually supportive interactions *between* **team members**, perhaps described as '**project** *actualizers*'.

Discussion will also encourage a fresh look at, and awareness of, traditional characterisations of leadership, and especially the questionable prestige and kudos afforded to charisma, while exposing the hidden costs associated with its historical acceptance. These conversations and discussions will serve to prompt all in project delivery to reframe and re-orient themselves as to their own roles, and not least their interdependence with their own **project leader**, whose function might be described as that of '**project** *activator*'.

'Actualizers' are those who deliver at the workface, whether physical or virtual, and may be deployed and dispersed across disciplines, professions and supply chain organisations. The project leader – known as *'activator'* are those carrying the responsibility for supporting *'actualizers'*, both as individuals, and nurturing the emergence of a collaborative team.

The enhanced role of *'actualizers'*, so defined, also serves to remove negative associations, and even stigma associated with the term 'follower', implying as it does reduced agency, capability, and status. At the same time, the role of *'activator'*, properly appreciated, represents an elevation in both function and status.

For project managers moving into the project leadership role of 'activator', any apprehensions or misgivings about 'losing' the perceived status of a command-and-control role can readily be put to rest.

It is vital that the opportunity to address this concern or challenge is not ducked or glossed over. It must be welcomed, and raised for all to consider. It opens the door to discussing and promoting an exciting vision and an opportunity to offer unequivocal proof of why project leadership is *more* effective and rewarding for all, including for the *'activator'*.

The power of project leadership

The 'activator', exercising project leadership, paradoxically, wields not less power, as may be initially perceived, but far <u>more</u> than that of the traditional project manager!

The activator ignites and unleashes a collective force far in excess of anything individual 'command and control' could ever be capable of. Its collective power has an agility and resilience best adapted to evolving delivery environments and emergent project complexity.

Well structured, the above exercises in 'setting the standard' through 'redefining roles' will serve to introduce and reorient all in project delivery to the wide-ranging need for collective acceptance of the new function of project management, as reflected in project leadership.

Facilitating transition to this new level of awareness also offers a unique opportunity to shift the commitment of all involved to an entirely new level. Changes in roles offer empowerment and opportunities for development to all. Communicating this also signals the increased levels of respect, commitment and support that '*actualizers*' are offered by organisations. This will in turn serve to encourage reciprocal commitment, engagement and ownership by those in delivery.

The benefits of achieving this dis-'illusionment' – leaving behind outdated and ineffective models of project management and leadership – extend far beyond the boundaries of project delivery. In the western world today, emergent populism heralds widespread disillusionment with traditional forms of political leadership. Similarly, the increasing impotence of command and control behaviours are becoming apparent in many increasingly complex fields of human endeavour. This is especially true of project delivery.

For those in project management, the problems now besetting society cascade into and 'complexify' project delivery environments already characterised and pervaded by the 'internet of increasingly inter-dependent things'.

The 'complexifying' challenges arising in project delivery may be biological, like the COVID-19 pandemic, or otherwise political, environmental, sociological, technological legal or, as Brexit portends, economic.

Addressing such challenges at the societal level are beyond the immediate scope of this book. It does, however, provide good evidence prompting re-examination of wider perceptions and assumptions as to the right, proper, relevant and therefore most effective function and forms of leadership.

Evolving project leadership

This book has sought to strip away the accumulated baggage surrounding portrayals of the function and forms leadership can take. It has also exposed and drawn out for scrutiny the profound changes in shifting, inter-dependent delivery environments experienced by project managers.

The widely accepted move from notions of 'stakeholder management' to 'stakeholder engagement' emphasises the extent to which project managers now have little line authority to 'command and control' integrated project teams comprising SMEs dispersed across extended, integrated project teams spanning multiple organisations.

Insight and Foresight inform a new Vision

This examination of the nature of traditional leadership; challenging its unquestioned application within project management, gave rise to the unexpected discovery of a growing gap between the function current forms of project management address, and what is now needed.

These Insights informed the project this book represents. Situational awareness of the gap between the function of project management now, and what is needed, helped forge this Vision of project leadership functioning in a form that is fit for purpose.

The 'Triple Catalyst', and 'Nine Steps' bridge the gap and offer Foresight and a structured approach to achieving project leadership as a function and organisational project capability.

Therefore, this newly envisioned function of 'project management', fostered to realisation by the 'Nine Steps' and 'Triple Catalyst', offers a 'Vision' of 'project leadership' in delivery, informed by 'insight', and inspired by 'Foresight', anticipating a better way for all to rise to the challenges ahead.

Appendix: Project leadership behavioural assessment

	Personal leadership behaviours	Status
a	Personal development plan: up to date. Third party informed and endorsed (i.e. organisational training department)?	
b	360° assessment informing CPD and development plan? What learning – how informed – how actioned?	
c	Targets for self-improvement – achieving excellence. What evidence of development to date and ongoing?	
d	Progress to plan and complete any mandatory role training. What evidence of development to date and ongoing?	
e	CPD log maintained, updated, and progressed? Activities?	
f	Networking – What undertaken to broaden organisational knowledge and awareness? Active/mentor? Evidence or endorsements?	
g	Insight and Foresight: situational awareness and understanding: *use* of personal measures of performance: i.e. Johari Window / Karpman Drama Triangle, emotional intelligence, Conversational intelligence, conscious awareness of personal weakness /vulnerability – mitigation measures.	
h	Personal or PM log (may include CPD) workbook.	
i	Documented planned rotation / succession?	
j	Evidences conscious informed deployment of appropriate behaviours: body language, tone, cadence, prosody etc. Informed by situational awareness and understanding. Examples and observations.	
k	What examples of successful stakeholder engagement and influence? i.e. setting the example of 'What good looks like'?	
l	Evidence reflecting active engagement, ownership and activation of the Triple Catalyst following each of the Nine Steps.	
m	Evidence of developing the Five Enablers of Interdependence.	
n	Line management endorsement.	

Appendix: Project leadership behavioural assessment

	Team leadership behaviours	**Status**
A	Has individual and team trajectory on **Tuckman continuum** been plotted, understood and managed?	
B	Has a **Belbin Team Role Assessment** been undertaken for team members?	
C	Have team member **development objectives** been discussed, documented and agreed?	
D	Have relevant **Integrated Project Team (IPT) team roles** been defined, assigned and shared?	
E	Has the **'Vision'** for team execution of the project (i.e. Project Execution Plan (PXP)) including The IPT organisational structure, culture, team building, been created, articulated (i.e. collaboratively?), and communicated? How? Project Charter.	
F	Has some form of **'Competence Assessment'** been carried out with team members?	
G	Is the project manager informing and aware of individual reports' **development plans**?	
H	Are **personal objectives** aligned with E) and F)?	
I	Responsible, Accountable, Consults, Informs (RACI) for self, and team?	
J	**Development plans in place**?	
	Evidence of developing team?	
K	Examples of **team and individual performance recognition**?	
L	Examples of collaborative leadership: **generating mutual trust and respect**?	
M	Does **stakeholder management plan** identify sources of **conflict / a plan to manage?** Concrete examples of how 'mutuality / collaboration achieved?	
N	How are project **challenges shared and discussed / brainstormed**?	
O	What has been done to establish an **environment** conducive to realisation of individual potential and team synergies?	
	Examples of team-building exercises.	
P	What evidence of **encouraging or supporting** additional team CPD: i.e. Academy courses, Project management foundation degree, ChPP?	

Appendix: Project leadership behavioural assessment

Q	What evidence of **mentoring**?	
R	What evidence of **coaching**?	
S	What evidence of facilitating candidate **workbook planning / completions**?	
T	**Stakeholder engagement and influence**: how do you set about this – what do you take into account? Results sought?	
U	What evidence of identifying and facilitating progression into the project management community from support etc?	
V	What activities planned and led to 'Lean' design/delivery? What effected?	
W	How was personal integrity and Vision communicated to the team?	
X	What activity best exemplified the way the team culture was planned, communicated and embedded?	
Y	What have you done to identify and address **under-performance**? What was the reason and how addressed?	

Application of the above should be aligned with complexity of project and level of project management leadership required of the role.

Index

'activator', 226–7
active (reflective) listening, 161–2, 165
'actualizers', 226–7
Aldrich, Howard, 'boundary spanner', 50
ambition, 27, 94, 104, 126, 205–6
APM Body of Knowledge 7th edition, 32–3, 42, 45, 90
    stakeholder engagement, 33, 38, 54, 119–20, 160
APM Research Fund, *'Project leadership: skills, behaviours, knowledge and values*, 73, 79–80, 82
aporia, 68, 96
artificial general intelligence (AGI), 46
artificial intelligence (AI), 46–7, 139
artificial narrow intelligence (ANI), 46
artificial superintelligence (ASI), 46
assertiveness, 22–3, 25, 28–34, 36, 166–7, 199, 207
assessments, 26, 59, 101–4, 115, 192, 195, 229–31
    leadership capability, 76–78
    project leadership effectiveness, 171–6
'asymmetric warfare', 67

behavioural assessments, project leadership, 229–31
Bentham, Jeremy, panopticon, 219
Berne, Eric, Transactional Analysis theory, 60–2, 61f, 81
body language, 28–9, 61, 112, 150, 161–2, 197, 220
bonsai, 129–30, 200–1
Bregman, Rutger, *Humankind: A Hopeful History*, 21–2
Building Information Modelling (BIM), 181, 183

Business Reporter, 'Mapping out the future', 45–6, 49

'calling to account', 62–4, 113
Call of the Wild, The (film), 137
charisma, 189, 219–23
climate change, 48
coaching, 5, 33, 43, 53–69, 153–5, 173, 180, 191, 209, see also Whitmore, Sir John, *Coaching for Performance*
cognitive empathy, 135
collaboration, achieving rapport, 164–71
command and control (C&C), 9, 10f, see also assertiveness
    costs and consequences of, 28–39
    reasons for inadequacy of, 45–52
communications, effective, 40, 76, 114, 119, 150
    digital, 205, 218–19
    vision, 41, 198
compassionate empathy, 135
Conan Doyle, Arthur, *A Study in Scarlet*, 118
conflict models, 120f
conflicts, 149–51, 169–70
    averting potential, 117–19, 120f, 170
continuing professional development (CPD), 116, 126, 169, 170, 177, 193, 229, 230
Covey, Stephen M. R., 85, 96, 211
    7 Habits of Highly Effective People, 57, 71
    'Public Victory', 73, 77
    At The Speed of Trust, 161
crisis situations, 9, 11–12, 189, 211, see also VUCA environments
curiosity, 165, 166–8, 212

Damasio, Antonio, *The Strange Order of Things*, 14, 35f, 162

Index

data, impact of increased volumes, 14, 37, 47, 49
decision making, 79–80
delegating, 5, 8, 37, 59, 128–9, 180, 198
   from direction to delegation (Hersey Blanchard), 37, 68, 153, 193
delivery environments, impacts of change, 45–52
digital communications, 205, 218–19
direction, 32–3, 37, *see also* coaching
diversity, 4, 40, 46, 98
domineering behaviours, 16, 57, 70, 113, *see also* assertiveness

eight project leadership survival skills, 73
emergent complexities, 7, 22, 45–8, 55, 87, 173, 183, 200–1, 204
emotional contagion, 141
emotional empathy, 135
emotional intelligence (EI), 13, 19, 21, 25, 64–5, 72, 81, 126, 137–43, 163–4
Emotional intelligence quotient (EQ), 21, 22
empathy, 50, 72, 86, 135–6
   absence of, 21, 25, 36
empowering, 33, 125–6, 191–2, 193–6, 198–201, 216–17
engagement, *see* stakeholder engagement
environmental challenges, 48–50, 204–5
evolutionary origins of behaviours, 12–14, 19, 32, 34, 162, 164

facilitation, 208–14, 224, 227
feedback, 26, 32–3
   360 assessments, 59, 115, 192, 195, 229
first impressions, unconscious bias, 102, 148, 162–3
five enablers of interdependence, 125–45
   emotional intelligence, 13, 19, 21, 25, 64–5, 72, 81, 126, 137–43, 163–4
   empathy, 50, 72, 86, 135–6
   motivation, 109–10, 126–8
   ownership, 128–34
   'we' before 'me', 126, 142–3, 151–3

followers, 10, 35–43, 81, 84, 215–17, 221–3
   inspiring, 33, 41–2, 80, 86
'Foresight', 11, 82, 83f, 87–90, 117, 134, 157–85, 228
   developing personal leadership behaviours, 159–76
   team members, 176–82
   team to synergy, 182–4
forming stage, 148–9, 177
Fundamental Attribution Error, 99–100

goals, 42, 65f, 66, 125, 182
Golding, William, *Lord of the Flies*, 22
Goleman, Daniel, *Emotional Intelligence* (EI), 19, 21, 64–5, 164
GROW model, 65–8, 65f, 125, 182

Hammarskjöld, Dag, 80
health indicators, traditional, 75, 77
Hersey Blanchard Situational Leadership, 37, 68, 153, 216–17
hiring, project leaders, 21, 100–4, 142–3, 204–5
humility, 128, 207–9

'Insight', 11, 83f, 87–9, 96–8, 107–55, 228
   challenges in developing, 93–5
   self as leader, 108–21
   team as individuals, 121–45
   unified integrated project team, 145–55
inspiring followers, 33, 41–2, 80, 86
integrated project team (IPT) as a unified team, 145–55
interdependence, shift from independence to, 57, 69–71, 70f, 73, 77, 85, 95–6, 210
   five enablers, 125–45
Intergovernmental Panel on Climate Change (IPCC) Special Report on Global Warming, 48
interviews, 20, 101–4

job titles, adopting new, 224–6
Johari Window, 59, 124, 192, 229
judgement, 73, 79–80

Index

Kahneman, Daniel, *Thinking Fast and Slow*, 162
Kilmann, Thomas, Conflict Model Instrument, 120

leadership
  behaviours, 7–22, 159–76, 205–8
  definitions, 32–3
  function and form, 39f
  primitive, 13–20
  stereotypes, 38, 109, 210, 215, 220–5
  styles, 10f, 57, 154, 217
  traditional, 12–13, 32–6, 38–9, 42 (*see also* command and control)
learning styles, 58, 114

Maslow's 'Hierarchy of Needs', 24, 57, 69–70, 179, 198–9
meetings, 122, 133, 139, 146–7, 175, 184, 197–8, 211–12
  one-to-one, 119, 193–5, 212–13
mentalisation, 124–5
mentoring, 37, 43, 58–9, 61, *see also* coaching
metrics, 76–78, 83–4, 131–2, 171–6
motivation, 109–10, 126–8
Murray, Henry, 165

Nine Steps to Delivery Team Leadership, 77, 82, 87–91, 91f, 107–202
  1 'Insight', self as leader, 108–21
  2 'Insight', team as individuals, 121–45
  3 'Insight', unified Integrated project team, 145–55
  4 'Foresight', developing personal leadership behaviours, 159–76
  5 'Foresight', team members, 176–82
  6 'Foresight', team to synergy, 182–4
  7 'Vision', personal transformation, 189–93
  8 'Vision', empowering team members, 193–6
  9 'Vision', measured informed ongoing intervention, 196–202

Nine Team Types, Meredith Belbin, 146
nocebo effect, 18
norming stage, 151–3
nudge approach, 19, 82, 96–100, 135, 168

observational bias, 102, 107, 148, 162–4
organisational foundations, enabling and supporting, 93–105
organisational intelligence (OI), 78–9
organisational transformation, 203–14
organisations
  adoption of five enablers, 144–5
  challenges for change, 24–8
  embedding the vision, 218–20
  role, supporting leaders, 20–3
ownership, 128–34

Performance Curve model, 57, 69–71, 70f
performing stage, 153–5
PESTLE (Political, Economic, Sociological, Technological, Legal and Environmental), 47–8
Plato, Socratic Dialogues, 68–9, 221
Powell, Colin, 80
primitive leadership, 13–20
project cultures, creating, 73, 80–2
project delivery environments, impacts of change, 45–52
project leaders
  behaviours and skills, 71–3, 85–8, 108–119, 128, 159–68, 190, 205–13
  functions, 11, 45–52, 53f, 54, 56, 189, 190, 204, 209
  hiring, 21, 100–4, 142–3, 204–5
project management capability (PMC) functions, 12, 21, 23, 50, 116, 131, 193, 218
project management office (PMO), 21, 116, 131, 177
Psychological First Aid (PFA), 126–7

rapport, 11, 41, 50, 136, 150–1, 164–71, 164f
  barriers to, 168–71
  building through coaching, 60

Index

recruitment, project leaders, 21, 101–4, 142–3, 204–5
reflective (active) listening, 161–2, 165
remote working, 218–19
reporting, 184
resistance, 26–7, 50, 94–7, 135–6, 150–1
rewards, 14, 19, 35f, 122, 136, 139–41, 143, 148–9, 163, 199
Rock, David, SCARF Model, 19, 34–5, 35f, 63, 72, 131
roles
    of organisation, supporting leaders, 20–3
    redefining, 224–6
Rumsfeld, Donald, 54

Sagan, Carl, 9, 164
SCARF Model, 19, 34–5, 35f, 63, 72, 131
self-actualisation, 24, 69–70, 108, 179, 198–9
self-awareness, 112–15
self-confidence, 57, 206–7, 220–23
self-esteem, 24–5, 57, 58, 60, 69–70, 96
situational awareness, 66, 88, 93, 107–12, 116, 124, 157–8, 171, 201–2
Situational Leadership, Hersey Blanchard, 37, 68, 153, 216–17
situational understanding, 88, 128, 157–9, 161, 167, 171, 187–202
skills, 73, 85–9, 121–4, 207–9, see also project leaders, behaviours and skills
SMEs (subject matter experts), 50, 55, 188, 204, 216, 224, 225
Socrates, 68, 221
Socratic Dialogues, 68–9, 221
special forces' operational culture, 67–8
Special report UK2030, 'Mapping out the future,' 46, 49
stakeholder engagement, 33, 38, 42, 119–21, 160–70
    identifying, 78–9, 159–60
    information gathering, 117–19
    modelling, 60–2
    through empowering, 216–17
STAR: Stop, Think, Act and Review, 138

stereotypes, leadership, 38, 109, 210, 215, 220–5
stories
    as force for change, 27, 97, 149, 196, 218
    of traditional leadership, 12, 16, 27, 95, 97, 207, 220–1
storming stage, 149–51
strengths and weaknesses
    project leaders', 108–21
    team members', 121–45, 136, 146, 182
subject matter experts (SMEs), 50, 55, 188, 204, 216, 224, 225
Sunstein, Cass R., Nudge concept, 19
survival skills, project leadership, 73
synergy, 50–1, 57, 82, 142, 182–3

team development stages, 146–55
    forming, 148–9, 177
    norming, 151–3
    performing, 153–5
    storming, 149–51
team members
    empowering, 193–6
    encouraging insight, 132–3
    fostering and nurturing 'Foresight', 176–82
    perceptions and role, 216–17
    self-assess relations, 133–4
    skills, 121–4
    strengths and weaknesses, 121–45
    synergy, 182–3
team types, 146–8
technologies, impact and significance, 45–9
Thaler, Richard H., Nudge concept, 19
threats, 14, 35f, 139–41, 143, 148–9, 163
360° assessments, 26, 59, 115, 192, 195, 229
traditional leadership, 7–10, 12–13, 32–6, 38–9, 42, *see also* command and control
Transactional Analysis theory, 60–2, 61f, 81
Triple Catalyst model, 75–90, 83f, 94, 98, 217
    Nine Steps to Delivery Team Leadership, 77, 82, 87–91, 91f, 107–202
    for project management leadership, 82–89

Index

Tuckman, Bruce, 'Forming and Storming to Norming 'and Performing', 146–7, 196

'Vision', 11, 32–3, 41, 82, 83f, 87–9
    articulating, 192–3
    empowering team members, 193–6
    ongoing intervention, 196–202
    personal transformation and delivery, 189–93
    voicing by stories, 97

VUCA (Volatile, Uncertain, Complex and Ambiguous) environments, 48, 58, 76, 103, 172

'we' before 'me', 126, 142–3, 151–3
wellbeing, 11, 39, 84, 131–2
Whitmore, Sir John
    Coaching for Performance, 37, 56, 58, 61, 68, 69, 108, 161
    GROW Model, 65–8, 65f, 125, 182
    Performance Curve model, 57, 69–71, 70f

WS - #0077 - 281223 - C0 - 246/189/11 - PB - 9781913305123 - Gloss Lamination